Writing Remains

Explorations in Science and Literature

Series Editors:
John Holmes, Anton Kirchhofer and Janine Rogers

Explorations in Science and Literature considers the significance of literature from within a scientific worldview and brings the insights of literary study to bear on current science. Ranging across scientific disciplines, literary concepts, and different times and cultures, volumes in this series will show how literature and science, including medicine and technology, are intricately connected, and how they are indispensable to one another in building up our understanding of ourselves and of the world around us.

Published Titles
Imagining Solar Energy, Greg Lynall
The Diseased Brain and the Failing Mind, Martina Zimmermann

Forthcoming Titles
Narrative in the Age of the Genome, Lara Choksey
Fictions of Prevention, Benedetta Liorsi
The Social Dinosaur, Will Tattersdill

Writing Remains

New Intersections of Archaeology, Literature and Science

Edited by
Josie Gill, Catriona McKenzie
and Emma Lightfoot

BLOOMSBURY ACADEMIC
LONDON • NEW YORK • OXFORD • NEW DELHI • SYDNEY

BLOOMSBURY ACADEMIC
Bloomsbury Publishing Plc
50 Bedford Square, London, WC1B 3DP, UK
1385 Broadway, New York, NY 10018, USA
29 Earlsfort Terrace, Dublin 2, Ireland

BLOOMSBURY, BLOOMSBURY ACADEMIC and the Diana logo are trademarks of
Bloomsbury Publishing Plc

First published in Great Britain 2021

Copyright © Josie Gill, Catriona McKenzie, Emma Lightfoot and Contributors, 2021

Josie Gill, Catriona McKenzie, Emma Lightfoot and Contributors have asserted
their right under the Copyright, Designs and Patents Act, 1988, to be identified
as Authors of this work.

For legal purposes the Acknowledgements on pp. xii–xiii constitute an extension
of this copyright page.

Cover design: Eleanor Rose
Cover image: © Jean-Claude Caprara / Getty Images

All rights reserved. No part of this publication may be reproduced or
transmitted in any form or by any means, electronic or mechanical,
including photocopying, recording, or any information storage or retrieval
system, without prior permission in writing from the publishers.

Bloomsbury Publishing Plc does not have any control over, or responsibility for, any
third-party websites referred to or in this book. All internet addresses given in this
book were correct at the time of going to press. The author and publisher regret any
inconvenience caused if addresses have changed or sites have ceased to exist, but can
accept no responsibility for any such changes.

A catalogue record for this book is available from the British Library.

A catalog record for this book is available from the Library of Congress.

ISBN: HB: 978-1-3501-0946-9
PB: 978-1-3502-0251-1
ePDF: 978-1-3501-0947-6
eBook: 978-1-3501-0948-3

Series: Explorations in Science and Literature

Typeset by Newgen KnowledgeWorks Pvt. Ltd., Chennai, India

To find out more about our authors and books visit www.bloomsbury.com
and sign up for our newsletters.

Contents

List of illustrations	vii
Series preface	viii
List of contributors	x
Acknowledgements	xii
Introduction: New intersections of archaeology, literature and science *Josie Gill, Catriona McKenzie and Emma Lightfoot*	1
Part I Genetics and human inheritance	21
1 New materialism, archaeogenetics and tracing the human *Jerome de Groot*	23
2 Jack London and *Before Adam*: Ahead of his time, or a cautionary tale in the study of prehistoric hominins? *James Walker and David Clinnick*	45
Part II Innovations in practice through collaborative projects	69
3 'Handle with care': Literature, archaeology, slavery *Josie Gill, Catriona McKenzie and Emma Lightfoot*	71
4 Creative facticity and 'hyper-archaeology': The spatial and performative textualities of psychogeography *Spencer Jordan*	95
Part III Literature, archaeology and layering the past	117
5 Deciphering the city: Ancient Egypt in Victorian London and psychogeographical archaeology *Eleanor Dobson*	119

6 From the Great Castle of the Hill to the Great Mound on the river: Imperialism and transatlantic archaeology in Thomas Hardy's 'Ancient Earthworks' *Anna West* 145

Part IV Narrative archaeology and the narratives of archaeologists 175

7 Something more than imagination: Archaeology and fiction *Robert E. Witcher and Daniël P. van Helden* 177

8 The death of the archaeologist: Imagining science, storytelling and self-understanding in contemporary archaeofiction *Anna Auguscik* 203

Index 225

Illustrations

Figures

5.1	Ross's route from Jermyn Street to Kensington Palace Gardens, passing the Egyptian Hall and the Albert Memorial	126
5.2	'Africa' group of Albert Memorial, September 2017	129
5.3	Cleopatra's Needle, August 2017	134
6.1	The escarpments of Maiden Castle	147
7.1	Michener's conceptualization of researching and writing a novel	192

Table

2.1	Passages from *Before Adam* (London 1907) that offer some type of trait-based distinction between different gradations of modernity and modern behaviours	54

Series preface

In spite of the myth of the 'Two Cultures', science and literature have always been shaped by one another. Many of our most powerful scientific concepts, from natural selection to artificial intelligence, from germ theory to chaos theory, have been formed through the careful – and sometimes careless – use of written language. Poets, novelists, playwrights and journalists have taken up scientific ideas, medical research and new technologies, exploring them, reworking them, at times distorting or misjudging them, but always shaping profoundly the wider culture's understanding of what they mean. This intimate and productive relationship between literature and science generated a steady stream of insightful scholarship and commentary throughout the twentieth century and has grown into a substantial field of study in its own right since the turn of the millennium. Where the idea of 'Two Cultures' does still have a hold, however, is in academic disciplines themselves. In schools and universities, we study science and arts subjects in different classrooms, taught by different people with different expectations. Literature and science studies has, so far, been largely a sub-discipline of literature, with only rare contributions from or addressed to scientific experts. In a world of ever-increasing specialization, failure to communicate across these disciplinary divides risks failing to appreciate the contribution that the study of literature can make to our understanding of science, medicine and technology; the uses that science makes of images, narratives and fictions; and the insights that scientists can bring to bear on literature and culture at large.

Explorations in Science and Literature aims to speak across this divide. It has a particular mandate to bring the insights of literary study to bear on science itself; to consider the significance of literature from a scientific point of view; and to explore the role of literature within the history of science. The books therefore examine the complex interrelations between science and literature in cross-disciplinary ways. They are written equally not only for scholars and students of literature and for scientists and science students but also for historians and sociologists of science, as well as general readers interested in science and its place in culture and society. By showing how each field can be enhanced by a knowledge of the others, we hope to enrich scientific as well as literary research and to cultivate a new cross-disciplinary approach to fundamental questions in both fields.

The series will encompass topics from across the physical, biological and social sciences, medicine and technology, wherever literature can inform our understanding of the science, its origins and its implications. It will also include books on literary forms and techniques that are informed by science, as well as studies that consider how science itself has been articulated. Along with literature in the broad sense of written texts, books in the series will also consider other cultural forms including drama, film, television and other arts and media.

John Holmes, Anton Kirchhofer and Janine Rogers

Contributors

Anna Auguscik teaches English Literature at the University of Oldenburg, Germany. She is the author of *Prizing Debate: The Fourth Decade of the Booker Prize and the Contemporary Novel in the UK* (2017). As a post-doctoral fellow of the research group Fiction Meets Science (funded by the Volkswagen Foundation) she was co-PI for a project on the media reception of science novels and has recently begun research on scientific expedition narratives in historical fiction.

David Clinnick is a lecturer in the Department of Biology at St Mary's College of California. His broad research interests include the Palaeolithic archaeology of early humans, Neanderthals and the history of prehistoric archaeology.

Eleanor Dobson is Lecturer in Nineteenth-Century Literature at the University of Birmingham, UK. Her work focuses on literature and culture of the nineteenth and early twentieth centuries, specifically focusing on representations of Egypt and Egyptology across this period.

Josie Gill is Lecturer in Black British Writing in the Department of English at the University of Bristol, UK. Her research concerns the intersections between contemporary literature, science and race and she is the author of *Biofictions: Race, Genetics and the Contemporary Novel* (2020). She was principal investigator of the interdisciplinary AHRC Science in Culture-funded project '*Literary Archaeology*': *Exploring the Lived Environment of the Slave*.

Jerome de Groot is Professor of Literature and Culture in the School of Arts, Languages and Cultures at the University of Manchester, UK. He is interested in the representation of history in contemporary popular film, television, drama and games and has published widely on historical fiction, historians, heritage and popular culture.

Daniël van Helden is a postdoctoral research associate in the School of Archaeology and Ancient History at the University of Leicester, UK. His research interests include the concept of identity in archaeology, formal mathematical approaches to archaeological knowledge representation and the relationship between fiction and archaeology.

Spencer Jordan is Assistant Professor of Creative Writing in the School of English at the University of Nottingham, UK. A writer and an academic, he is interested in historical and experimental writing, digital/hypertext fiction and literary geography, particularly as forms of affective intervention in response to critical social and cultural issues.

Emma Lightfoot is a Postdoctoral Research Associate in Biomolecular Archaeology at the McDonald Institute for Archaeological Research at the University of Cambridge, UK. Her research uses stable isotope analysis to investigate the social, cultural and environmental aspects of human food choice. Emma was co-investigator on the interdisciplinary AHRC Science in Culture-funded project *'Literary Archaeology': Exploring the Lived Environment of the Slave*.

Catriona McKenzie is a Senior Lecturer in Human Osteoarchaeology in the Department of Archaeology at the University of Exeter, UK. Her research is focused upon palaeopathology, funerary archaeology and medieval archaeology. Catriona was co-investigator on the interdisciplinary AHRC Science in Culture-funded project *'Literary Archaeology': Exploring the Lived Environment of the Slave*.

James Walker is a postdoctoral researcher on the Europe's Lost Frontiers project based at the School of Archaeological and Forensic Sciences in the University of Bradford, UK. His research interests include the archaeology of prehistoric hunter-gatherers, the history of archaeology, and questions of adaptation, migration and subsistence in prehistory.

Anna West is an independent scholar based in the United States and is the author of *Thomas Hardy and Animals* (2017).

Robert Witcher is Associate Professor of Archaeology at Durham University, UK. He has published widely in the fields of Roman archaeology and landscape archaeology with a focus on Italy and the Mediterranean. He is the editor of the world archaeology journal *Antiquity*.

Acknowledgements

This edited collection originated in discussions held at a conference at the University of Bristol – Writing Remains: An Interdisciplinary Symposium on Archaeology and Literature. The conference was supported by the Arts and Humanities Research Council Science in Culture theme under grant AH/N007107/1. We would like to thank all the participants who attended the conference for their contributions to a very memorable meeting. The work of Emma Lightfoot was supported by the TwoRains project which was funded by the European Research Council (ERC) under the European Union's Horizon 2020 research and innovation programme (grant agreement number 648609). We would also like to thank our anonymous reviewers and the series editors for their support in developing this project. Chapter 3 was originally published as Josie Gill, Catriona McKenzie and Emma Lightfoot (2019) 'Handle with care': literature, archaeology, slavery, *Interdisciplinary Science Reviews*, 44:1, 21–37 under a Creative Commons Attribution Licence. Minimal changes have been made from the original.

From James Walker and David Clinnick for Chapter 2

The authors wish to thank Miguel DeArce and Paige Madison for their discussions regarding their own work on the history of palaeoanthropology and Rob Witcher for encouraging our participation in the conference. We are especially grateful to the Writing Remains team (Josie, Catriona and Emma) for their patience and willingness to organize the conference where this chapter was first delivered. Any mistakes, of course, are our own.

From Josie Gill, Catriona McKenzie and Emma Lightfoot, for Chapter 3

This work was supported by the Arts and Humanities Research Council Science in Culture theme under grant AH/N007107/1.

We would like to thank Kristrina Shuler of Auburn University, Jonathan Santana at Universidad de Las Palmas de Gran Canaria and Hannes Schroeder of the University of Copenhagen for kindly allowing us to use their research for this project. We would also like to thank the writers, Edson Burton, Jenny Davis, Ralph Hoyte, Valda Jackson, Vanessa Kisuule, Ros Martin and Claudia Monteith, for their participation, enthusiasm and honesty throughout the project. We extend our gratitude to Ruth Hecht, Sue Giles and the team at Bristol Museums who supported us to deliver the public events at the MShed and Georgian House Museum in Bristol. We would also like to thank all of the people who attended the public events and made them so memorable. We would also like to thank our anonymous reviewers.

Introduction: New intersections of archaeology, literature and science

Josie Gill, Catriona McKenzie and Emma Lightfoot

In several interviews over a number of years, the Booker Prize-winning novelist Bernardine Evaristo has told and retold a story about her writer's residency at the Museum of London in 1999. Inspired by the Roman galleries by which she was surrounded during the residency, she began to contemplate writing a novel about the black presence in Roman London and approached the Museum's curators with her idea, only to be told that there was currently no bioarchaeological evidence (evidence from human skeletal remains) of any black people in London at that time (Evaristo 2016). Undeterred, Evaristo wrote *The Emperor's Babe* (2001), a verse novel about a black girl growing up in Roman London. Over the next few years Evaristo claims that 'Eventually the archaeologists caught up with fiction' (2017). Roman skeletons were reanalysed using new bioarchaeological techniques including stable isotope analyses and DNA analysis and people of colour were subsequently identified in the collections. 'This is a case', Evaristo contends, 'where the imagination came before the evidence, the scientific evidence' (2016).

When the editors of this volume – a literary scholar and two archaeologists – began working together, this account provided a means of thinking about the relationship between literature and archaeology; of considering how there have often been tensions between the disciplines around who can, and with what authority, write stories and create narratives about the past. In discussing whether to use this vignette, disciplinary differences around how to structure a piece of writing, what language and tone to use, what constitutes evidence and appropriate objects of analysis, and the value of different kinds of research, methods and writing became apparent. These are all things with which we have had to grapple in coming together as editors of this volume. They are also issues which come to the fore when exploring the subject of this collection: the intersections between archaeology and literature and how each imagines, theorizes and borrows from the other. As co-authors from these different disciplines, our project of exploring how and where archaeology and literary studies meet and diverge has had to begin with difficult discussions between ourselves about different disciplinary ways of working and thinking.

This practical form of interdisciplinarity is the driving force behind this collection, which brings together chapters by scholars from archaeological and literary studies, with the aim of bringing parallel scholarly debates and perspectives on the intersections of literature and archaeology into conversation with one another. An intersection is a place where things meet and cross; it denotes an overlapping and a commonality. The intersections in this book are textual, conceptual, spatial, temporal and material, and they are largely the result of discussions that began at a conference *Writing Remains: An Interdisciplinary Symposium on Archaeology and Literature* which took place at the University of Bristol in 2017. Our sense was that while each discipline is interested in the research, practices and theories of the other, there had actually been little in the way of real contact and conversation between archaeologists and literary scholars about their overlapping interests. We were motivated by the belief that such cross-disciplinary contact is crucial, particularly in an age when representations of archaeological knowledge and storytelling about the past are increasingly being weaponized, contested and debated in the public sphere. To take one recent example, in August 2017 Mary Beard, Professor of Classics, found herself at the centre of an online public Twitter row about a BBC children's cartoon which represented a Roman soldier as a black man. One commentator claimed that the depiction of Roman Britain as 'ethnically diverse' was historically inaccurate, to which Beard countered that the cartoon was in fact accurate, that people of various ethnicities, including those from Africa, lived in Roman Britain (Beard, *TLS*). In response, Beard received a torrent of online abuse, reflecting how, particularly in the context of post-Brexit Britain and an increasingly emboldened far-right, history is being publicly contested as a means of justifying racism in the present. Accepting that some Roman Britons were black would be to acknowledge the equality of black people with white and the long history of multiculturalism in Britain; instead, by claiming historians and experts to be motivated by political correctness, such debates call into question the ability of academics to tell true stories about the past. Several academics did intervene in the ensuing debate, drawing on bioarchaeological evidence as a means of consciously countering this incorrect narrative. Geneticist Jennifer Raff wrote in *The Guardian* that 'Roman Britain was indeed a multi-ethnic society ... Multiple lines of independent evidence, including isotopic analyses of teeth and bones, osteology, archaeology, and historical documents make this clear' (Raff 2017). An expert in human skeletal remains from the Museum of London, Rebecca Redfern noted that while bioarchaeological studies have shown that Roman Britain 'included newcomers and locals with black African ancestry', these findings have been 'rejected and ridiculed' particularly following the Brexit referendum in 'an atmosphere of growing nationalism' (Redfern 2018; for additional information about these cases, see Redfern 2017).

That archaeological findings are being dismissed – in line with wider attacks on academic expertise and on science – is of serious concern for archaeologists across the discipline. One kind of response might be to counter false narratives with hard, scientific fact, to close down the space for public discussion of science, to refuse the possibility that archaeology also involves creating narratives and telling stories. Yet archaeologists have instead recognized that harnessing the power of narratives about human history and consciously engaging with the stories generated by their discipline is the most productive way of engaging the wider public and political sphere. For as Ruth M. Van Dyke and Reinhard Bernbeck contend, 'archaeology is fundamentally about a critical discourse of evaluation, sorting through a multiplicity of truth claims. This process is as much bound to forms of narration as to equalities of different voices and listeners, that is, to the principle of maximizing the potential of participation by all those interested in the past' (2015: 19). Even when faced with a torrent of online abuse in which lay opinions appeared to be given as much weight as those of experts, Mary Beard, echoing the belief of many archaeologists,[1] wrote that 'I feel very strongly that talking about history isn't just for professional historians' (Beard, *TLS*). Narrative is central to engaging the public in 'ethical, and effective ways' as Alexis Boutin argues (2019: 283) in her call for archaeologists to 'break free from the traditional academic modes of interpretation, which sequester our research from the general public and encourage misperceptions of its broader utility, and experiment with new ways of writing about and disseminating our findings' (2019: 284). She argues for the creation, in the context of growing xenophobia and nationalism in the United States, of 'careful writing of widely accessible, fictional yet evidence-based, narrative interpretations of archaeological human remains' that 'can encourage empathy by rehumanizing both the subjects of our research and the practitioners of our discipline to the public' (Boutin 2019: 284–5). Yet the benefits of a conscious engagement with, and the creation of, stories within archaeology are not limited to better public communication; recognizing the power of narrative enables archaeologists to self-reflexively examine how their own disciplinary practices, and their history, might be variously implicated in the political narratives that archaeologists now seek to critique. As historical archaeologist Julia A. King puts it, 'while archaeology has the potential to produce new or alternative stories of the past, it can be just as challenging for archaeologists to escape old and familiar master narratives', narratives that have been told for so long that they now seem like facts (2012: 175). Recognizing how descriptive language and the naming of objects might perpetuate certain stories is a step towards upending 'myths about life in the past, often by providing a voice where none was heard before' (King 2012: 174).

This collection explores what role literature might play in these debates; how fiction variously participates in, contests, augments and anticipates the stories created by archaeologists, and how literary studies and approaches intersect with these archaeological concerns. As our opening example of Bernardine Evaristo's (2001) novel *The Emperor's Babe* makes clear, fiction has an important role to play in both challenging and supporting archaeological narratives and in voicing a past that, in this case, is increasingly disputed. However while Evaristo situates the disciplines in competition with one another, this collection is premised on the belief that both archaeologists and literary scholars can learn from one another's approaches to and understanding of narrative and storytelling about the past; and that in the face of an increasingly hostile political environment such conversation (rather than competition) is more needed than ever. Archaeological evidence is often at the forefront of debates about national and transnational origins, identities and cultures, operating to anchor particular narratives in the public's understanding of the past. This collection explores how literature and literary scholarship have informed and been informed by such archaeological discoveries and how tracing exchanges between archaeology and literary studies could lead to a better understanding of how such narratives about the past are formed.

To understand how literature and fiction are being interwoven in archaeological research currently, we need to first consider how the writing of archaeology has changed as the discipline has developed. In the eighteenth century, antiquarians recorded discoveries often in learned societies, through the medium of letters which contained sequential information about the excavations which were described in 'Imaginative and poetic terms' (Hodder 1989: 270). By the end of the nineteenth century and into the first half of the twentieth century, specialist archaeological reports were increasingly common (270–1). The aim of the specialist reports was to 'place the artefacts into constructed archaeological typologies' (271). During the 1960s and 1970s a number of new archaeological methods and techniques were being developed which emphasized the contribution that science could make to explain our understanding of the past, adopting logical positivism as a theoretical approach, in an era referred to as 'New Archaeology' or 'processual archaeology' (Harris and Cipolla 2017: 19). The research emphasis was on developing hypotheses about the past that could be scientifically tested with the ultimate aim of creating generalized laws (22). Archaeological reports and narratives were often presented without due consideration of the process of analysis and how this in turn may have influenced the interpretations and conclusions reached. Hodder describes reports from this time as 'increasingly distant, objective, impersonal and universal' (271). The reaction to processual archaeology in the 1980s and 1990s was led, in particular, by prominent archaeologists such as Ian Hodder, Christopher Tilley and Michael Shanks. These scholars, among others, recognized that processual archaeology failed to account for 'unique ways of being human' (Harris and Cipolla 2017: 22). They proposed a different theoretical approach known as 'post-processual archaeology' which recognized that there can be multiple 'readings' of the same material culture (26) and that political ideas and archaeology are often interwoven (24). Adopting this new approach to prehistoric field excavations at Leskernick on Bodmin Moor, Cornwall, Bender and colleagues argued, 'It is our job to be as rigorous as possible in defining, and assembling the evidence, as honest as possible in admitting when it goes against the grain of a prior interpretation, and as open as possible to rethinking and reconceptualising interpretation, narrative and evidence' (2007: 26). Through critical theoretical analysis, it has become increasingly clear that writing about the past is not straightforwardly transparent or value free (26), and 'All accounts, no matter how seemingly factual, how dryly presented, are, in reality, a sort of narrative, a sort of story' (26).

Since the 1990s archaeologists have been engaging with literature as a research method, with the writing of fiction changing the types of questions that researchers ask through a deeper engagement with the subject and evidence (Gibb 2000: 3). For example, imaginative techniques have been used in landscape archaeology (Pluciennik 1999, 2015; Wallace 2004; Bender, Hamilton and Tilley 2007), bioarchaeology (Boutin 2012, 2016), historical archaeology (Praetzellis 1998; Gibb 2000; King 2012; Van Dyke 2015), Roman archaeology (Witcher 2017) and archaeological theory (Shanks 1992, 2012; Thomas 2004, 2015). The benefits of writing archaeological fiction are documented by Gear who has been publishing archaeological evidence-based fiction since the early 1990s. He argues that readers not only 'want to learn something about human beings who lived in the past, and thereby discover something about themselves' (Gear and O'Neal Gear 2003: 24) but also that writing archaeological fiction is 'like crossing a minefield, writing fiction based on prehistory is fraught with challenges. You will find out just how little you actually knew about that time and place. The process will sharpen your wits and skills' (Gear and O'Neal Gear 2003: 27). Gibb agrees, '[fiction] … can provide a powerful analytical tool, an explicitly subjective, but rigorous, means of exploring archaeological and archival data' (2000: 3).

More recently, an extension of post-processual archaeology has occurred through the influence of the interdisciplinary new materialist movement. Michael Shanks asks, 'What if we didn't have disciplines? What would the study of material remains look like? How can science and art be combined in rigorous study and reconstruction [of the past]' (2012: 16). This new movement has elevated the significance of 'material "things"' while rejecting the privileged position of humans as 'masters and interpreters' of other beings and entities (Thomas 2015: 1287–8). Foregrounding material entities themselves, rather than the people who made, labelled or consumed them, objects become 'independent actors' that 'do not have to rely on people to animate them' (Thomas 2015: 1289). While this material turn is provoking new ways of conceiving of archaeological interpretation, premised on an interdependence of 'discursive practices and material things' (Marshall and Alberti 2014: 25, quoting Barad), its focus has largely been on material culture, although it is also concerned with human/non-human relations, and some are beginning to look at its potential for thinking about bodies in archaeology, through its disruption of more traditional distinctions between the organic and inorganic (Marshall and Alberti 2014).

The intersections of literature and archaeology that are the focus of this book not only build upon these developments but are also 'new' in a number of ways. First, this collection foregrounds a consideration of bioarchaeology, something which has often been absent from interdisciplinary studies of literature and archaeology. Despite the disciplinary changes in archaeology, noted above, in general there has been less investigation of the potential of narrative and of fiction in scientific archaeology (and particularly research focused on the analysis of human remains) with the exception of recent work by Boutin (2012, 2016, 2019; Boutin and Callahan 2019). As Joanna Sofaer argues, bioarchaeologists have on the whole 'failed to engage with recent developments in theoretical archaeology' (Sofaer 2006: 24), although there is evidence that this is beginning to change (see Buikstra 2019). At the same time, literary scholarship, while engaging with wider theoretical and conceptual developments, has been slower to address scientific archaeology. Archaeologist Julian Thomas notes that 'for as long as it has been recognized as a discipline, the word "archaeology" has been drawn on to describe forms of analysis that address origins, hidden realities, or fragments' (2004: 149–50), and this is certainly the case in literary studies, where writers and critics have drawn upon the archaeological metaphorically, exploring the significance of the buried, remains and fragments for thinking about a wide range of subjects in literature including history, memory and the body. Literary scholars and writers, following in the footsteps of theorists such as Freud and Foucault, often imagine their method as a kind of archaeological digging, as an excavation and reconstruction from archival or textual remains. Yet in this almost romantic view of what archaeology is, there is no space for the laboratories and chemical analysis of human remains, the increasing concern with the public communication and understanding of archaeology or the widespread archaeological anxiety about the ethics of voicing the dead (Van Dyke and Bernbeck 2015: 11), to name only a few facets of the discipline in the twenty-first century.

Rather than shy away from scientific approaches to human remains – approaches which in some senses are more distinct from the methodologies of historical and material archaeology than the latter is from the methods of literary studies – this collection seeks to reflect the full breath of the discipline and the intersections of a wide range of archaeological fields with literature. To this end, three chapters in the collection, including our own, explore how recent scientific developments within archaeology, including DNA, osteological and stable isotope analyses, are represented in and provoke new ways of imagining (past) individuals in literary fictions. If, as Casper and Currah contend, different 'disciplinary techniques ... squish and mold the biological material of a living being into a neatly bounded container – the individual' (Casper and Currah 2011: 4) then examining how these disciplinary techniques intersect offers new ways of understanding how both the historical and contemporary individual are shaped by new imaginings of and data about the body.

The intersections are also 'new' in the sense that this collection foregrounds literature itself – novels, short stories and poems – which represent the past peoples and cultures which are also the subject of archaeological investigation but which have until recently (see van Helden and Witcher 2020) been given less attention within archaeology. Explorations of archaeological storytelling have often involved collaborations with creative writers (see Elphinstone and Wickham-Jones 2012; Van Dyke and Bernbeck 2015; van Helden and Witcher 2020), but there has perhaps been less interaction, from within archaeology, with literary scholars and scholarship. Literary scholarship has, unsurprisingly, focused more on extant textual and the fictional sources, and on comparing literary and archaeological methods, in studies of the relationship between archaeological objects, narratives and methodologies and literature. For Philip Schwyzer, 'Literary scholars read messages from the dead in textual form, whilst archaeologists handle their physical artefacts and remains' (2007: 27) and

At the heart of each discipline, it would appear, lies a buried longing for the object of the other. Literary scholars have long dreamt of 'touching' their intangible texts. Pacing among their silent shreds and samples, archaeologists strain to hear voices. It is in this intersection of impossible desires that literary studies and archaeology may find themselves able to address one another. (2007: 28)

Foregrounding textual materiality, scholarship such as Schwyzer's has arisen from historically specific research on periods before archaeology as a discipline came into being.

In contrast, the literature discussed in this book is comparatively modern; the literary texts examined in each of the chapters were nearly all published in the twentieth century onwards, if not the late nineteenth century. While several are concerned with much earlier historical periods of archaeological interest, they represent literary engagements with archaeology which have occurred since archaeology emerged as a discipline and practice in the nineteenth century (although, as Warwick and Willis note, 'what might be called archaeological curiosity or wonder' existed prior to nineteenth century archaeological science (2012: 1)). In this, the collection departs from extant research in literary studies which has focused on earlier periods of literary production including the early medieval (Hines 2011), Arthurian (Snyder 2009), Renaissance (Schwyzer 2007), eighteenth century (Lake 2020) and nineteenth century (Pearson 2006; Zimmerman 2008; Malley 2012; Warwick 2017) or had a transhistorical focus (Hines 2004; Wallace 2004). The more modern focus of this collection means that it is concerned not only with how writers have 'responded to the material traces of the recent and distant past: ancient bones, ruined abbeys, exotic mummies and enigmatic urns' (Schwyzer 2007: 2) but also with how writers from the late nineteenth to the twenty-first century have engaged with archaeology as academic discipline and profession, with archaeologists as people practicing and creating a discipline embedded in particular historical and cultural circumstances. Indeed, the inception and formalization of archaeology as disciplinary practice cannot be separated from the geopolitical conditions which assisted its rise – namely, nineteenth-century imperialism which, through extensive and violent colonization, facilitated many of the archaeological 'discoveries' which fill Europe's museums today. The practices and narratives of archaeology which formed in this period were imprinted with 'colonial assumptions' and were characterized by a doubled discourse which struggled to reconcile labour and commodification with an older language of wonder and dreams (Warwick 2012: 85, 91). Warwick contends that 'In their reluctance to assert possession, the archaeologists underscore again the denial of production and commodification: objects are "finds" or "discoveries", that eventually become "gifts" or "bequests" or "acquisitions"' (2012: 93). For Warwick, 'The disturbance produced by archaeological objects is not the horror of the past, but of the recognition of the conditions of the present' (2012: 94), a colonial present which nineteenth-century archaeology elides but which is inescapable. Several of the chapters in this collection, particularly those of Dobson, Auguscik and West, explore how literature illuminates the imperial impulses and assumptions latent in late-nineteenth- and early-twentieth-century archaeological imagination and their legacies in contemporary archaeological and museal practice.

Both literary studies and archaeology are highly complex, diverse and inherently interdisciplinary, each encompassing a wide array of (often conflicting) methodologies, theories and approaches. We have attempted, within this collection, to capture some of the diversity of both disciplines, to capture not only different approaches to the literature/archaeology intersection but also the broad array of areas of inquiry in which such intersections occur. The chapters consider a wide range of texts including novels, short stories, poetry and social media and evince an equally broad approach to archaeology, including consideration of scientific analyses, museology and public communication and engagement, across prehistory, historical archaeology, bioarchaeology and landscape archaeology in a range of global contexts. We do not claim to cover all facets of modern literature and archaeology (an impossible task), and the different themes, periods, genres and methods presented here are by no means comprehensive. Rather what we offer is a range of perspectives – both archaeological and literary – not only on the common assumptions and preoccupations of the disciplines but also on their divergences, because 'multiple disciplinary perspectives in the humanities gain strength by their difference from one another and yet still have an ability to speak to one another – to hold tensions and varying viewpoints in suspension and therefore articulate complexity' (Willis 2012). As Hines also contends, there is no 'one formula for putting literary scholarship and archaeology together properly ... the potential interfaces between these two modes of cultural life are so multifaceted and multivalent' (2011: 980). The analysis by some of our authors may conflict with the conclusions of others, and stylistically there are differences between the chapters which to an extent reveal the disciplinary origins of their authors; for example, the contributions by archaeologists are all co-authored, and their chapters contain tables and diagrams, whereas those by literary scholars feature images. However, all are united in exploring the possibilities of fictional narrative as a point of new knowledge about archaeology as narrative and as practice, and as itself a source, object and site of archaeological investigation. We hope that this book will appeal to scholars in both disciplines and that the disciplinary differences between the chapters herein appear less important than the rich and diverse approaches to archaeology and literature that they offer.

The book identifies and is structured around four interlinked and interdisciplinary themes: Genetics and Human Inheritance; Innovations in Practice through Collaborative Projects; Literature, Archaeology and Layering the Past; and Narrative Archaeology and the Narratives of Archaeologists. Each theme acts as a way into understanding how the modern literary and archaeological imagination together shape understandings of human history, ancient and modern. The first part, 'Genetics and human inheritance', interrogates how the archaeology and bioarchaeology of human remains is altering our understanding of the past and how literature and literary critical approaches have shaped, and might inform, the interpretation of these data. Chapter 1 by Jerome de Groot explores how the development of high-profile scientific techniques has changed our understanding of, and interface with, prehistory. Focusing on advances in ancient DNA (aDNA) analysis, de Groot suggests that such scientific techniques prompt new ways of thinking about the human species, particularly about what it means to be human and the development of *Homo sapiens* through time. Connecting this new work in archaeogenetics with new materialist approaches to the body in the wider humanities, de Groot considers how the material and the imaginative are combined in discourses about aDNA. The chapter examines texts by Ali Smith, Carol Ann Duffy and Paul Beatty, exploring the ways in which these contemporary writers respond to the new definitions of the human emerging in archaeogenetics. De Groot argues that innovations in aDNA and new understandings of the body as multitemporal allow these writers to challenge normative structures of humanness as they address themes of roots, legacy, inheritance and archaeology. The question that is ultimately posed by the chapter is, 'Can literature enable us to reconcile – or at least comprehend – a seemingly profound epistemological shift towards understanding the human as and through data?'

This is a question to which Chapter 2 also partly responds but from the perspective of two archaeologists, rather than a literary scholar. Also concerned with changing archaeological understandings of the human, James Walker and David Clinnik focus in their chapter on the new species of *Homo* which have been discovered in the twenty-first century and on the closing of the gap between humans and Neanderthals following the discovery that interbreeding between them occurred. Their chapter explores how palaeofiction, specifically Jack London's *Before Adam*, appears to anticipate many of the discoveries now being made about the relationships between humans and Neanderthals and other hominins. Charting the ways in which London's portrayal of the relations between three distinct groups of ancestral beings complicates archaeological hierarchies and refuses to offer a definitive line of descent for present-day humans, Walker and Clinnik suggest that the traits and behaviours of London's characters disrupt older archaeological assumptions about what makes a modern human, while resonating with new, emerging archaeological understandings of human evolution. They also argue that the narrative form of the novel – which comprises a modern-day narrator dreaming the life of his ancestors – resonates with the way that archaeological narratives of early hominins have often been written with present-day humans as the benchmark against which other species are contrasted and compared. Rather than see this as a pitfall, Walker and Clinnik suggest that this closeness, as it is expressed in the novel, encourages empathy with non-humans of the kind that might enrich archaeological narratives.

The second part, 'Innovations in practice through collaborative projects', begins with a chapter also concerned with how bioarchaeological methods and processes might enhance and provoke new literary representations of the past, but is equally focused on how literature and creative writing might inform archaeological knowledge. The subject of Chapter 3 is slavery and the different methodologies employed by each discipline to understand what it was like to be enslaved. The chapter offers an account of an interdisciplinary, collaborative research project that brought the editors of this volume together, alongside seven black creative writers from Bristol, to explore how writing might not only communicate a history primarily understood through archaeological evidence but could itself inform approaches to that evidence. Offering an account of this experimental project and its methodologies, the chapter identifies two key themes that emerged from the project which acted as ways of opening up, rather than claiming, the past: conversation and caring. We suggest that these are themes which are also crucial to the success of such an interdisciplinary process, as it was only through attention to the relationships between academics and creative writers that each of us was ultimately able to reassess the nature of material in each of our disciplines.

Chapter 4 is an account by Spencer Jordan of another novel kind of research collaboration, which explores the interdependencies between fiction and archaeology using psychogeography as a methodology. For Jordan, a psychogeographical emphasis on the relationship between physical and subjective journeys enables the creation of new archaeological stories which are not simply textual but spatial, performative and technologically enabled. Arguing that the archaeological imagination – to which everyone has the capacity to contribute as part of placemaking activities – is increasingly digital, Jordan offers an account of the outcomes of the Walkways and Waterways research project, in which twenty members of the public participated in a psychogeographical walk through Cardiff, using Twitter to capture their creative responses in real time. A form of digital storytelling was the result, and Jordan encourages us to see the value of mobile phones and digital technology to democratize our engagement with place and allow us all to be psychogeographers. Recognizing that such democratization is increasingly necessary, but also difficult at a moment when distinctions between fact and fiction are being deliberately obfuscated, the chapter demonstrates how a psychogeographical, embodied exploration of landscape can thrive through new digital technology which is changing both archaeologists' and literary scholars' understanding of the relationship between narrative and place.

Part III, 'Literature, archaeology and layering the past', explores the ways in which landscapes, cityscapes, architecture and ruins have inspired artistic and archaeological reconstructions, and the role of place and space in the intersection of literature and archaeology. Continuing the psychogeographical theme of Chapter 4, Chapter 5 by Eleanor Dobson explores the possibilities of what she terms a 'psychogeographical archaeology' for comprehending the apparent collision between archaeological 'fact' and imaginative fantasy. However Dobson's emphasis is on the late Victorians, specifically the ways in which ancient Egyptian artefacts and symbolism came to influence popular fiction towards the end of the long nineteenth century. Focusing on Guy Boothby's *Pharos the Egyptian* (1899) and Bram Stoker's *The Jewel of Seven Stars* (1903), Dobson examines how the Egyptian spaces and artefacts represented in these novels exert an ancient magical power within the geography of contemporary London. Dobson suggests that with a basic understanding of the city's geography, combined with some Egyptological knowledge, readers of these novels can partake in 'psychogeographical archaeology' which invites them to decode cryptic fragments and bring to light hidden meanings lying just below the surface of the texts. Stoker and Boothby encourage such an approach to their novels, Dobson contends, rewarding both geographical knowledge of London and symbolic detective work that mimics the processes of the amateur archaeologist. However the spatial and temporal ruptures encoded in these texts are also revealing of the imperial anxieties of the period; the menacing reintroduction of ancient power into the modern world that the novels' heterotopic city spaces imagine reflects underlying anxieties about the consequences of the archaeological plundering of ancient Egyptological sites in the name of the British Empire. The novels underscore how archaeological fact and fantasy combine in the Victorian imagination through the blurring of fictional and real places that create dis-ease about an Empire through which so much modern archaeology was enabled.

It is the colonial history of the discipline that Anna West addresses in Chapter 6 in her consideration of how literary representations of archaeological sites and practices can illuminate not only archaeology's imperial mechanisms but also how their legacies are still manifest today. West's focus is also on the late nineteenth century, as she conducts a detailed analysis of 'Ancient Earthworks: And What Two Enthusiastic Scientists Found Therein', a short story by Thomas Hardy that was first published in the *Detroit Post* in 1885. The story, set at Maiden Castle, an Iron Age hillfort in Dorset, describes an illegal night-time dig conducted by an amateur archaeologist. West argues that although the story is set in Dorset, England, Hardy's critique of the destruction that archaeological endeavours can cause has a much wider reach and target. The publication of the story in the *Detroit Post*, West argues, connects it to the destruction of Native American burial grounds across the US Midwest, including the mounds and earthworks in Detroit: in this context the story becomes a satire of the Victorian imperialist values which drove archaeological digging (and destruction) of various sites, where, West demonstrates, the idea that earthworks could be Native American was denied in favour of a narrative which posited the earthworks' creation by 'ancient' cultures. The deliberate erasure of the true, Native American origins of the mounds was part of a wider colonial strategy of assimilation, designed to erase indigenous populations' tribal culture and identity (justified by their supposed savagery) and motivated by the desire to seize lands and resources. Read in this context, West contends that the multiple generic modes of Hardy's story problematize the relationship between Empire and archaeology, the legacies of which are apparent in current debates about how to decolonize museums.

While each chapter in the collection is concerned with the nature and possibilities of narrative in one way or another, the final part, 'Narrative archaeology and the narratives of archaeology', explores in more depth the connections between different narrative forms across fiction and archaeological writing and the changing role of the archaeologist in navigating these narrative terrains. Chapter 7 by Robert Witcher and Daniël van Helden investigates the relationship between scholarly archaeological accounts and fictional literature (particularly historic novels), addressing the long-standing archaeological concern with the distinction between fact and fiction. Outlining the potentials and pitfalls of archaeological research that engages with fiction, the authors argue in favour of greater archaeological engagement with fiction which might stimulate a more empathic view of the past and provoke insights and questions that might not otherwise have been raised. Through an in-depth analysis of James Michener's 1965 novel *The Source*, Witcher and van Helden argue that fiction about archaeology offers a reflection of, and model for, archaeological research, shedding light on different scales of analyses, human agency, multiple perspectives and historical causation. They demonstrate that both fiction and fictive techniques can be productively used as part of the research process to make archaeologists' ideas about the past 'actually work' (Elphinstone and Wickham-Jones 2012: 536) and argue for a more ambitious use of these approaches than there has been to date.

The final chapter of the collection, by Anna Auguscik, is an exploration of how contemporary fiction about archaeologists reflects upon the power of the archaeological imagination and the relationship between archaeology and its public. The chapter offers an in-depth analysis of two contemporary expedition novels, Barry Unsworth's *Land of Marvels* and Sarah Moss's *Cold Earth* (both 2009). Both novels place the lead archaeologists centre stage, revealing the blind spots of the protagonists who identify with the object of their research and build narratives in order to fill gaps in the data. By the end of each novel, both lead archaeologists die as a consequence of their obsession with protecting and preserving, as they themselves become the object of other characters' stories. Problematizing the trope of self-excavation, Auguscik, like West, shows how these novels expose archaeology as a metonym for Empire, where the archaeological imagination and storytelling are less progressive modes of interpretation than reflections of historically situated subject positions which cannot escape the colonial past. As the archaeologists in these novels become both subject and object, Unsworth and Moss depict how it is their stories that remain, rather than their sites, stories that are compromised and ultimately beyond the control of the archaeologists themselves. In so doing the novels evince how contemporary fiction can highlight the subjectivity of interpretation and the nature of archaeological knowledge-making.

Many universities throughout the world are currently encouraging interdisciplinary initiatives, recognizing that the 'most interesting questions and tough real-world problems are messy and don't fit neatly into academic disciplines' (Shanks 2012: 17). Although from two differing disciplines and backgrounds, both archaeologists and literary scholars approach the analysis of material culture and text in comparable ways – through description, interpretation and evaluation, placing both archaeological remains and texts within their broader contexts (Hines 2004: 26). We hope that the intersections outlined in this volume will make a significant contribution towards highlighting the potential for archaeology and literary collaboration and, by doing so, address some of the recent attacks on truth and knowledge, opening up the past so that we can all have a better understanding of our shared human history.

Note

1 For example, Christ Dalglish, who writes that 'there needs to be a shift away from the idea that the archaeologist's role is to correct a deficit of knowledge and competency amongst the public' towards a collaborative mode that avoids creating oppositions between one group and another (2013: 6).

References

Beard, M. (n.d.), 'Roman Britain in Black and White', *Times Literary Supplement*. Available online https://www.the-tls.co.uk/articles/roman-britain-black-white/ (accessed 3 March 2020).

Bender, B., S. Hamilton and C. Tilley (2007), 'Stone Worlds, Alternative Narratives, Nested Landscapes', in B. Bender, S. Hamilton and C. Tilley (eds), *Stone Worlds: Narrative and Reflexivity in Landscape Archaeology*, 16–35, New York: Routledge.

Boutin, A. T. (2012), 'Crafting a Bioarchaeology of Personhood: Osteobiographical Narratives from Alalakh', in A. Baadsgaard, A. T. Boutin and J. E. Buikstra (eds), *Breathing New Life into the Evidence of Death: Contemporary Approaches to Bioarchaeology*, 109–33, Santa Fe, NM: School for Advanced Research Press.

Boutin, A. T. (2016), 'Exploring the Social Construction of Disability: An Application of the Bioarchaeology of Personhood Model to a Pathological Skeleton from Ancient Bahrain', *International Journal of Paleopathology*, 12: 17–28.

Boutin, A. T. (2019), 'Writing Bioarchaeological Stories to Right Past Wrongs', in J. E. Buikstra (ed.), *Bioarchaeologists Speak Out: Deep Time Perspectives on Contemporary Issues*, 283–304, Switzerland: Springer Nature.

Boutin, A. T., and M. P. Callahan (2019), 'Increasing Empathy and Reducing Prejudice: An Argument for Fictive Osteobiographical Narrative', *Bioarchaeology International*, 3 (1): 78–87.

Buikstra, J. E. (ed.) (2019), *Bioarchaeologists Speak Out: Deep Time Perspectives on Contemporary Issues*, Switzerland: Springer Nature.

Currah, P., and M. J. Casper (2011), 'Bringing Forth the Body: An Introduction', in M. J. Casper and P. Currah (eds), *Corpus: An Interdisciplinary Reader on Bodies and Knowledge*, 1–20, New York: Palgrave Macmillan.

Dalglish, C. (2013), 'Archaeologists, Power and the Recent Past', in C. Dalglish (ed.), *Archaeology, the Public and the Recent Past*, Woodbridge: Boydell Press.

Elphinstone, M., and C. Wickham-Jones (2012), 'Archaeology and Fiction', *Antiquity*, 86 (332): 532–7.

Evaristo, B. (2001). *The Emperor's Babe*. New York: Viking Press.

Evaristo, B. (2016), *Free Thinking: Black British History*, [Radio Programme] Prod. Torquil MacLeod, BBC Radio 3, 9 November. Available online https://www.bbc.co.uk/sounds/play/b081tkr9 (accessed 3 March 2020).

Evaristo, B. (2017), 'There's Going to Be a Lot of Protest Literature after Trump and Brexit', interview with Kate Müser, *Deutsche Welle*, 26 January. Available online https://www.dw.com/en/bernardine-evaristo-theres-going-to-be-a-lot-of-protest-literature-after-trump-and-brexit/a-37265434 (accessed 3 March 2020).

Gear, W. M., and K. O'Neal Gear (2003), 'Archaeological Fiction: Tripping through the Minefield', *SAA Archaeological Record*, 3 (5): 24–7.

Gibb, J. G. (2000), 'Imaginary, but by no Means Unimaginable: Storytelling, Science, and Historical Archaeology', *Historical Archaeology*, 34 (2): 1–6.

Harris, O. J. T., and C. Cipolla (2017), *Archaeological Theory in the New Millennium*, London: Routledge.

Hines, J. (2004), *Voices in the Past: English Literature and Archaeology*, Woodbridge: Boydell and Brewer.

Hines, J. (2011), 'Literary Sources and Archaeology', in D. Hinton, S. Crawford and H. Hamerow (eds), *The Oxford Handbook of Anglo-Saxon Archaeology*, 968–85, Oxford: Oxford University Press.

Hodder, I. (1989), 'Writing Archaeology: Site Reports in Context', *Antiquity*, 63: 268–74.

King, J. A. (2012), *Archaeology, Narrative, and the Politics of the Past: The View from Southern Maryland*, Knoxville: University of Tennessee Press.

Lake, C. B. (2020), *Artifacts: How We Think and Write about Found Objects*, Baltimore: Johns Hopkins University Press.

Malley, S. (2012), *From Archaeology to Spectacle in Victorian Britain: The Case of Assyria, 1845–1854*, Farnham: Ashgate.

Marshall, Y., and B. Alberti (2014), 'A Matter of Difference: Karen Barad, Ontology and Archaeological Bodies', *Cambridge Archaeological Journal*, 24 (1): 19–36.

Pearson, R. (ed.) (2006), *The Victorians and the Ancient World: Archaeology and Classicism in Nineteenth-Century Culture*, Newcastle: Cambridge Scholars Press.

Pluciennik, M. (1999), 'Archaeological Narratives and Other Ways of Telling', *Current Anthropology*, 40 (5): 653–78.

Pluciennik, M. (2015), 'Authoritative and Ethical Voices: *From* Diktat *to the Demotic*', in R. M. Van Dyke and R. Bernbeck (eds), *Subjects and Narratives in Archaeology*, 55–82, Colorado: University of Colorado Press.

Praetzellis, A. (1998), 'Introduction: Why Every Archaeologist Should Tell Stories Once in a While', *Historical Archaeology*, 32 (1): 1–3.

Raff, J. (2017), 'If Mary Beard Is Right, What's Happened to the DNA of Africans from Roman Britain?', *The Guardian*, 9 August. Available online https://www.theguardian.com/science/2017/aug/09/if-africans-were-in-roman-britain-why-dont-we-see-their-dna-today-mary-beard (accessed 7 February 2020).

Redfern, R. (2018), 'The Roman Dead: New Techniques Are Revealing Just How Diverse Roman Britain Was', *The Conversation*, 24 May. Available online https://theconversation.com/the-roman-dead-new-techniques-are-revealing-just-how-diverse-roman-britain-was-95243 (accessed 7 February 2020).

Redfern, R. C., M. Marshall, K. Eaton and H. N. Poinar (2017), '"Written in Bone": New Discoveries about the Lives and Burials of Four Roman Londoners', *Britannia*, 48: 253–77.

Schwyzer, P. (2007), *Archaeologies of English Renaissance Literature*, Oxford: Oxford University Press.

Shanks, M. (1992), *Experiencing the Past: On the Character of Archaeology*, Oxon: Routledge.

Shanks, M. (2012), *The Archaeological Imagination*, California: Left Coast Press.

Snyder, C. A. (2009), 'The use of History and Archaeology in Contemporary Arthurian Fiction', *Arthuriana*, 9 (3): 114–22.

Sofaer, J. R. (2006), *The Body as Material Culture: A Theoretical Osteoarchaeology*, Cambridge: Cambridge University Press.

Thomas, J. (2004), *Archaeology and Modernity*, London: Routledge.

Thomas, J. (2015), 'The Future of Archaeological Theory', *Antiquity*, 89 (348): 1287–96.

Van Dyke, R. M. (2015), 'The Chacoan Past: Creative Representations and Sensory Engagements', in R. M. Van Dyke and R. Bernbeck (eds), *Subjects and Narratives in Archaeology*, 83–99. Boulder: University Press of Colorado.

Van Dyke, R. M., and R. Bernbeck (2015), 'Alternative Narratives and the Ethics of Representation: An Introduction', in R. M. Van Dyke and R. Bernbeck (eds), *Subjects and Narratives in Archaeology*, 1–26, Colorado: University of Colorado Press.

van Helden, D., and R. Witcher (eds) (2020), *Researching the Archaeological Past through Imagined Narratives: A Necessary Fiction*, Abingdon: Routledge.

Wallace, J. (2004), *Digging the Dirt: The Archaeological Imagination*, London: Duckworth.

Warwick, A. (2012), 'The Dreams of Archaeology', *Journal of Literature and Science*, 5 (1): 83–97.

Warwick, A. (2017), 'Ruined Paradise: Geology and the Emergence of Archaeology', *Nineteenth-Century Contexts*, 39 (1): 49–62.

Warwick, A., and M. Willis (2012), 'Introduction: The Archaeological Imagination', *Journal of Literature and Science*, 5 (1): 1–5.

Willis, M. (2012), 'Open Fields? The Future of Interdisciplinary Studies in the Humanities', Keynote Lecture Mount Allison University, 11 February. Available online https://www.academia.edu/1491885/The_Future_of_Interdisciplinary_Studies_in_the_Humanities (accessed 10 March 2020).

Witcher, R. E. (2017), 'The Globalized Roman World', in T. Hodos (ed.), *The Routledge Handbook of Globalization and Archaeology*, 634–51, Oxon: Routledge.

Zimmerman, V. (2008), *Excavating Victorians*, Albany: University of New York Press.

Part I

Genetics and human inheritance

1

New materialism, archaeogenetics and tracing the human

Jerome de Groot

In May 2019 the Centre Pompidou in Paris opened its 'Préhistoire: Une énigme moderne' exhibition. The exhibition outlined multiple encounters between artists and ideas of the ancient past, arguing that modernist work in particular was highly influenced by archaeology, fossil reclamation and ideas of prehistory:

> Nourrie des découvertes archéolgiques, mais loin d'en être simplement le reflet, cette idée commune de 'préhistoire' déborde sa stricte définition scientifique, centrée sur l'émergence de l'humanité jusqu'à l'invention de l'écriture. Elle modèle les horizons mentaux de la modernité, où elle fonctionne comme une puissant machine à remuer le temps.[1]

Aesthetic engagement with the prehistoric past is hardly new, then. However the development of innovative new techniques for reading ancient human DNA (aDNA) has dramatically changed our understanding of, and interface with, prehistory. This chapter explores these new high-profile scientific techniques for understanding the human and considers the aesthetic response. The chapter suggests that archaeogenetics, particularly improvements in the sequencing of aDNA, prompts new ways of thinking about the human species and its relationship to the past. These developments have the potential to change the ways in which we think about the disciplines of archaeology, history and literary studies. The chapter considers archaeogenetics in the light of new theories of materialism that have arisen in the humanities. In particular I look at the ways that the use of genetic science in archaeological investigation forces a reconsideration of the 'human' and its history. I argue that a key element of this reconfiguring of the species relates to the human in time. Despite the wealth of research into DNA we have little sense of how what Nadia Abu El-Haj terms the 'genetic historical imagination' functions (El-Haj 2012: 20). The chapter works towards a final discussion of several contemporary writers and the ways that they have approached ideas of roots, legacy, inheritance and archaeology in their work in response to the new definitions of the human emerging in archaeogenetics. Can literature enable us to reconcile – or at least comprehend – a seemingly profound epistemological shift towards understanding the human as and through data?

Ancient DNA and the 'human'

Investigation of aDNA is changing our understanding of what it means to be human and how *Homo sapiens* developed over time (see, for instance, Furholt 2018). The genetic analysis of archaeological samples has been common since the 1990s, driven by technological innovations such as next-generation sequencing, which has enabled whole genomes to be sequenced at relatively high speed. The clarity and scope of this work have enabled new assertions to be made about the development of human groups, as well as revealing species of the *Homo* genus that had hitherto been unknown (see Reich et al. 2010). Such research has seemingly transformed the field of archaeology and will shortly begin to impact upon historical investigation of areas other than prehistory as geneticists Marc Haber et al. put it: 'Findings from aDNA research are currently transforming our understanding of human history at an ever-increasing pace' (Haber et al. 2016).

Ancient DNA has been used to investigate the human in history through its application within archaeogenetics, that is, the use of genetic science practices of varying kinds in the creation and analysis of data found at archaeological sites (often in comparison with modern DNA). This has led many geneticists to argue that such data can change the way we understand the human and the past. Joseph Pickrell and David Reich, two leading figures in archaeogenetics, argued in 2014 that improved technology and analysis techniques lead directly to new ways of understanding 'human history':

> Because of these technological advances, the past few years have seen a dramatic increase in the quantity of data available for learning about human history. Equally important has been rapid innovation in methods for making inferences from these data. We argue here that the technological breakthroughs of the past few years motivate a systematic re-evaluation of human history using modern genomic tools – a new 'History and Geography of Human Genes' that exploits many orders of magnitude more data than the original synthesis. (Pickrell and Reich 2014: 377)

Their claim is that the DNA they investigate and the modes of interrogation – the upgrade in technique and opening up of quantity – lead to a richer understanding of how the human species develops over time. The rhetoric is about accuracy, density of data, innovation and the way that this allows a more textured understanding of 'human history'. Ancient DNA investigation conceives of *Homo* as data and considers ways of understanding, narrating and articulating this data. The geneticist-historian produces the information – through sampling, sequencing and considering the genetic materials – and then reads it. The amount of data being produced by aDNA investigation is vast and such research is intervening in debates about population, migration, cultural development, evolution and the definition of the human (see Mathieson and Skoglund 2018). Much of this is driven by improvement in investigative techniques. The revolution of next-generation sequencing means that acquiring the entire genome is now much cheaper. Increase in computing power and developments in bioinformatics have made the process much quicker, and this has led to increased resolution and texture to results. The data is seemingly better and much more detailed. For Pickrell and Reich this leads to something of an epistemological shift: knowing the human differently, as much as a shift in understanding what there is *to know* about the human.

The impact of aDNA investigation on archaeological practice, and hence on wider public understanding of the past, has been significant. These technological, genetic developments have contributed to a number of public events reported widely in the press and around the world. The most high-profile moment was during the discovery, exhumation and examination of King Richard III's remains in 2012 (Buckley et al. 2013). The remains were found under the site of a car park in Leicester and identified through laborious DNA investigation connected with other types of archaeological analysis. The investigations prompted a set of popular discussions in the press and beyond about the nature of lineage, the contemporary world's relationship with heritage and the ethics (and legality) of disinterring human remains. The bones took on a kind of material substance as they were proven to be those of Richard III, shifting their physical nature into something to be celebrated and dreamed of, something that had relation to the contemporary world. The discovery of the king's remains suggested that archaeogenetics might allow the identification of 'truth' in the past, particularly in relation to physical identity. The investigation into Richard III's remains was a complex project intellectually, scientifically and ethically (King et al. 2014). The work on the DNA of the skeleton was crucial in establishing the veracity of the bones. The body of the king was reinterred in Leicester Cathedral after a year of legal wrangling about the final burial site, including a final judicial review and decision made by the High Court. The five days of events celebrating the reinterment situated the event at the intersection of heritage performance, nationalistic memorial service and historical re-enactment.

Two years later the remains of the boy known as 'Anzick-1' were reburied with much less attention although with some public discussion in the wider press. The child's remains were discovered on a farm in Montana in 1968, buried with artefacts identified as part of the Clovis culture. Named after the family that owned the farm, the remains, which had been buried around 12,000 years ago, were sampled for DNA sequencing in 2014 before being reinterred. The investigation suggested that Anzick-1 was both a direct ancestor of contemporary Native Americans and also had Asian ancestors. In this way:

> The Anzick-1 data thus serves to unify the genetic and archaeological records of early North America, it is consistent with a human occupation of the Americas a few thousand years before Clovis, and demonstrates that contemporary Native Americans are descendants of the first people to settle successfully in the Americas. (Rasmussen et al. 2014: 229)

The sequencing of the DNA was part of the final process of investigating the remains before they were reinterred. The ceremony was brief and low-key but still provoked some debate about the use and excavation of human remains. Shane Doyle, an academic who made arrangements for the reburial, argued that 'From a tribal point of view, this is a big part of reclaiming our history, reclaiming our dignity for our kids' (French 2017). The same article in the local *Billings Gazette* quotes Armand Minthorn of the Umatilla Tribe (now located in Oregon): ' "These are our ancestors' remains, they are not artefacts. I hope that the people who come after us remember this, as well." ' The reinterring of Anzick-1 formed part of an ongoing reclamation of ancient memory in the Native American community (see Tallbear 2013).

The investigative team in this case, based at the Centre for Geogenetics at the University of Copenhagen, have worked on a variety of projects including ancient plant DNA and the controversial Kennewick Man (a prehistoric skeleton found in Washington, United States, which was the subject of a dispute over whether the man was Native American). Their director, Eske Willerslev, was profiled in the *New York Times* in an article which argued that 'The findings have enriched our understanding of prehistory, shedding light on human development with evidence that can't be found in pottery shards or studies of living cultures' (Zimmer 2016). DNA, the article suggests, can contribute more to our understanding of what is at present a relatively unknown past, through the interpretative clarity of science. The article echoes the claims of Pickrell and Reich and points to the increasing public awareness of the transformative potential of archaeogenetics and bioarchaeology.

The innovative work being done by the Centre for Geogenetics and elsewhere on aDNA seeks to investigate the human past as accurately as possible using contemporary techniques that are not engaged with historiography. The work involves high-level DNA analysis, statistical investigation, mathematical modelling, consideration of previous studies (in particular radiocarbon dating) and population genetics and often incorporates physiological techniques such as cranial morphology. The work begins with the sample itself but soon expands to take in morphology, population genetics and statistical analysis. This is scientific archaeology, excavation, moving from one technique to another, sifting, comparing, analysing. Numerous techniques are brought to bear on the sample, but the purpose of the work is to exemplify it and give it meaning. This meaning allows the sample to live as both ancient stuff and contemporary signifier; it is both old and in the now, interpreted and inert. The research is painstaking in revealing, through investigation and analysis, new possibilities about the human. One of Willerslev's early high-profile successes was the sequencing of the 'Inuk' or Saqqaq genome from hair dug out of the permafrost in Qeqertasussuk, Greenland, in 1986 (Rasmussen et al. 2010). The genome was so complete that the team could suggest hair colour, baldness and facial features. An image of the Saqqaq was produced by Nuka K. Godtfredsen, a Greenlandic comic artist, and used around the world as a representation of a common ancestor. This visualization was key in the communication of the image of the 4,000-year-old DNA. Such analysis allows us to see a human not only as data but also as image, as something idealized and specific. This instance also demonstrates the power of the image over the genetic data and the trust that is being invested in the scientific community. Much of the complex work that is done by Willerslev's team is well beyond the capacity of a layperson to understand. The conclusions are worked through in exacting bioinformatic detail, but the knock-on effect, through media coverage and the circulation of things like the Saqqaq image, is far less subtle and leads to more popular discussion that warps the original information.

The huge increase in the use of scientific techniques and in particular aDNA sequencing provokes significant challenges to normative understanding of disciplinarity, materiality and epistemology, although this is not necessarily new. Colin Renfrew argues that science transformed the archaeological field some time ago; 'it was not until the availability of science-based dating techniques some fifty years ago that a secure chronology could be established for the development of human culture' (Renfrew 2008: x). Renfrew argues that the study of the human past 'before' history involves a great deal of data collection and a multitude of techniques:

> Prehistory, or prehistoric archaeology, is a field of study involving an extensive battery of techniques used to study the material remains that document the human past. The distinction is important, because the study of prehistory turns out to be a difficult task. Gathering the data is hard enough, involving painstaking archaeological excavations in different and often remote parts of the world. But the task of interpretation is even more difficult. For prehistory is the science of us. It is the discipline by which we study ourselves and investigate the way we have come to be as we are. The prehistorian keeps on having to re-evaluate what might seem to be the easiest proposition in the world: Who are we? Or rather, What are we? What

does it mean to be human? What at first might seem obvious becomes, on examination, a more difficult question. (Renfrew 2008: ix)

For Renfrew, understanding 'prehistory' is key to understanding the human. The difficulty of interpretation is inflected by the interpreter being part of the data set, by archaeology being the 'science of us'.

Renfrew's is one of a plethora of contemporary popular archaeology books accounting for the development of the species and, in particular, keenly interested in the thing that makes *Homo sapiens* distinct from other hominids. Yuval Noah Harari argues that *Homo sapiens* are one of many hominid species that at points lived together, that 'the truth is that from about 2 million years ago until around 10,000 years ago the world was home, at one and the same time, to several human species' (Harari 2015: 8). An intersection between 'prehistory' and DNA investigation allows assertions to be made about 'humanness' as the popular understanding of 'prehistory' changes. In particular, these popular texts are interested in reconfiguring the relationship between the human, history and time. For many popular writers the distinction between pre- and 'history' is the development of the mind: 'For history to begin, people required the modern mind – one quite different to that of any human ancestor or other species alive today. It is a mind with seemingly unlimited powers of imagination, curiosity and invention' (Mithren 2003: 3). Renfrew's *Prehistory: The Making of the Human Mind* proposes 'to understand the formation of mind' (Renfrew 2008: xi) and his 'Cognitive archaeology' seeks to understand the shift that seemingly took place between c.100,000 and 50,000 BCE. This involves the human becoming inserted into 'history', as Yuval Noah Harari argues: 'About 70,000 years ago, organisms belonging to the species *Homo sapiens* started to form even more elaborate structures called cultures. The subsequent development of these human cultures is called history' (Harari 2015: 3). The sense that before 'history' was something more amorphous, events occurred in time but were not somehow 'organized' into chronology is common in popular books of the science of the human. Steven Mithen differentiates it from evolution:

> Human history began in 50,000 BC. Or thereabouts. Perhaps 100,000 BC, but certainly not before. Human evolution has a far longer pedigree – at least three billion years have passed since the origin of life, and six million

since our lineage split from that of the chimpanzee. History, the cumulative development of events and knowledge, is a recent and remarkably brief affair. (Mithen 2003: 3)

This is a profound distinction in the sense that it links 'the human' to the species *Homo sapiens* and within that argues for a subset of understanding or knowledge that might be termed 'history'. The human is therefore defined through their relationship to history and the evolution of a particular type of cognitive function. To be human is to be 'conscious' and to be in history – to be before this is to be something else. The distinction between what is biological – evolution – and what is human – history – is for Mithen related to psychology and to commemorative practice. Popular books about the development of the human, then, conceptualize a time of 'prehistory', which is before the resultant sweep of 'history'. Ancient DNA evidence helps to locate the species in deep time and to precisely pinpoint the moment that it became 'human'. This in turn demonstrates the way that genetic evidence becomes an historical marker. Before this moment evolution was occurring but 'history' was not. In popular archaeology the moment after the advent of the 'human' often then becomes part of a developmental progress towards the now.

Ancient DNA analysis enables the trajectory of these narratives of the development of *Homo sapiens* and the investigation of what it is to be human. As Harari suggests, there is even more plurality to come when other parts of the human family are analysed. Work on the 430,000-year-old bone fragments from the Sima de los Huesos hominin suggested that these early *Homo neanderthalensis* were separated from *Homo sapiens* earlier than was thought and hence were living at the same time for longer (Meyer et al. 2016). *Homo sapiens* was one of several *Homo* species on the planet for quite some time.[2] Hence evidence is being presented through genetic analysis of archaeological materials that is shifting the ways of thinking about the evolution of *Homo sapiens* and about when the recognizable 'human' comes into being. This aDNA investigation is transforming the edges of the human species, interrogating understanding of what 'humans' are and what their relation to their genus might be.

Renfrew concludes his overview of current thinking in archaeogenetics with the claim that 'I predict that over the next twenty years or so a more coherent synthesis of the data from genetics, archaeology and linguistics is likely to emerge than we can yet envisage' (Renfrew 2010: 162). Others are more circumspect, suggesting that 'DNA is a valuable addition to the interdisciplinary toolbox for studying past human societies, but this research cannot be done in analytical isolation or inductively' (Johannsen et al. 2017: 1120). However many scientists and geneticists are already presenting themselves as historians in practice, as for instance this assertion in Frei et al. about the Bronze Age 'Egtved Girl': 'Our study provides evidence for long-distance and periodically rapid mobility. Our findings compel us to rethink European Bronze Age mobility as highly dynamic, where individuals moved quickly, over long distances in relatively brief periods of time' (Frei et al. 2015). These projects use genetic data to intervene into 'historical' debate, positing their evidence as transformational.

The development of enhanced genetic tools for analysing ancient materials has led to an acceleration of information regarding human evolution and development. It also has concomitant impact on the way that culture thinks about and visualizes humanness and prehistory. If DNA holds within it historical possibility, if through its interpretation history can be 'told', then its analysis, visualization and rendering by scientists would be a form of historiographical practice. Isolating, studying and engaging with DNA sequences would be a form of historical endeavour. It would be possible for historians to map the historical genre of the DNA sequence. Furthermore, if DNA is conceived as a library archive, then the scientist looking at a particular element or aspect would be the historian, reading the evidence to make a particular point. Considering the use of genetic information in historical and archaeological investigations takes us back to key issues in historiography: evidence, analysis, narrative, materiality, interpretation. The work that is being done is historical investigation of a kind and the genetic scientist is increasingly intervening into a set of debates that seek to understand humanness and to present the investigation of the past as the acquisition, organization and interpretation of data. Genetic science, therefore, is establishing a sense of historicity – linear, structural, networked, factual – that interacts with evolutionary science, molecular biology, statistical analysis and data mining. It is contributing to a redefinition of time within evolutionary contexts, augmenting our sense of population development and, at its most baroque, arguing for a new way of thinking about humanness, kinship and history.

New literary approaches for understanding the new human

How does this new understanding of the human body in time drive theoretical shifts in the humanities? As we have seen, huge claims for *Homo sapiens* are being made. Literary and humanities scholars have striven to conceptualize the place of such scientific technology and theory in the wider humanities and to integrate these developments into their work. Among others, Paul Gilroy has suggested a 'new humanism' as a consequence of biotechnological advance, something that might render redundant older definitions of identity: 'At the smaller than microscopic scales that open up the human body for scrutiny today "race" becomes less meaningful, compelling, or salient to the basic task of healing and protecting ourselves' (Gilroy 2000: 37). Kinship, race, ethnicity, identity, history, self – each of these humanistic concerns might be considered to function anew or differently with this newly generated data and the new forms of knowledge arising from it (see Nelson 2016). As Nikolas Rose points out, the body is increasingly being theorized as a material entity after years of 'constructionism' (Rose 2013: 3). Similarly, Shital Pravinchandra argues that 'Simply put, research in the life sciences is challenging humanities scholars to recalibrate our now customary suspicion of essentialist and deterministic explanations of human society' (Pravinchandra 2016: 28). Scholars have begun to develop what Catherine Malabou calls 'a materialist approach of the interaction between the biological and the cultural' (Malabou 2017: 43). Malabou's focus is the philosophy of neuroscience, and she argues for a relationship between physiology and culture where 'the brain is not the natural ideal of globalized economic, political, and social organization: it is the locus of an organic tension that is the basis of our history and our critical activity' (Malabou 2008: 81). Her insight here is that the interrelationship between that described by 'science' materially (the brain) and the 'world' is not neutral. This is part of a broader attempt to develop critical and philosophical models that take account of the material, the physical and the biological. The most elaborated of these models is affect theory, which traces what Brian Massumi terms 'irreducibly bodily and autonomic' phenomena via an interpretation of basic emotions (Massumi 2002: 28). Ruth Leys, in her criticism of affect, points out that the neuroscience is easy to challenge and articulates why people are looking at this in the first place: 'They seek to recast biology in dynamic, energistic, nondeterministic terms that emphasize its unpredictable and potentially emancipatory qualities' (Leys 2011: 440). These studies look at the interrelationships between human, self, mind, material, object and the formation of something called 'history' (Malafouris 2013).

This work on the interrelationship between the scientifically material and the cultural/political/social often invokes the theories of Bruno Latour. In particular Latour's 'Actor Network' theory seems to offer humanities scholars an opportunity to think about the interrelationship between the material, social and temporal. As Rita Felski argues, 'Cross-temporal networks mess up the tidiness of our periodizing schemes, forcing us to acknowledge affinity and proximity alongside difference, to grapple with the coevalness and connectedness of past and present' (Felski 2011: 597). Felski quotes Jonathan Gil Harris and his discussion of the anti-temporal: 'What do we do with things that cross temporal borders – things that are illegal immigrants, double agents, or holders of multiple passports? How might such border crossings change our understanding of temporality?' (Gil Harris 2008: 579). Gil Harris's influential reading of the philosopher Michael Serres focuses on the 'polychronic and multitemporal' nature of the object (Gil Harris 2008: 3). His point is that there is an ethical and political duty to provoke a new discussion in the humanities through a consideration of multiple contending temporalities. Gil Harris derives his argument from philosophy of science to make the case that 'an object is never of a singular moment but instead combines ingredients from several times' (Gil Harris 2008: 3). Building from Latour's idea of the 'polytemporal', his contention is that in considering the multiple times of the object the scholar can begin to evade linear norms and directional templates of thinking (Latour 1993: 75). As Latour argues, 'We do have a future and a past, but the future takes the form of a circle expanding in all directions, and the past is not surpassed but revisited, repeated, surrounded, protected, recombined, reinterpreted and reshuffled' (Latour 1993: 75). This sense of the interrelationship between the 'thing' or event (what Latour calls 'elements') and the multitemporal relationships between them and the ways they might be arranged allows a reconceptualization of the material and its status in 'time'. To illustrate this Latour turns to genetics, in a famous passage: 'Some of my genes are 500 million years old, others 3 million, others 100,000 years, and my habits range in age from a few days to several thousand years … it is this exchange that defines us' (Latour 1993: 5).

Latour's work, as is shown by Gil Harris's reading, is foundational in a shift towards what many have termed 'new materialism' (Adeney Thomas 2012: 802). This movement has drawn from actor network theory, posthumanism, feminism and postcolonialism to stage an engagement between contemporary science and the 'new humanities'.[3] This synthesis is a place that we can link the new work undertaken by archaeogenetics with practice and methodology in the wider humanities. Karen Barad, one of the key proponents of the 'new materialist' movement, argues that she seeks

> an epistemological-ontological-ethical framework that provides an understanding of the role of human and non-human, material and discursive, and natural and cultural factors in scientific and other social-material practices, thereby moving such considerations beyond the well-worn debates that pit constructivism against realism, agency against structure, and idealism against materialism. (Barad 2007: 26; see also Kirby 2013)

The challenge is to look at the way that the material and the imaginative are combined in discourses relating to aDNA. How we account for the very real problem of the materiality of aDNA – both physically material and imaginative – is crucial in our understanding of the ways in which this discourse is popularly understood. What is the legibility of aDNA, how does it relate to our understanding of ourselves and our conception of time? Is it something polytemporal, multiple, existing in and out of human time and perception? Can we aestheticize and understand it outside of the scientific discourse? What is the political dimension of this data (or is it simply 'truth')? Can we 'read' it? How does aDNA intervene into our understanding of the past and the present? The 'human' that emerges from these conceptualizations is both concrete and imagined, conceptualized and constructed. Understanding aDNA as somehow simultaneous – 'simultaneously a matter of substance and significance' – entails positing the 'epistemological-ontological-ethical framework' that Barad seeks.

Ancient DNA can itself be considered as a nexus point enabling this simultaneity. Christine Kenneally contends:

> DNA and our life experiences make our bodies palimpsests. As we learn how to interpret the body in the context of its genetic code, we begin to understand how the hand of fate, the choices of families, and the enormous journey of DNA through deep time affect our lives right now. (Kenneally 2015: 264)

What was remote is now intimate; what is 'science' is also now 'life'. The body exists in 'deep time' and in the present, both palimpsest and also a solid, contemporary living object. Our genetic make-up allows an enormous historical perspective to open up. The question of our individual relation to 'humanness' is provoked by DNA investigation and in particular by individual sequencing. Kenneally's outlining of the multiple temporality of DNA is suggestive of Latour's outline, conceiving of the body as carrying markers of a variety of chronologies within it. Latour and his followers' theorizing of the cross-temporal seems highly apposite for beginning to understand how to 'read' DNA more generally. DNA seems clearly to work as an intertemporal conceit in the popular imagination, at once something static but also exploding definitions of ontological time, agency and situatedness. DNA's value for this type of thinking is its multi-materiality and its status as simultaneous data and flesh, old and new. DNA is something that is now and not-now, as something that is self and other, as something that is immigrant and migrant and refugee all at once. Our bodies are contemporary, of the moment, now, but created by something that has an incredible legacy and temporal reach. We might begin, as Latour does, to consider DNA as something that is multitemporal and our analysis and understanding of it to be aware of this shifting complexity. DNA is something that suggests, following Latour, that 'we have never been modern'; indeed, the concept of modernity is problematic and unethical, and does not allow us to consider our actual, polytemporal natures. We might also look at the little-quoted section of Latour's work that comes slightly earlier:

> Let us suppose, for example, that we are going to regroup the contemporary events along a spiral rather than a line ... Elements that appear remote if

we follow the spiral may turn out to be quite nearby if we compare loops. (Latour 1993: 73)

The challenge to linearity that Latour outlines here is a line that lives in two plane dimensions, which bears some resemblance to a helix (helix is sometimes translated into French as 'spirale'). In this telling the event is a flexible thing, flickering in and out of temporal actualization. In later work Latour discusses 'idealized materialism' in his attack on the way that the whole 'machine' is conceptualized (Latour 2007: 139). He points out that the relationship between the idealized image and the material thing itself is crucial, and the interrelation between the two states – material and rendered – highlights the problems of iteration. This ability to hold something as simultaneously real/now and conceptual/then points to a complexity of comprehension and a fundamental ambiguity inherent in these new theoretical positions.

How have these opportunities and theoretical insights gained over the past decade been applied in practice? How might we 'read' the new human articulated by aDNA and archaeology using these tools? Many writers have turned to new archaeological and aDNA data in order to think carefully about what it means to be human, from Doris Lessing's transhistorical undermining of anthropocentric gender in her plotless last novel *The Cleft* (2007) to Nicola Barker's timeslip DNA structures in *Darkmans* (2007) and Kazuo Ishiguro's meditation upon prehistoric trauma in *The Buried Giant* (2015). In order to reflect upon the impact of archaeological innovation and aDNA on literary aesthetics, I conclude with three brief examples that each conceive of temporality in new ways through a consideration of the interrelationship between DNA, race and human identity. I examine writing by Ali Smith, Carol Ann Duffy and Paul Beatty, to think about the ways that literary texts engage with and open up debates about the self in relation to time, genetics and history. In particular these writers respond to the new information being created by aDNA investigation, drawing on the polytemporality of DNA to reflect new modes of understanding the human. Each of these writers uses the innovations and insights of aDNA to understand the human as a multitemporal, conflicted and conflicting thing. They challenge normative structures of conceiving of humanness and of thinking of the human's relation to temporality. This challenge, I contend, is enabled by innovations in archaeogenetic practice.

Paul Beatty's prize-winning 2015 novel *The Sellout* is a highly aggressive and difficult satire on the notion of post-race as a concept. Beatty considers a variety of ways that 'race' might be challenged and discussed in the contemporary moment. Towards the novel's conclusion a black political activist attempts to gain white students entrance to a Los Angeles school that has been designated 'black only'. Foy Cheshire, subversive re-author of books like *The Pejorative-Free Adventures and Intellectual and Spiritual Journeys of African-American Jim and His Young Protégé, White Brother Huckleberry Finn, as They Go in Search of the Lost Black Family Unit* (95), is attempting to prove the 'blackness' of white students by appealing to a shared ancestry:

> Foy stepped to the head of the pack to take over negotiations, magically producing a small stack of DNA results. Flapping them, not in Charisma's face, but directly into the lens of the nearest TV camera. 'I have in my hand a list of results that show each one of these children has maternal roots tracing their ancestries back thousands of years to Kenya's Great Rift Valley.' (Beatty 2015: 254)

Foy attempts to make the white students black by showing their DNA to be traceable to Africa, as all humans eventually are. In order to challenge a racially based entrance premise (only black students can attend the school), Foy seeks to demonstrate that 'white' students have black antecedents. The children that Foy attempts to integrate are given 'new' identity by their DNA link to the past. They are able, in his formulation, to challenge contemporary race construction. Race becomes something subsumed by genetic signification, not external but somehow internal and related to deep history. Foy invokes a kind of warped deep history, and consequently Beatty's novel begins to suggest the possibility of the destruction of black/white binaries. The students are polytemporal, both now and then, and this in-betweenness – this potentiality – might impact upon them in the contemporary world. It also enables Foy to challenge the binary of race which Beatty attacks throughout *The Sellout*. The political purpose of the novel is the reimagining and contestation of black identity as something continually shifting, in contrast to whiteness that is considered to be a fixed, comprehendible, rational, identity. Turning this notion on its head in this section, Beatty satirizes the equation of whiteness with fixity by applying popular ideas of genetics and identity to it, ideas more often invoked around discussions of blackness. In so doing, Beatty demonstrates the redundancy of contemporary identity signifiers like race. Beatty's purpose in presenting these questions about identity and archaeologically inflected definitions of self is to suggest that 'whiteness' is not integral or even original. Indeed, the prehistorical context ensures that race is not innate but constructed. Structural racism and economic deprivation are the drivers of inequality, and these are highlighted by Beatty's use of DNA as a link to a central humanness. The newly defined human enabled by aDNA is potentially challenging to normative understanding of race and identity. At the same time, Foy's intervention is a joke, so Beatty also suggests the problems inherent in using DNA tests to construct a way of understanding the human.

A more experimental and theoretically self-aware way of engaging with time, history and genetics is found at the fractured conclusion of Ali Smith's *How to Be Both*. This book seems to use genetics as a way out of mainstream realism, as a way of destroying normative aesthetic categories. As such it presents the postgenomic human in conflict with the historical. The novel is divided into two distinct but related narratives. One details the grief of a contemporary girl, George, and her attempts to understand the death of her mother. The other, more experimental, section, voices Francesco del Cossa, a fifteenth-century artist that Smith conceives of as a girl brought up as a boy and further imagines as a kind of disembodied ghost in the book. In half of the print run of the book one narrative comes first; in the other half the other narrative comes first. Therefore experiences of the book are different, around two poles of possibility. By reading them in one order the reader imposes a kind of temporal ordering, a hierarchy of precedence. This challenge to temporal linearity is common in contemporary fiction, seen in Sarah Waters's reverse narrative in her novel *The Nightwatch*. Like Waters, Smith has a desire to subvert the heteronormative novel form and in one sense the dual narrative is simply an experimental strategy to highlight this genre's concerns with control, linearity and becoming.

While the majority of the book is written in prose, the more experimental section told in the sixteenth-century artist's voice uses a kind of poetry at the beginning and end of this narrative. As the voice swims into existence the prose figures itself as a helix. In the final section of the text the writing disintegrates again and there are three pages of helix curl:

> the curve of the eyebone
> of the not yet born
> hello all the new bones
> hello all the old
> hello all the everything
> to be
> made and
> unmade
> both (Smith 2014: 372)

This section seems to dramatize Latour's thoughts about simultaneity quoted earlier, suggesting that DNA is the conduit by which we might move between then and now. The voice is old and new, then and now, whole and fragmented; it is 'both'. Smith's conclusion seems to dramatize the potentiality of understanding history as genetic – not as linear and progressive and purposeful but as winding and strange and simultaneous. Smith's prose poem is simultaneously fragmenting as it is producing meaning, formally disintegrating while pointing towards something ineffable. The form mimics a helix, emphasized by the dual-narrative structure of the book, two stories nested within one another but never touching. The book is overtly concerned with 'real-world' rendering of DNA, as one protagonist finds a memorial to the discovery of DNA, an inlaid pathway that one can follow through the Cambridgeshire countryside. DNA is literally a linear, directional path in the novel, something that might give physical shape to one's movement (geographical and temporal) through the world. With her conclusion and her twinned narratives Smith puts pressure on this linearity and on the form of the novel, particularly the importance of realism and coherence, in order to conceive of an historical experience somehow material and ethereal, simultaneous and particular, 'made and/ unmade/ both'. How to render this new 'human', at once past and present, textual and imagined, ghostly and material, is the challenge that Smith presents us with. DNA gives the human a new dimensionality, and the novel's fragmentary form suggests that DNA enables a complex, multitemporal understanding of the human.

The ways that literature might conceive of the interrelation of science and human might be seen in Carol Ann Duffy's sonnet 'Richard', read as part of the ceremony of reinterment of Richard III. At the service the British actor Benedict Cumberbatch performed the poem written by Duffy, the former UK poet laureate. This event was an extraordinary conflation of the material, the imagined and the nationalistic. Cumberbatch was preparing to play Shakespeare's Richard III for the BBC when he was asked to perform at the ceremony; it was also widely reported that he was directly related to the 'real' Richard. These interlinkings – genealogical, aesthetic, historical, imagined – show the strange new materiality of the king in the contemporary world. The multiple, uncanny echoes of the event are explored by Duffy's poem which exists in, and meditates upon, this multitemporality, particularly in its address to Richard III's body as a 'human braille' (Duffy 2015). Read aloud at the televised church ceremony and then published afterwards in *The Guardian*, Duffy's public poem is a sonnet, a historically inflected form that lives with multiple echoes. It is surely meant to recall the most famous of Richard III's 'writers' and a key sonneteer, William Shakespeare. It refers to The strangeness of the interment of the king and to his being dug up and, most importantly, publicly *defined*, in new contexts and with new tools, both intellectual and physical. Duffy's poem considers the human and the genetic, conceiving of something in-between, material and ghostly, indistinct and scientifically physical. Richard is conjured by archaeogenetics, but must live somehow in the imagination, and Duffy's poem attempts to understand this life/non-life. The sonnet as a form is material and an echo, part of a long tradition of poems articulating the difficulty of rendering humanness in words. The poem explicitly references the actuality of Richard's body being brought up from the mud:

> My bones, scripted in light, upon cold soil,
> a human braille. My skull, scarred by a crown,
> emptied of history. (ll. 1–3)

The sense of the interrelation between language, skeleton, writing, mud and 'braille' figures the complexity of Richard in the now, as a thing and a dream, something imaginary, a ghost, material and imaginary. This very physical (although textual) representation of the body as raised from the mud, and then defined by science, evokes the interrelation of the scripted, the imagined, the material and the genetic. Duffy's poem opens by taking the material out of the discourse of history. The body is interpreted and written, both earthy and human. Richard is interpreted into being, made into an event, identified and given identity. Yet the end of the poem, shifting after the volta, considers an interrelationship between then and now. Duffy invokes something uncannily atemporal, suggestive of both Macbeth's Witches and a strange performance of identity:

> or I once dreamed of this, your future breath
> in prayer for me, lost long, forever found;
> or sensed you from the backstage of my death,
> as kings glimpse shadows on a battleground. (ll. 11–14)

Richard interacts physically with the present but is a shadow, an afterimage. Like Smith, Duffy uses seeming paradoxes ('lost long, forever found') to emphasize the strange simultaneity of existence. The poem is infused with Shakespeare, particularly the idea of what is lost being found from *The Winter's Tale*, but his influence is particularly invoked in 'the backstage of my death'. This is a kind of afterlife place, suggesting a relationship between the death event, the afterlife representation and the current moment of ceremony. New types of data, new modes of investigation and new epistemologies presented by biological, biogenetic and biochemical research are challenging our models of the human. As these writers demonstrate, this new information is undermining more traditional understandings of history and identity. In particular, ways of conceiving of the human using aDNA investigation are both tremendously exciting – they might allow challenges to temporality, gender, race – while at the same time troubling and worrying given the associated return of racist science and essentialist categorization. These authors mobilize this emerging space in order to critique race, linearity and epistemology. Through briefly considering their work we can see how aDNA is shifting ways of understanding and representing the human. Duffy and Smith respond to a new fragility in the body of the human, a translucent quality that DNA contributes. They point out the increasing contradictions of which our bodies are now made up, the new multitemporalities that are defined at a molecular, genetic level. Beatty reminds us that the physical must always live in the structural, inasmuch as the human body is never simply science, never just DNA, always more than the sum of its genetic parts. Archaeology, genetic science and narrative aesthetics are all struggling to define the human in a new set of contexts, data and methodology. The legibility of our species is increasingly blurred, as new information and discovery lead more to complexity than to clarity.

Notes

1 'Driven by archaeological discoveries, but far from being simply a reflection of them, the idea of "prehistory" goes beyond the strict scientific definition (which generally centres on the emergence of humanity until the invention of writing). In this alternative reading "prehistory" shapes the imagination of modernity, enabling a means to challenge notions of temporality' (Debray, Labrusse and Staavrinaki 2019: 14, my translation).
2 Recent research suggests various different types of hominin groups interbred including Neanderthal and Denisovans, see Teixeira and Cooper (2019).
3 See the essays of Coole and Frost (2010).

References

Barad, K. (2007), *Meeting the Universe Halfway*, Durham, NC: Duke University Press.
Beatty, P. (2015), *The Sellout*, London: OneWorld.
Buckley, R., M. Morris, J. Appleby, T. King, D. O'Sullivan and L. Foxhall (2013), '"The King in the Car Park": New Light on the Death and Burial of Richard III in the Grey Friars Church, Leicester, in 1485', *Antiquity*, 87: 519–38.
Coole, D., and S. Frost (eds) (2010), *New Materialisms: Ontology, Agency, and Politics*, Durham, NC: Duke University Press.
Debray, C., R. Labrusse and M. Staavrinaki (2019), 'Introduction', in C. Debray, R. Labrusse and M. Staavrinaki (eds), *Préhistoire: Une Énigme Moderne*, 14–27, Paris: Éditions Pompidou.
Duffy, C. A. (2015), 'Richard', *The Guardian*, 26 March. Available online https://www.theguardian.com/books/2015/mar/26/richard-iii-by-carol-ann-duffy.

El-Haj, N. (2012), *The Genealogical Science*, Chicago, IL: University of Chicago Press.

Felski, R. (2011), 'Context Stinks!', *New Literary History*, 42 (4): 573–91.

Frei, K., U. Mannering, K. Kristiansen, M. E. Allentoft, A. S. Wilson, I. Skals, S. Tridico, M. L. Nosch, E. Willerslev, L. Clarke and R. Frei (2015), 'Tracing The Dynamic Life Story of a Bronze Age Female', *Scientific Reports*, 5 (10431): doi:10.1038/srep10431.

French, B. (2014), 'Remains of Ancient Child Ceremoniously Buried', *Billings Gazette*, 28 June. Available online http://billingsgazette.com/news/state-and-regional/montana/remains-of-ancient-child-ceremoniously-reburied/article_3fcc174d-6f01-55b9-9923-96c9223ecda8.html (accessed 5 July 2017).

Furholt, M. (2018), 'Massive Migrations? The Impact of Recent aDNA Studies on Our View of Third Millennium Europe', *European Journal of Archaeology*, 21 (2): 159–91.

Gil Harris, J. (2008), *Untimely Matter*, Philadelphia: University of Pennsylvania Press.

Gilroy, P. (2000), *Against Race*, Cambridge, MA: Harvard University Press.

Haber, M., M. Mezzavilla, Y. Xue and C. Tyler-Smith (2016), 'Ancient DNA and the Rewriting of Human History: Be Sparing with Occam's Razor', *Genome Biology*, 17 (1): 10.1186/s13059-015-0866-z.

Harari, Y. (2015), *Sapiens: A Brief History of Humankind*, New York: Harper Collins.

Johannsen, N., G. Larson, D. Meltzer and M. Vander Linden (2017), 'A Composite Window into Human History', *Science*, 356 (6343): 1118–20.

Kenneally, C. (2015), *The Invisible History of the Human Race*, Harmondsworth: Penguin.

King, T. et al. (2014), 'Identification of the Remains of King Richard III', *Nature Communications*, 5 (5631): doi:10.1038/ncomms6631.

Kirby, V. (2013), *Quantum Anthropologies*, Durham, NC: Duke University Press.

Latour, B. (1993), *We Have Never Been Modern*, trans. C. Porter, Cambridge, MA: Harvard University Press.

Latour, B. (2007), 'Can We Get Our Materialism Back, Please?', *ISIS*, 98: 138–42.

Leys, R. (2011), 'The Turn to Affect', *Critical Inquiry*, 37: 434–72.

Malabou, C. (2008), *What Should We Do with Our Brains?*, trans. S. Rand, New York: Fordham University Press.

Malabou, C. (2017), 'The Brain of History or the Mentality of the Anthropocene', *South Atlantic Quarterly*, 116 (1): 39–53.

Malafouris, L. (2013), *How Things Shape the Mind*, Cambridge, MA: MIT Press.

Massumi, B. (2002), *Parables for the Virtual*, Durham, NC: Duke University Press.

Mathieson, I., and Skoglund, P. (2018), 'Ancient Human Genomics: The First Decade', *Annual Review of Genomics and Human Genetics*, 19: 381–404.

Meyer, M. et al. (2016), 'Nuclear DNA Sequences from the Middle Pleistocene Sima de los Huesos Hominins', *Nature*, 531: 504–7.

Mithen, S. (2003), *After the Ice: A Global Human History*, London: Orion.

Nelson, A. (2016), *The Social Life of DNA*, Boston, MA: Beacon Press.

Pickrell, J., and D. Reich (2014), 'Toward a New History and Geography of Human Genes Informed by Ancient DNA', *Trends in Genetics*, 30 (9): 377–89.

Pravinchandra, S. (2016), 'One Species, Same Difference? Postcolonial Critique and the Concept of Life', *New Literary History*, 47 (1): 27–48.

Rasmussen, M. et al. (2010), 'Ancient Human Genome Sequence of an Extinct Paleo-Eskimo', *Nature*, 463: 757–62.

Rasmussen, M. et al. (2014), 'The Genome of a Late Pleistocene Human from a Clovis Burial Site', *Nature*, 506: 225–9.

Rasmussen, M. et al. (2015), 'The Ancestry and Affiliations of Kennewick Man', *Nature*, 523: 455–8.

Reich, D. et al. (2010), 'Genetic History of an Archaic Hominin Group from Denisova Cave in Siberia', *Nature*, 468: 2053–60.

Renfrew, C. (2008), *Prehistory: The Making of the Human Mind*, New York: Random House.

Renfrew, C. (2010), 'Archaeogenetics – Towards a "New Synthesis"?', *Current Biology*, 20 (4): 162–5.

Rose, N. (2013), 'The Human Sciences in a Biological Age', *Theory, Culture & Society*, 30 (1): 3–34.

Slon, V. et al. (2018), 'The Genome of the Offspring of a Neanderthal Mother and a Denisovan Father', *Nature*, 561: 113–16.

Smith, A. (2014), *How to Be Both*, London: Hamish Hamilton.

TallBear, K. (2013), *Native American DNA: Tribal Belonging and the False Promise of Genetic Science*, Minneapolis: University of Minnesota Press.

Teixeira, J., and A. Cooper (2019), 'Using Hominin Introgression to Trace Modern Human Dispersals', *PNAS*, 116 (31): 15327–32.

Thomas, J. (2012), 'Not Yet Far Enough', *American Historical Review*, 117 (3): 794–803.

Zimmer, C. (2016), 'Eske Willerslev is Rewriting History with DNA', *New York Times*, 16 May. Available online https://www.nytimes.com/2016/05/17/science/eske-willerslev-ancient-dna-scientist.html (accessed 5 July 2017).

2

Jack London and *Before Adam*: Ahead of his time, or a cautionary tale in the study of prehistoric hominins?

James Walker and David Clinnick

When prehistoric archaeologists and palaeoanthropologists describe the evolutionary line of descent for humans, they create a narrative. In this respect, they are often comparable to storytellers and authors as interlocutors of the human past. Writers of fiction, of course, are not always constrained to scientific facts, whereas the narratives told by archaeologists and palaeoanthropologists are tied closely to the framework provided by available scientific data. Traditionally, this data has been derived from fossil remains and artefactual evidence, although more recently, palaeogenetics and other means of enquiry have contributed significantly to the investigative repertoire at our disposal (e.g. Krings et al. 1997; Green et al. 2010). This chapter explores how works of fiction may seemingly pre-empt narratives told by contemporary science. What can palaeofiction (a unique blend of science fiction and prehistorical fiction) offer to academic palaeonarratives of human evolution, especially now that we know that there were once other hominins who looked like us, and maybe acted like us too? In an act of seeming prescience, one such story – *Before Adam*, by Jack London, serialized between 1906 and 1907 – portrays a prehuman history that reflects many traits now understood as crucial indicators of modern and uniquely human behaviour. Can such a novel tell us anything about the current state of our knowledge, or how we construct it? How was it that London was able to seemingly anticipate these issues, and what does it say about our modes of inquiry as archaeologists and palaeoanthropologists that he had this ability?

What is a modern human?

New findings in archaeological and palaeoanthropological research mean that our understanding of what it means to be a modern human is constantly being updated. The recent discovery and acceptance of at least three new species of *Homo* in the twenty-first century (*floresiensis*, *naledi* and in 2019 *luzonensis*) have all prompted major reconsiderations of previously accepted theories of human evolution and the history of our genus. Within the species of *Homo sapiens*, archaeologists and anthropologists have traditionally distinguished between anatomically modern *Homo sapiens* (AMHS) and behaviourally (or cognitively) modern *Homo sapiens* – that is to say, fully modern humans. Other species of hominin are differentiated from *Homo sapiens* in terms of their anatomical morphology and their behavioural traits. Yet the differences used to distinguish ourselves and our more recent ancestors (*Homo sapiens*) from other species of hominin – or our non-modern ancestors – have become increasingly complicated.

Archaeologists who distinguish between anatomically (early/archaic *Homo sapiens*) and behaviourally modern (later/modern *Homo sapiens*) humans have done so through artefacts or features of the archaeological record which they argue could only have been produced by beings with certain (human) traits (Galway-Whitham, Cole and Stringe 2019: Fig. 2). The artefacts are seen as indicative of behaviours, and the appearance of new behaviours is seen as a reflection of changes in our cognitive capacity, and thus elevated in significance (Hoffecker 2017: 94). But why should, for example, the appearance of a particular stone tool type, or personal ornamentation, be considered as indicative of cognitive ability? Their significance relies on the assumption that they represent watershed moments in the past: the first evidence of a capacity, or need, for expression of interpersonal style; an ability to conceive of a raw material in a fundamentally different way; the earliest evidence of the imagination necessary to create and appreciate artistic forms; the ability to adapt culturally rather than genetically (Noah Harari 2014). Discussions of human modernity have also often entailed comparison to hominins deemed as non-modern, most frequently, as our closest extinct relatives, *Homo neanderthalensis*. Neanderthals are often described as being anatomically different from early modern humans, even though an increasing amount of evidence suggests that they had the cognitive capacity for at least some of the behaviours that were traditionally seen as the preserve of modern humans.[1] The apparent 'cognitive gap' between our ancestors and their contemporaries is increasingly contested (Villa and Roebrooks 2014: 7).

The relatively recent revelation that *neanderthalensis* did indeed interbreed with *Homo sapiens* (Green et al. 2010) further closes the gap between our species and theirs – evidencing a closeness between the two that many had previously been reluctant to countenance. While Neanderthals have often been seen as our morphologically more robust, if not intellectually lacking, cousins, we, that is to say, modern humans (*Homo sapiens*), had ancestors who were as biologically human as we are today, yet seemingly lacked the cognitive faculties for what are deemed modern behaviours. The earliest fossil remains of individuals agreed to be AMHS lack the accompanying artefactual evidence typically held as indicative of these behaviours (Tattersall 2019). Throughout much of the latter half of the twentieth century, it was widely held that modern behaviour developed when *Homo sapiens* spread to Eurasia around 40,000 years ago, under what was called the 'Human', 'Upper Palaeolithic' or 'Cognitive' Revolution. It is still widely believed that the modern humans who arrived in Europe in the Upper Palaeolithic possessed a capacity for complex behaviours beyond that of the native Neanderthal population (Papagiani and Morse 2015: 156). However, it has now been recognized that the Upper Palaeolithic was not the point in time when our ancestors became modern. Consequently, terms such as Human, Palaeolithic or Cognitive Revolution have become rarer in archaeology in recent years, especially in the wake of several influential critiques (McBrearty and Brooks 2000; Gamble 2007; Mellars et al. 2007).

Despite growing arguments for comparably sophisticated intelligence among Neanderthals in the face of mounting archaeological evidence that they (and perhaps other species of hominin too) possessed behavioural complexity (e.g. Villa and Roebrooks 2014), the idea of a cognitive revolution between forty and thirty thousand years ago has remained an enduringly popular narrative, among both the public and some in the academic community (see, e.g. Noah Harari's formulation of the hypothesis in his 2011/14 work of popular science *Sapiens*). Although it has become more common among archaeologists, since the work of McBrearty and Brooks (2000), to look for evidence of human modernity emerging in Africa tens of thousands of years prior to humans' dispersal into Europe, various elements of the Cognitive Revolution model have endured, and there remains an attachment to the idea that at some point in our history our ancestors developed a capacity for behaviours that are uniquely and definingly human (behaviours such as visual art and music) – those which distinguish us from other *Homo* species (see Hoffecker 2017: 97). It has proved difficult for many to let go of the idea that complex social behaviours are the preserve of humans and that the appearance of modern *looking* humans did not necessarily align with the appearance of behaviours that we deem to be characteristic of a modern brain (see Hoffecker 2017: 12, 97 for summary). In this view, Neanderthals become the yardstick against which our own success is measured. As Papagianni and Morse remark in *The Neanderthals Rediscovered*: 'From our perspective as *Homo sapiens*, it can be tempting to look back on human evolution with a sense of triumph and destiny' (2015: 11).

There is clearly a strongly emotive appeal in viewing the past in this way. The idea that there is a fundamental difference between us and other hominins offers a potential explanation for how it is that we came to be the only species of our genus left alive on the planet. Many narratives of the final steps we took towards the present day in our evolutionary journey have often been inextricably tied to the narratives of demise associated with our closest relatives, the Neanderthals (e.g. Pfeiffer 1969). The poor and simple Neanderthals didn't stand a chance, so the story goes, even if they did possess some semblance of our own faculties, their brains were no match for ours. This story, however, has proved to be incorrect. As reflected in the titles of recent popular science books such as *The Humans Who Went Extinct* (Finlayson 2010) and *Neanderthals Rediscovered* (Papagianni and Morse 2015), the relationship between *Homo sapiens* and Neanderthals is more complex than was previously understood. We now know that Neanderthals could interbreed with some *Homo sapiens* (Green et al. 2010). Moreover *Homo sapiens* and Neanderthals cannot always easily be distinguished on the basis of physiology, as Matt Cartmill contends, 'Anatomically modern human has no clear or established meaning, and is basically a scientific sounding way of evading the fact that there is no agreement on the list and distribution of the defining autapomorphies of the human species' (2001: 104). Hackett and Dennell argue in a similar vein that 'Neanderthals illuminate what we are [because] we are defined osteologically by their (alleged) non-Neanderthal traits, or by their alleged "modern" behaviour, even though we know the boundaries are blurred' (2003: 825). There are even some cases where, prior to the spread of *Homo sapiens* throughout Eurasia, Neanderthals appear to have succeeded (if not out-competed) humans in the Levant, highlighting both the complexities of the palaeoanthropological and archaeological data, and indeed the relationship between our ancestors and their Neanderthal brethren (Shea 2003). That one species won out in the long run seems clear, but that one was superior to another seems, at best, increasingly conditional.

What makes a modern human, and thus what makes *us* human as we understand ourselves today, is no longer immediately clear. However, even if there were significant differences between Neanderthals and our ancestors, it is we, in the here and now, who decide what constitutes evidence of modern behaviour and label this as what it means to be fully human. The idea of the Neanderthal often serves as a mirror, an image, both of ourselves and of what we might have been. Fiction has had a role to play in how other hominins have been constructed as what historians of science and literary critics call the 'other' (Madison 2016: 430) or, in the case of Neanderthals, 'same but other' (Drell 2000: 20). Stringer and Gamble argued that 'many authors have used Neanderthals to explore the present', often with the result that they are expelled from the human category (1993: 31). Yet it is telling that the overwhelming majority of palaeofiction is devoted, if not to early modern humans then to our Neanderthal cousins (Hackett and Dennell 2003), who unlike a more visibly removed species of hominin (such as the more ancient and much smaller *Homo habilis*), appear to have much more in common with ourselves. It is easy to see that the idea of a creature that not only looked and acted much like us but was also, at some fundamental level, unlike us, is inherently appealing for authors of palaeofiction, especially as depictions of our ancestors and hominin relatives in fiction and other media are often projections of ourselves and our current social values (Drell 2000; Hackett and Dennel 2003; McNaab 2012; Madison 2016). Given that, as McNaab notes, science fiction both reflects and shapes the public's views of evolution (2012: 335), how might palaeofiction from another era intervene in current debates about what it means to be a modern human, and how we relate to Neanderthals and other hominins?

Jack London's *Before Adam*

Jack London has been described as 'the first great writer in the English language to give his full sympathetic attention to prehistoric fiction' (Ruddick 2009: 43). However his 1907 novel *Before Adam* is one that, with a few exceptions (see Sommer 2005), has largely been overlooked by archaeological and anthropological professionals interested in palaeofiction, even though it continues to provoke discussion among literary critics concerned with London's portrayals of race, species and the deep past (Bender 2011; Wahida 2012; Nichols 2013; Hsu 2019). *Before Adam* is about an ancestral being (in an unspecified location) who was not among the most primitive of humans but also not among the most advanced – those who are implied in the novel as being those that gave rise to humans today. In this respect, it is the story of a missing link, connecting something that is barely human, to something that is comfortably so. The novel tells the story of Big Tooth and his day-to-day existence within the Folk, whose evolutionary status is above the arboreal Tree People and beneath the technologically sophisticated Fire People. While the Tree People symbolize nature, the Fire People are symbolic of culture (Ruddick 2009: 43). The Folk are somewhere in between. Big Tooth struggles to survive alongside the brutish and oppressive Red Eye, an atavistic member of the Folk who terrorizes any who dare not appease him, while the Folk also struggle to survive the threat posed by the encroachment of the more advanced Fire People.

The story of Big Tooth's adventures with his friend Lop Ear, and love interest the Swift One, is told through a modern-day narrator, who dreams that Big Tooth is his distant ancestor. The idea that it was possible to remember experiences of ancestors via a racial memory or dream was popularized in the early twentieth century by psychoanalysts Freud and Jung (Sommer 2005). In the novel, the narrator imagines that 'there must be a medium whereby these memories are transmitted from generation to generation […] It carries the memories of the whole evolution of the race [...] some strains of germplasm carry an excessive freightage of memories – [and] are, to be scientific, more atavistic than other strains; and such a strain is mine' (London 1907: 10). It is through this narrative device that London first complicates the apparent hierarchies of the groups in *Before Adam*; while it is implied that the Folk face imminent extinction and that the Fire People are the ancestors of modern humans, this cannot be the case if London is recalling Big Tooth's memories as those of his ancestor (cf. Pankake 1976: 46).

London often courted controversy in his writing and sought to defend his position through professing scientific credentials. He is notable as one of the most iconic authors of the Progressive Era in early-twentieth-century North America and was one of the first to achieve fame within his own lifetime. His works were received with both acclaim and scorn and have continued to divide critics long after his death in 1916. He is known to have been an avid reader of various scholars and intellectuals, including Darwin, Huxley, Spencer, Haeckel, Marx, Nietzsche, Freud and Jung (Harpham 1975; Qualtiere 1982; Lindquist 1997; Berkove 2004; Ruddick 2009; Nichols 2013), and prided himself on his reading of contemporary science; he referred to his own library of books that he read for the preparation of his writings as his 'tools' (Sommer 2005). London was challenged over the originality of *Before Adam* by Stanley Waterloo, author of '*The Story of Ab: A Tale of the Time of the Cave Man*' published in 1897, a work of palaeofiction that Waterloo argued London had plagiarized. London's characteristically belligerent rebuttal was that his own work was partly a response to Waterloo's: an attempt to amend the lack of scientific rigour in his accuser's work (Hensley 2002).

While he saw himself as a communicator of contemporary science, London's work must also be understood in the context of his complex political and social views. He was renowned for his socialist ideals, and *Before Adam* was the first of his works to be authorized for publication in the Soviet Union (Pankake 1976: 39). He was so well known there that Lenin's wife Krupskaya read London's *Love of Life* to Lenin on his deathbed (Berliner 2008: 72). London was also well known, however, for his racism, having once infamously declared himself to have been 'first of all a white man and only then a socialist' (see Hopkins 2003: 91). He was also among the most celebrated of novelists to advocate Spencerian notions of Social Darwinism (Mitchell 1998: 317), which had become popular in some quarters of American society in the early twentieth century (Bettinger, Garvey and Tushingham 2015: 21). This mixture of beliefs permeates much of his writing, meaning London has come to be regarded, often disdainfully, as 'one of the most representative men of a confused and uncertain generation' (Harpham 1975: 23) or a 'materialist, Socialist, Darwinian, Nietzschean, [attempting to ride simultaneously] upon the backs of all these horses, even when they were galloping furiously in different directions' (Wagenknecht 1952: 224 in Berliner 2008: 55). His racism has proved particularly unpalatable for some, being dismissed as 'a prototype of the violence-worshipping Fascist intellectual if ever there was one' (Kazin 1942: 111 in Hopkins 2003: 98), but other critics have acknowledged more nuance in his views, noting his 'empathetic portrayals of racial others, and at other times, jarring crudities about white superiority' (Reesman 2009).

London's conflicting and changing views on race are reflected in *Before Adam*, in which his portrayal of evolutionary progression as a transition from natural primitiveness to relative sophistication mirrors contemporaneous narratives about the perceived humanity of native Americans. London exhibited great curiosity about the 'discovery' of Ishi, the so-called 'last wild Indian' in 1911, and was interested in Ishi's portrayal by the media as a civilized relic of a past primitiveness (Crow 1996). Ishi inspired London's character Ushu, the archer, lost from his own people but taken in by others in *The Star Rover* (1915). Although the Ishi case did not arise until after the publication of *Before Adam*, it is clear that London saw, in his narrative dialectics of wild and domestic, natural and human, a displacement of contemporary humanity from its natural environment, setting or home, of the sort that Ishi came to represent (Crow 1996). In his study of London's interest in Ishi, Charles Crow highlights the incongruity of London's apparent racism and affinity for Social Darwinism with his apparent disdain for the Fire People in *Before Adam*, although it has been argued that by this time he was eschewing Spencerian evolution in favour of a Huxleyan stance on ethical progress (Berkove 2004: 244–6). Crow notes the irony of the clear parallel between the Fire People's attack on the Folk and the colonial violence of nineteenth-century America, violence of the kind which led to the destruction of Ishi's village in 1865 (1996: 50). Describing the Fire People as 'the most terrible of all the hunting animals that ranged the primeval world' (1907: 85) – at least from the perspective of the persecuted

Big Tooth – London appears to reject the trope of the racially pure hero pitted against inferior villains (Martin 1983: 41). Although he refrains from making the Fire People the moral superiors of the story, London nevertheless places them at the top of a technological if not cultural and cognitive progression hierarchy, and in doing so created one of the first literary representations of a tripartite division of human prehistory.

Modern facts and old stories

What makes *Before Adam* a prescient story for more recent scientific narratives of human evolution? London's prehuman categorizations are not directly analogous to the tripartite divisions used for European prehistory – Palaeolithic, Mesolithic and Neolithic – but his conceptualization of arboreal (primitive archaic?), fire (fully modern?) and folk (something in between?) is striking when viewed as a linear evolutionary chain, with a primitive ape, a precociously modern ape and an evolutionary missing link in the form of the Folk that we assume must have existed between ourselves and our seemingly more primitive relatives. By incorporating three distinct but contemporaneous groups of ancestral beings through his take on the tripartite system, London's tale invokes comparisons between them. This makes various details given about the different groups comparable to more recent archaeological and palaeoanthropological narratives of human evolution, as London is not simply describing a single form of primitive human but multiple gradations thereof. Furthermore, a number of these differences – some buried within the descriptive narrative of the plot – anticipated various landmark traits among more contemporary scientific accounts of what makes humans fully modern (Table 2.1).

In contemporary archaeological and palaeoanthropological studies of human evolution, the cognitive capacity for advanced human behaviours has often been identified as what constitutes a fully modern human (e.g. Deacon and Deacon 1999: 100), 'the final stage of what made hominids human' (Willoughby 2008: 182), something, it is regularly assumed, that will be evident in the archaeological record (Hoffecker 2017). Although our notions of what, where and when to look for archaeological evidence of traits that signify

Table 2.1 Passages from *Before Adam* (London 1907) that offer some type of trait-based distinction between different gradations of modernity and modern behaviours

Trait	Passage	Page	Explanation
Control of Fire After observing the Fire People around a campfire and the protection it afforded from nocturnal predators, Big Tooth and Lop Ear attempt to emulate them by stoking the embers once left and inadvertently start a forest fire.	'We too were Fire-Men, we thought, as we danced there, white gnomes in the conflagration. The dried grass and underbrush caught fire, but we did not notice it.'	40	Although the control of fire is not a trait of exclusively modern behaviour, it is nevertheless regarded as an important innovation, particularly with regard to the consumption of cooked meat and the changes this made to brain development.
Forward Planning and Teamwork Although lacking fire, the Folk are able to evade predation through rudimentary teamwork. The Fire People are capable of even more advanced coordination.	'Behind the Fire People I could see the little wizened old hunter directing it all.' 'but they had order and plan, while we Folk had none.'	95 and 90	Complex social networking behaviours and the advanced planning strategies they can afford have often been assumed to be the preserve of 'modern' cognition.
Compassion and Empathy Marrow-Bone, an elder among the Folk, is unable to fend for himself, being weak in body and gentle in disposition. He is tolerated if not assisted by many of the Folk, and even regarded by Big Tooth with affection.	'Sometimes old Marrow-Bone had sick spells and was unable to leave the cave. Then it was that the Hairless One filled the gourd [with water] for him.'	42	Evidence of compassionate care for the elderly and infirm, especially if assumed to be a strain on resources, has been argued in the past as denoting complex social relations typical of modern behaviours.
Storage Marrow-Bone, who is also arguably the cleverest and most experienced of the Folk, in addition to being the eldest, uses gourds to store water.	'He kept a supply of drinking-water in his cave, which cave belonged to his son, the Hairless One, who permitted him to occupy a corner of it.'	42	Storage is often read as evidence of planning for times of need in the future, and thus evidence of advanced planning strategies, and the ability to speculate if not predict the future.

Trait	Passage	Page	Explanation
Domestication of the Dog Big Tooth plays with a wild dog until Lop Ear's gluttony gets the better of him.	'I might have brought about the domestication of the dog. And this was something that the Fire people […] had not yet achieved.'	44	Although the domestication of the dog is not a distinguishing feature of behavioural modernity among humans (note the Fire People do not possess this), it is certainly the case that we regard animal domestication as solely the preserve of fully modern humans.
Communication of Knowledge and Learning After observing Marrow-Bone using the gourd to store water, Big Tooth and other members of the Folk also begin this practice.	'It never entered my head to fill the gourd with water and carry it into my cave.' and 'Imitation was strong in the Folk, and first one, and then another and another, procured a gourd and used it in a similar fashion.'	42	Transmittance of knowledge and different patterns of learning are often seen as key to the successful adoption and spread of innovations of the sort that comprise the archaeological trait-list used to assess modern behaviours.
Advanced Social Hierarchy The atavistic Red Eye, in many respects the most primitive of the Folk, may act with impunity as none can (or dare) stand up to him. By contrast, the Fire People are marshalled by an older individual with a limp, implying rank or respect rather than strength or physical ability as important for the Fire People.	'One of the Fire-Men was the wizened old hunter who limped.' and 'Behind the Fire People I could see the little wizened old hunter directing it all.'	84 and 95	Evidence of social stratification is difficult to see archaeologically but has sometimes been assumed to have been at least more prevalent if not more developed among modern humans than more archaic hominin groups.
Exploitation of Marine Resources In further evidence of trial-and-error-based learning, Big Tooth and Lop Ear learn first how to fish and then how to use rudimentary rafts after being forced by necessity. The Fire People, at the novel's end, are described as piloting a catamaran.	'Here we spent many hours each day, catching fish and playing on the logs, and here, one day, we learned our first lessons in navigation. The log on which Lop-Ear was lying got adrift.'	56	Exploitation of marine resources (particularly shellfish) has been linked to developments in the brain that have been suggested as possibly connected to the emergence of modern behaviours. Furthermore, coastal migration routes are increasingly invoked in suggestions of migrations and diaspora of modern humans around the world.

(continued)

Table 2.1 Continued

Trait	Passage	Page	Explanation
Gendered Divisions within Society Female and male members of the Folk behave differently according to gendered expectations.	'By and by, except on unusual occasions, the men never carried any water at all, leaving the task to the women.'	43	This reinforcement of the tropes of 'man the hunter' and 'woman the gatherer' reflect gendered divisions that are sometimes argued to have been important in the management of extended social networks associated with modern humans.
Advanced Language London describes the quality of language in each of his three groups. While the Folk manage better than the Tree People, their communication falls short of full linguistic ability, which London links to a capacity for abstract thought.	'As I have said, our language was extremely meagre.' and 'But we Folk of the Younger World lacked speech.'	21 and 79	Advanced syntactical language and communication is often believed to be a correlate (cause or result) of behavioural modernity.
Structuration of Space The Folk inhabit caves, while the Fire People have constructed dwellings, organized into structured settlements. They are also comfortable exploring new territories.	'Sometimes the men and women tied tough vines about bundles of ferns and branches that they carried to the caves to sleep upon.'	43	More clearly structured use of space (such as divisions among domestic space) is often seen to become more pronounced and developed if not emergent as a result of behavioural modernity.
Composite Technology The Bow and Arrow, often regarded as a significant technological breakthrough, is a technological innovation unique to the Fire People.	'But he carried something in his hand that I had never seen before. It was a bow and arrow. But at that time a bow and arrow had no meaning for me. How was I to know that death lurked in that bent piece of wood?'	37–38	The ability to connect multi-component tools or multiple moving parts within a single technological device is often seen as an indication of advanced cognition necessary to comprehend abstract functionality.

Trait	Passage	Page	Explanation
Body Hair and Clothing Not only are the Fire-folk more hairless than the Folk, and certainly the Tree Folk, they possess clothing too. The Folk meanwhile have not invented clothes but are aware of their modesty.	'the next and inevitable step would have been the weaving of cloth. Clothes would have followed, and with covering our nakedness would have come modesty.'	43	Body hairlessness is not associated with modern humans, but likely happened at some point earlier in our ancestry. Certainly at the time at which London was writing, it was commonly imagined that other prehistoric hominins would have had thick body hair. Clothing, meanwhile, as much as becoming an expression of stylistic choice and identity, would have also served as a fundamental adaptation to harsh and cold climates.
Artistic Expression and Music While the Folk are capable of unifying to produce simple coordinated rhythms and communal vocalizations, this is neither complex nor melodious and seemingly unplanned.	'Some one seized a stick and began pounding a log. In a moment he had struck a rhythm. Unconsciously, our yells and exclamations yielded to this rhythm. It had a soothing effect upon us.' and 'whenever we were so drawn together we precipitated babel, out of which arose a unanimity of rhythm that contained within itself the essentials of art yet to come. It was art nascent.'	79	Artistic expression is often presumed to be predicated on a capacity for symbolic thought. This, in turn, it is often posited, is only possible with fully developed cognition.
Anatomical Physiology London describes differences in anatomical physiology between the three apes. The Tree Folk are similar in appearance to chimps or orang-utans in their stature, while the Folk have narrower hips than the Fire People.	'His hips were thin; and the legs, lean and hairy, were crooked and stringy-muscled. In fact, my father's legs were more like arms.'	15	Anatomy remains the cornerstone of palaeoanthropology and the main means by which humans are distinguished from other species of hominin in the fossil record. Craniometry in particular remains a frequently used metric to discuss aspects of prehistoric cognition.

(continued)

Table 2.1 Continued

Trait	Passage	Page	Explanation
Belief Systems Although London falls short of proscribing an actual religious system, he contrasts the fears of the Folk (predation) with those of the Fire People (the unknown).	'We had no germs of religion, no conceptions of an unseen world.' and 'As imagination grew it is likely that the fear of death increased until the Folk that were to come projected this fear into the dark and peopled it with spirits. I think the Fire People had already begun to be afraid of the dark in this fashion; but the reasons we Folk had for breaking up our hee-hee councils and fleeing to our holes were old Saber-Tooth, the lions and the jackals.'	80	The capacity for abstract thought allows the Fire People not only to fear the unknown but also to speculate about future scenarios in a way that is beyond the reasoning capacity of the Folk. The capacity for religious thought and the various behaviours associated with it (e.g. aspects of many mortuary rites) have often been seen to be indicative of advanced cognition.
Interbreeding It is strongly implied that Big Tooth (Folk) and the Swift One (Fire People) procreate.	'The Swift One and I managed to bring up one child, a boy.'	102	Animals of different species are typically described as being unable to create viable offspring. The discovery (in 2010) of Neanderthal DNA in modern-day humans was a surprise to many who had believed them to be a discretely different species to ourselves.

behaviours distinctive of behaviourally modern humans have changed over time, what has remained common is that archaeologists have wished to know why we survived and no other hominin did. With the realization that there were extinct beings closer to us than any currently living primate, archaeologists and palaeoanthropologists have felt compelled to define prehistoric hominins in terms of what they are not (i.e. us). In this sense, *Before Adam* explores uncomfortable territory that Darwin himself was (at least initially[2]) reticent to explore – 'human origins, and the extent of their continuity with other animal life' (Hopkins 2003: 99).

Many of the traits outlined in Table 2.1 do not correlate neatly with a binary division of modern or non-modern behaviours. The domestication of the dog, while only known among populations regarded as modern, is not itself associated with this transition. Equally, bipedal locomotion came long before our ancestors approximated anything that might be called behaviourally (or indeed anatomically) modern. London is not concerned with portraying any being as behaviourally modern (at least not in an explicit sense) but rather in distinguishing between three classes of ape on a spectrum of humanness. That Big Tooth is born a member of the Tree People, becomes a member of the Folk and reproduces with a probable member of the Fire People could betray some Lamarckian belief in transmutation, but equally it might serve to highlight the fluidity and ease with which London felt that a being may transition, perhaps even biologically, from beastliness to civility; 'were the Folk, before their destruction, in the process of becoming men? And did I and mine carry through this process? On the other hand, may not some descendant of mine have gone in to the Fire People and become one of them?' (London 1907: 241).

This reading is supported by the prevalence of atavism and recapitulation, not only in *Before Adam* but also in the science of the time in which he was writing (Sommer 2005). Red Eye, the tyrannically atavistic member of the Folk, is more at home among the Tree People by the end of the novel, while Big Tooth has progressed to become among the more intellectually enlightened of the Folk, despite his origins among the Tree People. For London, raw savagery and animal nature were still present in some, hidden beneath a veneer of civility, and while the Fire People are clearly the most advanced of these prehistoric hominins, London nevertheless accentuates the evolutionary remoteness of this people, including them with the Folk and the Tree People in the narrator's description of their doings as something that we would understand only as a 'screaming incoherence' (1907: 2). He is deliberately vague about how his characters relate biologically and how evolutionary descent works (Hopkins 2003: 98); they may represent different (albeit closely related) species (Nichols 2013) but London avoids providing a definitive answer (Hensley 2002: 36).

The narrative of *Before Adam* comprises a present-day narrator who dreams or 'remembers' his ancestor Big Tooth's life and thus tells the story with the knowledge of what would come to be, of how humans would develop: for example, 'And thus, in a fight, ended one of the earliest attempts to domesticate the dog' (London 1907: 47–8) and 'if once we wove withes into baskets, the next and inevitable step would have been the weaving of cloth. Clothes would have followed, and with covering our nakedness would have come our modesty' (1907: 43). Through this narrative technique, we know that whatever befell Big Tooth and his lineage, it ended up culminating in the narrator, who cannot but help relay the story of his ancestors through his own image, before stripping away certain elements. The narrator is simultaneously both a modern human and a descendent of Big Tooth, and his relationship with Big Tooth, if not his status in the here and now, is frequently confused: 'I often wonder about this line of descent. I, the modern, am incontestably a man; yet I, Big-Tooth, the primitive, am not a man' (London 1907: 104).

This conflation has parallels with the way that, as Hackett and Dennell have argued, both scientists and writers have built our own self-image by defining ourselves in terms of what our extinct relatives were not (2003). Without any closer point of reference for comparison, we, in the present, become the de facto benchmark against which we compare prehistoric hominins. Even when attempting to elicit these hominins' evolutionary history, and not our own, their stories are often told within the context of how they fare relative to either ourselves or other living primates. Tasked with explaining why our ancestors survived, and why other prehistoric hominins did not, scientific narratives of our own history elevate the significance of whatever causal factors were responsible. London does something similar in *Before Adam*, but by focusing on the individual, and changes that occur at a group level, he emphasizes chance and luck involved in making, repeating and communicating a discovery or innovation that will eventually lead to humanness. While concerned with the relationship between ourselves and our ancestors, London does not provide a neat answer as to what makes us human and does not seek to invoke any major single event or process as a catalyst for widescale behavioural development, as is often the case in scientific grand narratives (e.g. Hoffecker 2017: 94), although the parallel between the persecution (to possible extinction) of the Folk by the Fire People does parallel the enduringly popular notion that Neanderthals were driven to extinction by the arrival of modern humans in Eurasia.

Before Adam resists the temptation to set its ape-characters (early hominins) entirely apart from humans and instead encourages readers to empathize with their non-human ancestors. As John McNabb writes in his excellent account of British palaeofiction from the late nineteenth century:

> Fiction is an exploration of the human condition. It achieves its aim by placing imaginary characters in a variety of testing situations, and in so doing achieves a better understanding of human nature through the reactions of those characters. Thus authors invite readers to examine what their own reactions might have been. Science fiction simply pushes the envelope further. These writers define what it is to be human by testing their characters' humanity against ever more exotic challenges and extra-ordinary backgrounds. (2012: 289)

In communicating the story of Big Tooth, the Swift One and Lop Ear through a human narrator, London inflects the narrative with empathy that allows readers to relate to beings that are humanlike, if not actually human. For example, London imagines a scene where Lop Ear helps a wounded Big Tooth while fleeing the Fire People: 'the two of us, half grown-cubs, in the childhood of race, and the one mastering his fear, beating down his selfish impulse of flight, in order to stand by and succor the other' (London 1907: 40). Evidence that such care and compassion existed among Neanderthals is apparent from the remains of a male Neanderthal from Shanidar, in Iraq, which showed evidence of having sustained, and recovered, from a debilitating injury that demonstrates that this individual was looked after and cared for by others (Spikins, Rutherford and Needham 2010). London encourages his readers to see the human in the non-human and, in so doing, encourages empathy in a way that scientific considerations of the past are often loath to explore.

This is not to say that empathy is uniquely human – indeed evidence of empathy has been observed in other living primates (de Waal 2010) and contended in other prehistoric hominins (Wilson 2020) – but London uses empathy to allow us to relate to his characters as human, even while we are simultaneously being told how different they are from ourselves. Frequently throughout *Before Adam*, the narrator comments in frustration at Big Tooth's shortcomings and, as Hensley points out (2002: 34), confuses them for his own: 'But it was our inconsequentiality and stupidity that especially distresses me when I look back upon that life' (London 1907: 42). The narrator describes Big Tooth, at times, as though they are one and the same and, even when denigrating his intellect or status, does so from a position of a human contemporary serving as a referent. Scientists, understandably, seek to avoid straying into the realm of fiction, but London's novel acts as a reminder that empathy is an important aspect of narrating the past. Indeed all archaeologists, as Matthew Johnson explains, construct narratives built around empathy when they talk about the past, whether they realize they are doing so or not (2020: 114). For example, as Rob Foley wrote in *Humans Before Humanity*, 'the compassion inspired by the latent humanity in the eyes of a gorilla is testimony to the close affinities humans have with apes' (1995: 32).

Before Adam, like many other works of palaeofiction, gives readers a means of accessing connections between themselves and other species of hominin that scientific narratives, and particularly those concerned with emphasizing our own uniquity, rarely do. As Steven Mithen has surmised: 'Because their lifestyles are so alien to us, it seems clear how they should be studied: once we have reconstructed the behaviour of the earliest *Homo*, for instance, we try to understand it as if we were an ecologist trying to understand the behaviour of any other primate species' as opposed to when dealing with a being that approaches sufficiently modern levels of humanness, at which point we 'try to be more like an anthropologist than an ecologist' (1998: 129). Such biases, conscious or otherwise, may be as counterproductive as they are useful for understanding the history of our species in contrast to that of our closest relatives.

Conclusion

Chris Stringer and Clive Gamble once contended that, on the subject of our Neanderthal cousins, the 'scientific and popular worlds seem set on separate paths, with little exchange' (1993: 30–1). Certainly, archaeologists have sought to stress their own scientific credentials, sometimes in contraposition to purveyors of fiction: 'authors pictured our prehistoric ancestor as a kind of gorilla, violent and cruel, almost completely devoid of intelligence and tradition. Prehistoric archaeologists, who work with facts and scientific methods, more and more are able to substitute some degree of certain knowledge and probable hypotheses for these earlier fantasies' (Leroi-Gourhan [trans. Jacobson] 1989: 1). While it is true that authors of fiction do not have to keep their stories rooted in fact, it is also true that fiction has the capacity to reveal the stories, and ways of storytelling, that are integral to science. Misia Landau was one of the first to critically examine the role of narratology in the science of human evolution, noting that the narrative is integral to understanding any relationship or sequence, meaning that it is an unavoidable component of discourse: 'Consequently, they [scientists] may be unaware of the narrative propositions that inform their science' (1984: 262). Landau's analogy (1991) of human origins to myths, legends and fairy tales has continued to resonate among historians of science interested in the history of palaeoanthropology (Rees 2016) and has paved the way for several critiques of Neanderthal evolution from a similar perspective (Drell 2000; Hackett and Dennell 2003; Papagianni and Morse 2015). That the subtext of London's *Before Adam* foreshadows the development of an archaeological trait list for constituting behavioural modernity and that, through the telling of Big Tooth's story, he is able to invoke empathy for his characters while simultaneously informing readers that they are not comparably human to ourselves reveals underlying similarities in the narratology of palaeofiction and emerging scientific narratives of human evolution. As Ruth Tringham argues (albeit not directly about other hominins), archaeologists attempt 'to put words in the mouths of prehistoric actors, knowing that these words say more about us than they do about prehistory' (2019: 338). The apparent prescience of *Before Adam* in reflecting subsequent scientific enquiry into hominin evolution is a reminder that *we* determine what it means to be modern or fully human and also that whenever we seek to tell the story, fictional or non-fictional, of a hominin ancestor or relative, it is inevitably, in large part, our own story that gets told.

Notes

1 See the title of Joao Zilahão's *Anatomically Archaic, Behaviourally Modern: The Last Neanderthals and Their Destiny* (2001).
2 The prospect of human evolution was barely touched upon in *Origin of Species*.

References

Bender, B. (2011), 'Darwin and Ecology in Novels by Jack London and Barbara Kingsolver', *Studies in American Naturalism*, 6 (2): 107–33.

Berkove, L. I. (2004), 'Jack London and Evolution: From Spencer to Huxley', *American Literary Realism*, 36 (3): 243–55.

Berliner, J. (2008), 'Jack London's Socialistic Social Darwinism', *American Literary Realism*, 41 (1): 52–78.

Bettinger, R. L., R. Garvey and S. Tushingham (2015), *Hunter-Gatherers. Archaeological and Evolutionary Theory*, New York: Springer.

Cartmill, M. (2001), Taxonomic Revolutions and the Animal-Human Boundary', in Corbey, R. and Roebroeks (eds), *Studying Human Origins: Disciplinary History and Epistemology*, 97–106. Amsterdam: Amsterdam University Press.

Crow, C. L. (1996), 'Ishi and Jack London's Primitives', in L. Cassuto and J. C. Reesman (eds), *Rereading Jack London*, 46–54, Stanford: Stanford University Press.

Deacon, H. J., and J. Deacon (1999), *Human Beings in South Africa: Uncovering the Secrets of the Stone Age*. Cape Town: David Philip.

De Waal, F. (2010), *The Age of Empathy. Nature's Lessons for a Kinder Society*, London: Crown Publishing, Potter Style.

De Waal, F. (2016), *Are We Smart Enough to Know How Smart Animals Are?*, New York: W. W. Norton.

Drell, J. R. R. (2000), 'Neanderthals: A History of Interpretation', *Oxford Journal of Archaeology*, 19 (1): 1–24.

Finlayson, C. (2010), *The Humans Who Went Extinct: Why Neanderthals Died Out and We Survived*, Oxford: Oxford University Press.

Foley, R. (1995), *Humans before Humanity*, London: John Wiley.

Galway-Whitham, J., J. Cole and C. Stringer (2019), 'Aspects of Human Physical and Behavioural Evolution during the Last 1 Million Years', *Journal of Quaternary Science*, 34 (6): 355–78.

Gamble, C. (2007), *Origins and Revolutions: Human Identity in Earliest Prehistory*, Cambridge: Cambridge University Press.

Green, R. E. et al. (2010), 'A Draft Sequence of the Neandertal Genome', *Science*, 328 (5979): 710–22.

Hackett, A., and R. Dennell (2003), 'Neanderthals as Fiction in Archaeological Narrative', *Antiquity*, 77 (298): 816–27.

Harari, Y. N. (2014), *Sapiens: A Brief History of Humankind*, London: Harvill Secker.

Harpham, G. (1975), 'Jack London and the Tradition of Superman Socialism', *American Studies*, 16: 23–33.

Hensley, J. R. (2002), 'Eugenics and Social Darwinism in Stanley Waterloo's "*The Story of Ab*" and Jack London's "*Before Adam*"', *Studies in Popular Culture*, 25 (1): 23–37.

Hoffecker, J. F. (2017), *Modern Humans: Their African Origin and Global Dispersal*, New York: Columbia University Press.

Hopkins, L. (2003), 'Jack London's Evolutionary Hierarchies: Dogs, Wolves, and Men', in L. A. Cuddy and C. M. Roche (eds), *Evolution and Eugenics in American Literature and Culture, 1880–1940: Essays on Ideological Conflict and Complicity*, 89–100, London: Associated University Presses.

Hsu, H. L. (2019), 'Paleo-Narratives and White Atavism, 1898–2015', *Interdisciplinary Studies in Literature and Environment*, 26 (2): 296–323.

Johnson, M. (2020), *Archaeological Theory: An Introduction*, London: Wiley-Blackwell.

Kazin, A. (1942), *On Native Grounds: An Interpretation of Modern American Prose Literature*. New York: Harcourt Brace.

Krings, M., A. Stone, R. W. Schmitz, H. Krainitzki, M. Stoneking and S. Pääbo (1997), 'Neandertal DNA Sequences and the Origin of Modern Humans', *Cell*, 90 (1): 19–30.

Landau, M. (1984), 'Human Evolution as Narrative', *American Scientist*, 72: 262–8.

Landau, M. (1991), *Narratives of Human Evolution*, London: Yale University Press.

Leroi-Gourhan, A. (1989), *The Hunters of Prehistory*, trans. C. Jacobson, New York: Atheneum.

Lindquist, B. (1997), 'Jack London, Aesthetic Theory, and Nineteenth-Century Popular Science', *Western American Literature*, 32 (2): 99–114.

London, J. (1907), *Before Adam*, New York: Macmillan.

London, J. (1915), *The Star Rover*, New York: Macmillan.

Madison, P. (2016), 'The Most Brutal of Human Skulls: Measuring and Knowing the First Neanderthal', *British Journal for the History of Science*, 49 (3): 411–32.

Martin, S. (1983), *California Writers*, Basingstoke: Macmillan.

McBrearty, S., and A. Brooks (2000), 'The Revolution that Wasn't: A New Interpretation of the Origin of Modern Human Behavior', *Journal of Human Evolution*, 39 (5): 453–563.

McNabb, J. (2012), *Dissent with Modification: Human Origins, Palaeolithic Archaeology and Evolutionary Anthropology in Britain 1859–1901*, Oxford: Archaeopress.

Mellars, P., K. Boyle, O. Bar-Yosef and C. Stringer (eds) (2007), *Rethinking the Human Revolution*, McDonald Institute Monographs: McDonald Institute for Archaeological Research.

Mitchell, L. C. 1998. '"And Rescue Us from Ourselves": Becoming Someone in Jack London's *The Sea Wolf*', *American Literature*, 70 (2): 317–35.

Mithen, S. (1998), *The Prehistory of the Mind: A Search for the Origins of Art, Religion and Science*, London: Orion Books, Phoenix.

Nichols, R. L. (2013), 'Missing Links: Genre, Evolution, and Jack London's "*Before Adam*"', *Studies in American Naturalism*, 8 (1): 6–20.

Pankake, J. (1976), 'Jack London's Wild Man: The Broken Myths of "Before Adam"', *Modern Fiction Studies*, 22 (1): 37–49.

Papagianni, D., and M. A. Morse (2015), *The Neanderthals Rediscovered. How Modern Science Is Rewriting Their Story*, London: Thames and Hudson.

Pfeiffer, J. (1969), *The Emergence of Man*, New York: Harper and Row.

Rees, A. (2016), 'Introduction (Special Section: Paleonarratives and Palaeopractices: Excavating and Interpreting Deep History', *British Journal for the History of Science*, 49(3): 383–6.

Reesman, J. C. (2009), *Jack London's Racial Lives: A Critical Biography*, Athens (US): University of Georgia Press.

Ruddick, N. (2009), *The Fire in the Stone. Prehistoric Fiction from Charles Darwin to Jean M. Auel*, Connecticut: Wesleyan University Press.

Qualtiere, M. (1982), 'Nietzschean Psychology in London's "The Sea Wolf"', *Western American Literature*, 16 (4): 261–78.

Shea, J. J. (2003), 'Neandertals, Competition, and the Origin of Modern Human Behavior in the Levant', *Evolutionary Anthropology*, 12 (4): 173–87.

Sommer, M. (2005), 'How Cultural Is Heritage? Humanity's Black Sheep from Charles Darwin to Jack London', in S. Muller-Wille (ed.), *A Cultural History of Heredity III: 19th and Early 20th Centuries*, 233–54, Berlin: Max-Planck-Institut für Wissenschaftsgeschichte.

Spikins, P. A., H. E. Rutherford and A. P. Needham (2010), 'From Homininity to Humanity: Compassion from the Earliest Archaics to Modern Humans', *Time and Mind: The Journal of Archaeology, Consciousness and Culture*, 3 (3): 303–26.

Stringer, C., and C. Gamble (1993), *In Search of the Neanderthals: Solving the Puzzle of Human Origins*, London: Thames and Hudson.

Tattersall, I. (2019), 'Human Intelligence and How It Was Acquired', *Sistemi Intelligenti. Rivista Quadrimestrale di Scienze Cognitive e di Intelligenza Artificiale*, 31 (1): 71–86.

Tringham, R. (2019), 'Giving Voices (Without words) to Prehistoric People: Glimpses into an Archaeologist's imagination', *European Journal of Archaeology*, 22 (3): 338–53.

Villa, P., and W. Roebroeks (2014), 'Neandertal Demise: An Archaeological Analysis of the Modern Human Superiority Complex', *PLoS One*, 9 (4): e96424.

Wagenknecht, E. (1952), *Cavalcade of the American Novel*. New York: Henry Holt.

Wahida, H. (2012), 'Hegemonising Intellectual Imperialism: Speciesism in Jack London's', *Call of the Wild*', *Journal of Humanities and Social Science*, 4 (5): 13–18.

Waterloo, S. (1897), *The Story of Ab: A Tale of the Time of the Cave Man*, New York: Doubleday, Doran.

Wilson, S. (2020), 'Empathy, Cognition and the Response to Death in the Middle Palaeolithic: The Emergence of Postmortemism', in J. Walker and D. Clinnick (eds), *Wild Things 2. Further Advances in Palaeolithic and Mesolithic Research*, 109–22, Oxford: Oxbow Books.

Willoughby, P. R. (2008), 'Review: Origins and Revolutions: Human Identity in Earliest Prehistory', *Canadian Journal of Archaeology*, 32 (1): 182–4.

Zilhão, J. (2001), *Anatomically Archaic, Behaviourally Modern: The Last Neanderthals and Their Destiny*, Amsterdam: Stichting Nederlands Museum voor Anthropologie en Praehistoriae.

Part II

Innovations in practice through collaborative projects

3

'Handle with care': Literature, archaeology, slavery

Josie Gill, Catriona McKenzie and Emma Lightfoot

In an interview in 2010, the black British novelist Andrea Levy considered the problem of how to understand the life of an enslaved person from their own perspective, articulating an issue with which writers concerned with the era of transatlantic slavery have grappled for some time: 'I know my ancestors were slaves, but what did they do? How did they live? How did they manage to survive it? We know so little and very little of what we do know comes from them' (Levy 2010). For Levy, 'The only way you can go any further is through fiction' and her 2010 novel about Jamaican plantation slaves *The Long Song* sets out to recreate the world in which her ancestors lived. African American writer and Nobel Laureate Toni Morrison has also addressed this lacuna in knowledge. Morrison contends that historical narratives, including autobiographical narratives written by slaves, are limited in their ability to convey the inner lives of enslaved people because they often had their purpose and style determined by a popular taste which 'discouraged writers from dwelling too long or too carefully on the more sordid details of their experience' ([1987] 2008: 69). She writes:

> Whatever the style and circumstance of these narratives, they were written to say principally two things. One: 'This is my historical life – my singular, special example that is personal, but that also represents the race.' Two: 'I write this text to persuade other people – you, the reader, who is probably not black – that we are human beings worthy of God's grace and the immediate abandonment of slavery'. (66)

In the face of narratives written to persuade a white readership that slavery should be brought to an end, Morrison understands her role as a contemporary black writer as being to attempt to access what is absent from these narratives, namely, the 'unwritten interior life' which she approaches using her 'own recollections' and 'the act of imagination' (71). This is a method she describes as 'a kind of literary archaeology' where 'on the basis of some information and a little bit of guesswork you journey to a site to see what remains were left behind and to reconstruct the world that these remains imply' (71).

Morrison's use of archaeology here is metaphorical, following a long line of twentieth-century thinkers and theorists including Freud and Foucault.[1] As a writer she is involved in digging, unearthing and reconstructing a vanished past from archival fragments and artefacts, in much the same way as an archaeologist digs for physical evidence of past lives. Yet it is also the case that archaeologists themselves have been increasingly concerned with the question of how to understand the inner lives of enslaved people. Research initiatives such as the EUROTAST project, which was set up to bring together researchers from historical studies, archaeology, anthropology and population genetics to consider the transatlantic slave trade, have made the 'identities and lived experiences of individuals displaced by the slave trade' (Abel and Sandoval-Velasco 2016: 173) a central point of investigation, seeking to 'cast light upon histories that have long been suppressed by trauma, displacement and silence' (150). Archaeologists working on the New York African Burial Ground project aimed to 'tell a rich and absorbing story of the lives of enslaved Africans in colonial New York' (*The New York African Burial Ground* 2009) through examining their remains. Such projects utilize bioarchaeology in their approach to understanding the lives of enslaved Africans, analysing graves, bones and teeth to gain information on the sex, age, health and cultural practices of enslaved individuals (2009). Many archaeologists have viewed research into slave life as 'a moral mission', a mission 'to tell the *story*' (our emphasis) of the 'poor, powerless and "inarticulate" – who had been forgotten by the written record' (Singleton 1999: 1). That archaeologists and creative writers both aim to understand the inner lives of enslaved Africans is clear, but while each discipline 'invoke[s] the other as a metaphor for its own practice' (Schwyzer 2007: 6), there has been little interaction between these fields of inquiry, despite their similar objectives.[2]

This chapter offers an account of an interdisciplinary research project, *'Literary Archaeology': Exploring the Lived Environment of the Slave*, which was a collaboration between a literary scholar and two archaeological scientists. The project set out to examine the relationship between literary and archaeological approaches to slavery and to investigate where and how the methods and priorities of each discipline might inform each other in understanding what it was like to be enslaved. Our aim was to explore how contemporary fiction and archaeological data might be brought together to create a literary archaeology that is more than metaphorical, a method where writers begin with physical remains, and imagination, memory and living bodies become ways of making sense of the archaeological information revealed by the bones of long dead enslaved people.

While there has been some excellent research on the relationship between material culture and literary studies, there has been much less attention given to the dynamic between scientific archaeology and literature.[3] Within archaeology, there have been projects which seek to 'give voice' to people who left few textual traces through collaborations with artists (Schwyzer 2007: 31–2). However, Joanna Sofaer (2006) argues that such phenomenological approaches often fail to account for the materiality and specificity of the body. Sofaer suggests that scientific (osteological) approaches, which have sometimes been negatively viewed as treating bodies as fixed specimens, need to come together with experiential approaches to form a 'theoretical and methodological space in which many kinds of bodies can be drawn together' where 'the physicality of the archaeological body forms the locus of this incorporation' (11). Our project sought to create such a space, a space in which we could work towards a new approach to the experiences of enslaved people and think through what it means to try to recover these experiences – a full understanding of which can arguably never be known. In what follows we discuss how we developed an interdisciplinary research process using science and creative writing as a means of approaching this complex and painful past. It is our intention that this chapter should be accessible to scholars working in each of our fields who are interested in interdisciplinary working across the sciences and the humanities, as well as to those interested in working with community groups. As Felicity Callard and Des Fitzgerald (2015) note, 'accounts of what interdisciplinary projects are like in practice are still relatively few in number, and most people are still reticent about the quotidian experiences that characterize them' (7). We hope that this chapter goes some way towards filling this gap in knowledge.

Beginnings, background and methods

The '*Literary Archaeology*' project was set up after the investigators met during an AHRC Science in Culture event for early career researchers from the humanities and the sciences. We realized that we were all interested in understanding the lives of enslaved people and in exploring the relationship between our disciplinary approaches to this subject. We created an interdisciplinary project focused around the following research questions:

1. Can literary engagements with slavery stimulate new lines of enquiry in the analysis of human skeletal remains and aid or inform the interpretation of archaeological data?
2. How might archaeological methods, data and physical remains inspire and enhance literary attempts to reconstruct past slave environments and literary critical ways of thinking about slavery and the relationship between archaeology and literature?
3. Can a synthesis of literary and archaeological perspectives enhance public understanding of the experiences of enslaved Africans?

We commissioned seven black creative writers affiliated with the Bristol-based writers' collective *Our Stories Make Waves* to work with us. The aim was to create an environment in which writers, scientists and literary scholars could interact, exchange questions and ideas, identify gaps in knowledge and stimulate new ways of thinking that could potentially impact upon each of our disciplinary approaches. The writers would produce new creative works in response to the science, while the archaeologists would be inspired to consider new perspectives which could inform what they do and look for in the laboratory.

We held two workshops, the first of which was led by the academics. Gill gave an overview of transatlantic slavery and of some of the ways black creative writers have approached writing about slavery. McKenzie and Lightfoot presented information on archaeological approaches to slavery using two case studies: slave burial grounds at the Newton Plantation in Barbados and Finca Clavijo in Gran Canaria, where the remains of individual slaves have been subject to osteoarchaeological and chemical analysis. As this was an exploratory project, we considered it appropriate to use published data, enabling us to explore this new avenue of research while not disturbing burial grounds or bones unnecessarily.[4] The Barbados study was chosen as the Newton Plantation is a site where human skeletal remains have been subject to extensive bioarchaeological analysis, while the Gran Canaria study was selected as Lightfoot had been part of the scientific team and had undertaken the isotopic analysis of the remains. The presentations provided a broad overview of slavery in Barbados between the seventeenth and nineteenth centuries and in Gran Canaria in the late fifteenth and sixteenth centuries. McKenzie and Lightfoot presented information compiled from the published literature about four individuals from each site. The individuals selected encompassed a range of males and females, from young adolescents to older adults, a mixture of individuals who had been captured and moved during their lifetimes and people who had been born on the plantations. Information was provided about the completeness and preservation of the remains, sex, age at death, stature and all pathological lesions and cultural modifications which could be identified in the bones. The chemical analysis identified the likely diet of each individual, alongside evidence of geographical movement. McKenzie and Lightfoot brought human skeletal remains to the workshop: a cranium (from a different context) and a rib from the Gran Canaria population which the writers were able to handle during the day. The afternoon was set aside for questions and discussion.

The writers were commissioned to produce new creative works in response to the case studies and we held a second workshop three months later, led by the writers, who talked about their feelings about the project and presented first drafts of their writing. Gill, Lightfoot and McKenzie shared their reflections on the process and discussed the answers to questions that the writers had posted on an online forum which had been set up to facilitate communication between workshops. Across the course of the project, everyone was encouraged to write blog posts to record their thoughts and ideas as the process unfolded. The completed creative pieces were published on the project website and were read at public events in two museums in Bristol in October

2016. The workshops and public events were filmed and a short documentary was produced about the project and the public response to it. The work of the project took place in the city of Bristol, where there is an ongoing public debate about how the transatlantic slave trade should be acknowledged and remembered. Given that archaeology has the power to challenge 'orthodox or hegemonic historical narratives by grounding history in the remains of the past, the unedited evidence for past lives' (Shanks 2012: 10), it was important that we opened our project up to local communities in Bristol and began a dialogue with them which focused around our core idea: how writing might not only communicate a history primarily understood through archaeological evidence but could itself inform approaches to that evidence.[5]

Our experimental, interdisciplinary approach, which involved face-to-face interaction with creative writers, discussion, creativity, dialogue, reflection, memory and intuition, moved each of us away from the normal methods of our disciplines: laboratory work, in the case of archaeological science, and textual analysis, in the case of literary studies. It was important for us to move beyond our usual approaches in order to avoid what Callard and Fitzgerald (2015) call 'the normative weight that this prefix – inter- – has come to carry' where 'a kind of transgression is apparently achieved by working between one discipline and another – and yet fundamental assumptions (e.g. about what an experiment might be, about who does it, about how its objects are produced, and so on) are left quite unquestioned' (4). In order to understand if and how our disciplines could inform each other, we needed to establish an environment in which not only new approaches to slavery could take shape but also our very ideas about what constitutes knowledge and research in this area would be open to challenge, a way of, as Callard and Fitzgerald put it, 'marking, folding, and perturbing the existing order of the world' (44). Indeed, we were aware that the normative weight that interdisciplinary research has come to carry includes assumptions about the location of knowledge (i.e. that it is to be found in academia) and its producers (i.e. usually white, often male, university academics). Interdisciplinary research, particularly science–humanities collaborations, has rarely engaged the (critical) work of black thinkers or black communities. We didn't want our project to be about academics telling or explaining, about scientists simply using the humanities to communicate their work or humanities scholars critiquing science under the assumption that the scientist is a 'crude empiricist', 'blithely washing sociological histories away with her all-conquering brain machine', an attitude Callard and Fitzgerald contend has sometimes characterized cross-disciplinary interaction (34).

Working together equally, and with a group of local black writers many of whom had rarely, if ever, been involved in university-level research, meant that we could begin to bring our disciplinary expertise into dialogue with creative practitioners for whom the bodies under consideration evoked a range of critical and emotional responses. Whereas the role of universities has traditionally been to produce a corpus of knowledge where 'the corpus to be produced was not the human body but a body of knowledge, profoundly disembodied' (Currah and Casper 2011: 3), our project foregrounded the physical, biological body – both of the living participants and the dead – as a means of creating new forms of knowledge that could be brought within institutional walls. Accounting for the role of the body of the researcher in the bodies of knowledge they produce is something which Tim Ingold (2016) contends has been missing in science where, he argues, the sensations and bodily experiences of the scientist doing research have become somewhat removed from the scientific method (9). He argues instead for 'a relation of *correspondence*' between things and people, where the objective is 'not to accumulate more and more data *about* the world, but to better correspond *with* it' (10-11). We wanted to explore how such calls for a different mode of embodied knowing might work in practice, to test how our sensations, experience and feelings as individuals and as a group could cohere around the human remains of enslaved people, remains which are at once object and subject.[6] In so doing we hoped to correspond with the material and with each other and thus to begin the process of interdisciplinary working in earnest.

Findings

The results we present here are organized around the two main themes which emerged from the research process and the creative writing: Conversing with Bones and Caring for Bodies. Rather than attempting to map the impact of the project onto each discipline, we present the implications of interdisciplinary working for each of the disciplines within each theme and draw some tentative conclusions about the benefits of working together. There is not space here to discuss all the creative writing produced, so we have based our analysis on two examples which address the emergent themes while pointing in interesting and significant ways to how literature and archaeology together can shape our understanding of the experience of enslaved people.[7]

Conversing with bones

The first workshop began with a round of introductions, where everyone was encouraged to share their initial thoughts about the project. The writers felt at once excited to work with scientific information, while at the same time apprehensive and nervous – both about approaching the subject and about working with university academics. McKenzie and Lightfoot voiced similar feelings of trepidation about approaching the subject of slavery, conscious that the writers might be disappointed with the small amount of information which could be derived from the analysis of each of the skeletons. We were acutely aware that many of the questions that the writers had about the enslaved individuals – about how they lived and died – could not be answered through the analysis of the skeletal remains. Among archaeologists there are serious reservations about extrapolating too much from the physical evidence. As Rogers and Waldron (1995: vii–viii) suggest 'palaeopathologists owe it to themselves, and to those on whose behalf they work, to do what they *can* do well. They do this best by not exaggerating the claims for their discipline, and by ensuring that the information that they do provide is soundly based'.

They continue:

> In addition to general details such as age, sex, and height about the individuals they have recovered, archaeologists would like to know what diseases the individuals suffered from, what they died of, what their occupation was, what their state of nutrition was, and as much as possible about their way of life, and the health of the population of which they were once a part. It is dismal to have to say that, in actual fact, very little such information is going to be forthcoming, and we have the distinct impression that a great many bone reports are a profound disappointment to their recipients. (1995: vii)

The uncertainty that often accompanies archaeological interpretations has resulted in some nervousness in archaeology around giving 'voices' to the bodies it considers. This concern is articulated several times in Van Dyke and Bernbeck's (2015) book on narrative in archaeology: 'We must tread carefully as we attempt to imagine – but not speak for – the people who populate our imagined pasts' (2). They write, 'We can use our fantasies to produce imagined past individuals and motivations for their actions, but real past people can't reply by doing the same with us' (5). Considering the ethics of voicing the dead they ask, 'are recognition of past subjects and respect for them achieved through the construction of "human faces" with sensory experience, emotion, and meaning, or is this merely one further way for archaeologists to appropriate and subjugate past peoples?' (10). The concern is that in the face of the impossibility of ever gaining a full picture of past lives from archaeology, the narratives which archaeologists create could be in danger of misrepresenting the 'truth' of those past lives.

By contrast, writers, particularly black writers tackling the subject of slavery, have typically been much less anxious about voicing the past and have been explicit, rather than worried, about the way those voices connect to people in the present. Saidiya Hartman (2007), for example, writes of her attempts to uncover the lives of her enslaved ancestors in the face of having little information about them. As she goes 'in search of people who left behind no traces' (15), she begins to question her attempt, asking herself, 'Was the experience of slavery best represented by all the stories I would never know? ... I was determined to fill in the blank spaces of the historical record and to represent the lives of those deemed unworthy of remembering, but how does one write a story about an encounter with nothing?' (15–16). For Hartman, the solution begins with imagining herself as a 'vestige of the dead' (18). Indeed, closing the space between the living and the dead is one of the ways in which black writers – perhaps most famously Morrison in her 1987 novel *Beloved* – have tried to 'fill in the blank spaces' and in so doing recover the voices of long dead slaves.

Yet the dynamic that emerged at the workshops was not one where the writers simply took the responsibility of 'voicing' away from archaeologists who, perhaps in lacking an ancestral connection to the remains, might have concerns about the ethical implications of attempting to narrate their stories. Rather, what emerged was a literary anxiety about voice akin to the archaeological concerns expressed above, an anxiety encapsulated in Vanessa Kisuule's (2016) spoken word poem *The Slave, The Sea, The Static, The Silence*, which she wrote in response to the project. Kisuule dramatizes her encounter with the bones, focusing on the question of how to describe them, on how to create a voice for the person whose body parts she holds. The poem proceeds as a kind of conversation between the poet and the dead slave, the latter responding to the faltering descriptions of the former as the poet imagines how a long dead slave might respond to their body being analysed and the bones speak back:

> I see your bones
>
> Markings
>
> Lesions
>
> This honeycomb skull
>
> > *Huh?*
>
> No, brittle snap skull
>
> > *Come again?*
>
> No, concrete sponge skull
>
> No, just a skull
>
> I grip it
>
> Waiting for answers
>
> That won't come

The poet struggles to find a language which is authentic but ends up speaking plainly and directly 'just a skull', searching for 'the least wrong words' as each attempt to voice the slave leads the poet back to uncertainty and self-doubt about whether the description, despite its basis in archaeological science, is true:

> *I have worms in my bowels*
> *Tight tight feeling in the knee and the hip*
> *The times I come slowly down to my knees*
> *Dreamed that death come upon me*
> *Merciful and sweet*

Is this right? Is this true?
Truth and fiction walk shoulder to shoulder
Scheming to tear each other's hair out
Interrogating eachother
Interrupting eachother
Fiction asks truth a question
And truth responds
With yet another question

> *Why these people*
> *Asking me these questions*
> *In a language (I?) me don't know*
> *Can't you see here,*
> *I'm resting*
> *Don't I get no rest, even now?*

Truth and fiction are personified as slave and poet, squaring up to each other with more questions than answers, yet the scene also evokes something of the interaction of the archaeologists with the writers at the workshops, the overlapping and jostling of fact and fiction 'Interrogating eachother / Interrupting eachother'. The poet appears allied neither to the scientist nor to the slave, both of whom appear to have greater claims and access to truth than she. Yet at the same time the poet is also one of 'these people' asking questions 'in a language' which is foreign through being academic, as the ancestor and later the poet herself situate science and poetry as coming from the 'hallowed halls' of 'high academia' where 'we desperately, arrogantly / Try and approximate you'. Poetry and science are as one in their mutual attempts to enliven bodies: 'I am a gravedigger/ Atavistic Frankenstein / Trying to make a beautiful thing / From monstrous parts of history.' While the poet's job is to piece together a human from parts and remains in a way that is 'beautiful', she increasingly fears that her words are just more of the 'many alien sounds' that 'have been attached to you' – aligned to the scientific language that has labelled the skeletal remains 'Individual N52'.

The poem thus emphasizes how both scientist and writer share responsibility for, and must justify, their intrusion into the lives of the dead and their attempts to create voices or narratives for people who don't necessarily want to speak or be heard; '*They peerin in at me / They dig and dig and dig but / No dignity in this*'. Meaningful connection and communication appear elusive to each as they attempt to fill a gap in knowledge (represented by the space in the middle of the page) but in so doing only emphasize the past as an ultimately unknowable void, 'But we rewrite history every time we cast our eyes back / The more elusive the past, the larger the gap for all / These jangling words to fall into.' Yet just as the poet seems to be giving up on language and on science, questioning the point of the whole exercise, the conversation starts to focus on the orifice which makes conversation possible – the mouth:

Ol teeth ache like

Like what – what would his teeth ache like?

Like sunsets

No

Like fist fights

No, that's not right either

Like,

what?

Like,
what? Like,

what?

Feels like a dream
Thinking of this place I was taken from
This place where I could come and go
Lay my head down where I please

The past is losing its teeth
It opens up its mouth to tell the truth
And a million sugar rotted, rum corroded
Teeth fall out in breathless staccato

I am losing my teeth
I feel em dancing around in my mouth
When I go to eat my saltfish

> *I spit em out into my Guinea corn*

I cannot sink my teeth into this story
I am met with things that crumble
On contact

Until this point, the interaction has been characterized by looking and sight, 'I see your bones', 'Can't you see here', 'we cast our eyes back', a conversation based on regarding one another at a distance. However, by shifting focus to the mouth, the poet starts to come to terms with what it might mean to allow the past to talk. For although the poet struggles once again to find the right language, it is in the *attempt* to communicate, to speak and to listen, that understanding and connection is made. The poet imagines the rotten and neglected teeth of the slave as preventing the slave – and by extension the past – from speaking 'the truth', the past losing its bite and becoming instead 'like a dream', something which the poet is unable to sink her own teeth into. Yet the past of this section is also the slave's past, the dream of 'the place I was taken from' remembered only in the music of the 'breathless staccato' and 'dancing' of the teeth now falling out in the anxiety dream-cum-nightmare that is slavery. In order for the poet to speak of the past (an act performed through the spoken word delivery of her poem), the dead must also speak of their past, a past revealed through science in their teeth. Voicing the past is thus revealed to be not about trying to 'speak for' the dead or trying to tell their truth but about conversing with them about the past through conversations formed and informed by their mouths.

What the poem points towards is the ongoing, unfinished nature of this conversation where 'Each time it comes to rest on the shore / It is sent back on itself' in a never-ending cycle of call and response. The poem thus speaks to archaeological anxieties about voicing the dead by suggesting that it is uncertainty which is to be embraced, that emotion and meaning are not fixed by description or narrative but endlessly reimagined in the process of engaging with the remains of enslaved people. The science can provide detail about what the person ate, 'Guinea Corn', about the place they were taken from, but rather than securing the person in history, the science informs an ongoing dialogue in which what is 'fact' and 'fiction' shifts like the ebb and flow of the sea. The reciprocity foregrounded by the poem is therefore not only that between poet and slave but between scientist and poet and scientist and slave; conversing with the past is also a way for science and literature to converse with one another in the present, a conversation which the poem enables through its incorporation of science, and suggestion that archaeology might let the past speak through poetry. It was ultimately through listening and speaking, both to the past and to each other at the workshops, that we could begin to address shared concerns around voicing past people and by doing so begin to unlock 'the power of the disembodied and the stories that those who forcibly undertook the Middle Passage are still yearning to tell, five centuries later' (Alexander 2006: 6).

Caring for bodies

While we had anticipated that most of the writers' initial questions would focus on the scientific process, on how accurate the science could be and on what information the analysis can and cannot provide, there was also a lot of interest in the archaeologists as people. How did it feel for Lightfoot and McKenzie to handle human skeletal remains? What was their motivation? What were the academics getting out of this project and what were their universities getting out of it? Such questions placed both intellectual and emotional demands upon us that we initially found startling: we were doing this, we thought, to develop new approaches to slavery across academic and creative boundaries. Yet it became clear that these kinds of questions were closely interrelated with the writers' feelings towards the case studies. They were interested in how the archaeologists engaged with human skeletal remains and the ethics of excavation. As Jenny Davis put it in a blog post following the workshop:

> what is the proximity, in terms of time, when human remains, the excavated dug up bones are simple pure bone, yielding itself up for analysis, a microscope, objective scientific enquiry? When is it simply two milligrams of bone, and when is it ancestor? Is time simply the measure here? Or does memory determine this? (2016)

Such questions were, for Ros Martin, directly linked to the dynamics of how we would work together as a group:

> These are our ancestors are they not yours and part of complex and painful intertwining histories of a global human community? Or are these mere bones, dug up, isotoped to discover what is it we do not yet know? What are we anticipating or hoping it will yield? And the yet to be acknowledged: black artists white scholars coming together ... What of our own unique histories will we examine and bring into consideration in studying this period, these sites? (2016)

There was a desire to find common ground, to think of ourselves as fellow human beings rather than as scientist, writer, scholar; yet questions of power and ownership of the research process circulated alongside this as the writers began to identify a gap between the academics' affective relationship to the individual case studies and their own:

> The archaeologists offer a pile of bones. There's evidence of tooth decay, malnutrition, hard manual labour. Some individuals were born in Barbados, others were not. Overall, they deliver small answers to big questions. It's as if the bones are saying - after all I've been through, you wait a few hundred years and now you ask what it was like? Can't blame them for holding out. Maybe that is just as it should be. What did we expect? (Monteith 2016)

The challenge for the writers was how they could be part of this process, whether they could or should reconcile the knowledge derived from archaeological science – as information and as method – with their own craft.

While these frictions made for some interesting discussions at the workshops they were a necessary part of our interdisciplinary exploration, as the creative pieces which the writers produced as a result demonstrated. Indeed, it was the creative writing which began to suggest a way forward. Valda Jackson's (2016) poem 'How I Feel', which she shared at the second workshop, addressed the issue of the scientific reduction of the human body to bone directly, beginning with a description of the unfamiliar experience of handling human remains:

> We pass around human remains.
>
> I hold a person's skull in my hand.
> Feel its roundness,
> toughness, It's weight
> and texture, small pits and dents.
> Like a thing hand-made.

Modeled in clay.

Sculpted ivory.

The scientific stuff of facts and supposition float in the air.

While I, cupping my hand atop the crown, marvel at its size, its density.

Compact.

Handled.

And so, so small.

I compare its scale to those of the living-breathing people around me.

There is much mass in flesh and fluids, skin and hair.

Weight and substance.

There is volume in breath …

In life.

Through the first line of the poem, the poet establishes not only the unusualness of the exercise which is being undertaken but that it is physical contact between bodies – living and dead – which is to provide the means by which the science is comprehended. The poet's first contact with the skull involves, perhaps surprisingly, its reduction from a 'human' to a material object, something the poet imagines having been 'hand-made', 'modeled' or 'sculpted', its 'pits and dents' assessed almost aesthetically, as an initially artistic response is contrasted with 'the scientific stuff'. Yet the poet takes on a scientific perspective as her observation extends to the people in the room, whose 'mass', 'weight' and 'volume' is assessed in relation to the skull. Making the living the object of scientific investigation, while the skull is a source of sensory experience and feeling, the poem not only establishes a sense of continuum between the bodies of the living and the dead but inverts the scientific gaze onto the bodies of the scientists themselves. In so doing it is the poet who gains power over the process; science becomes ephemeral and loses its weight as 'facts and supposition float in the air' – only the 'weight' of the skull, of the flesh and breath of the living, is real.

Yet the weight which the poet feels is also the weight of responsibility: holding, handling, comparing and feeling, the poet must turn the object once again into subject, a body that is not owned, over whom nobody, including the poet, has power. The poet cannot retreat from this responsibility when, as she examines a piece of rib 'A sprinkling / that escapes its plastic entombment remains / caught / in the fold of my open book / The centrefold'. The poet must bring the boxed bones to life, which she does later when she describes 'Rubbing my finger slowly down the inner spine / I feel the gritty uneven texture of ground bone'. Here, the poet's body, her book and bone are fused together as the way in which the poet will care for the bones comes into view: the rubbing of the spine (of the book) points towards the later verses, voiced by anonymous, numbered individuals, where in the aftermath of the whipping of a slave, another slave attempts to care for the injured slave. The whipped slave 'cannot bear a touch. / I cannot stand another hand / laid on me' but she watches her carer 'take my feet in your two hands / gently'. In the next verse, which is from the carer's perspective, the carer says 'I will not let you be un-held. Cannot.' The act of almost religious devotion with which one enslaved person cares for another is what the poet attempts to replicate through her own sensory experience of massaging their bones. The poet's care for the bones is an analogue for the healing touch of her ancestor, and she must craft her writing with equal care as her book's spine becomes that of the slave, her poem a physical, breathing body where language is its fluid and its shape is a twisting, noduled spine.

While, as the poet notes, the scientists present the bones in boxes marked 'handle with care' (which all involved in the process do), the poem suggests that real care for these bones involves something more – a care for subjectivity, a subjectivity which Sian Jones and Lynette Russell argue has often been stripped away by scientific archaeology which instead has sought 'to locate fragments of knowledge deemed to be of real (objective) historical value' (2012: 272). Jackson's response to the stripped back fragmentation of the archaeological object is to develop a kind of artistic care which builds up rather than scrapes away: She is also an artist and made a film to accompany the poem in which she paints a picture of two women as her poem is read aloud. The film foregrounds a relationship of care between the body of the living (artist) and the dead, even though time stands between them, a disjuncture conveyed through the time lapse technique the film employs where Jackson's creative process is shown from beginning to end.[8]

The poet-artist's care for the remains and her evocation of caring relationships between enslaved people points towards two possible directions for future bioarchaeological analysis in this field. The first is the potential to investigate methods of care among enslaved people. What do the bones reveal not just about how the person worked and what they ate, but also how they were cared for? What can bones reveal about healing practices and about relationships between different people? Can touch be accounted for? While care has become an emerging theme in bioarchaeology we are not aware of such questions being asked in the context of slave burial grounds.[9] Yet considering caring practices also has the potential to inform archaeological analysis by bringing into view the archaeologist's relationship to the human fragments she handles and analyses. Knowledge and caring are, as María Puig de la Bellacasa (2012: 202) contends, relational, a recognition which highlights the collectivity of knowledge-making that is often undervalued in academia. Ingold contends that in science 'curiosity has been divorced from care' and he writes that 'We are curious about the well-being of people we know and love, and never miss an opportunity to ask them how they are doing. That is because we care about them. Should it not be the same for the world around us? Is curiosity a way of caring?' (19). Was Lightfoot and McKenzie's very presence on the project, and interaction with writers, not a way of caring? A care enacted through their curiosity, but perhaps not articulated as such? If Jackson's poem evoked care for the object and subject, the dead and the living, as interchangeable and continuous, then the care taken for the living in the space of the workshop suggested new ways of caring for the dead in the bioarchaeology of slavery; a care for the feeling, emotion and connection evoked by the bones and by the writers' responses to them.

Conclusion

We live in an era in which the meaning and significance of transatlantic slavery is perhaps more contested than ever. Global protest movements call for the removal of colonial statues and iconography which commemorate those involved in the slave trade and call upon institutions built on the profits of the trade to publicly recognize the fact. In Bristol, a local group of activists called

Countering Colston recently made international headlines when Bristol's Colston Hall announced it would be changing its name, removing that of the infamous slave trader who bequeathed tremendous wealth to the city. The group state on their website that they wish to 'Acknowledge and repair, as far as possible, the negative effects in the present day of historical slavery' and in so doing recognize the continuing impact of how slaves lived on black lives and identities in the present.

Yet there is debate about the degree to which the lives of enslaved people can or should be linked to experiences in our contemporary moment. This debate has not only arisen within archaeology where, as we have discussed, there is concern that giving a 'voice' to individuals could be seen as invasive. There has also been some critique within literary studies of the way 'many scholars have staked their own critical agency on a recovery of the political agency of the enslaved, making the slaves' "hidden history" a vital dimension of the effort to define black political goals' (Best 2012: 453). Stephen Best asks, 'Through what process has it become possible to claim the lives and efforts of history's defeated as ours either to redeem or to redress?' (454). What Best queries is why we try to recover the past of slavery; if it is for ourselves, to make sense of our present situation, then literary scholars and writers must question the ethics of such an enterprise, much as archaeologists continually do when considering the purpose and effects of their interpretations.

There are no easy answers to such questions, yet we would like to suggest that interdisciplinarity could be one way of beginning the search for answers, if not of keeping these problems in view. For what our project found is that bringing literary and scientific disciplines together did not result solely in a focus on the experience of individual enslaved people in the past and on what they might mean to us in the present. Rather, our project highlighted the relationships between things, relationships among enslaved people, relationships between the living and the dead, relationships between scientist, writer and literary scholar, the relationship between the public and academia. The creative writing produced from the project focused not on what we can know about the lives of long dead slaves but on how and why we might begin to know it, and in doing so suggested two relational dynamics – conversation and caring – as ways of opening up, rather than claiming, the past. In turn, these methods suggested ways in which to approach interdisciplinary working, conversation and care for one another being crucial to our shared project. Callard and Fitzgerald argue that

> emotional dynamics can have great power in enabling and closing down the pursuit of particular interdisciplinary research trajectories. To treat the emotional economy of interdisciplinary collaborative work as epiphenomenal to – rather than a significant shaper of – those cross-disciplinary research trajectories would be a mistake. (114)

The results of our project demonstrate just how closely intertwined the emotions and relationships of those involved can be with the approach to the subject under consideration. It was ultimately through attention to our relationships with each other that we were able to begin to rethink the material basis of each of our disciplines and to understand the overlapping, interdependent nature of information, facts, thoughts and feelings, in both literature and science.

Notes

1. For a discussion of archaeology as metaphor in literary and critical theory, see Schwyzer (2007: 6–9).
2. Archaeologists have been concerned about the appropriation of archaeological concepts by thinkers in the humanities, who often detach such concepts from an engagement with things and the earth (González-Ruibal 2013: 1), while there have been tensions between black communities and archaeologists over the archaeological analysis of slave burial grounds (Nelson 2013: 529; Blakey 2001: 400).
3. In addition to Schwyzer, work in the former category includes Wallace (2004), Hines (2004) and Van Dyke and Bernbeck (2015).
4. The cases studies were based on articles by Santana et al. (2015) and Schroeder et al. (2009). The entire project was approved by the University of Bristol Faculty of Arts Research Ethics Committee.
5. Unfortunately there is not space here to discuss the public aspects of the project in detail.
6. The importance of understanding the interconnected nature of animate and inanimate bodies has been highlighted in work within the new materialist movement as well as by black feminist scholars (see Alexander 2006; Coole and Frost, 2010; Marshall and Alberti 2014).

7 For the full texts of these and the other works produced, please see our project website http://www.bristol.ac.uk/arts/research/literary-archaeology/creative-writing/.
8 To view the film please go to http://www.bristol.ac.uk/arts/research/literary-archaeology/creative-writing/.
9 See Tilley (2015).

References

Abel, S., and M. Sandoval-Velasco (2016), 'Crossing Disciplinary Lines: Reconciling Social and Genomic Perspectives on the Histories and Legacies of the Transatlantic Trade in Enslaved Africans', *New Genetics and Society*, 35 (2): 149–85.

Alexander, M. J. (2006), *Pedagogies of Crossing: Meditations on Feminism, Sexual Politics, Memory, and the Sacred*, Durham, NC: Duke University Press.

Best, S. (2012), 'On Failing to Make the Past Present', *Modern Language Quarterly*, 73 (3): 453–74.

Blakey, M. L. (2001), 'Bioarchaeology of the African Diaspora in the Americas: Its Origins and Scope', *Annual Review of Anthropology*, 30: 387–422.

Callard, F., and D. Fitzgerald (2015), *Re-thinking Interdisciplinarity across the Social Sciences and Neurosciences*, Hampshire: Palgrave Macmillan.

Coole, D., and S. Frost (2010), 'Introducing the New Materialisms', in D. Coole and S. Frost (eds), *New Materialisms: Ontology, Agency, Politics*, 1–46, Durham, NC: Duke University Press.

Currah, P., and M. J. Casper (2011), 'Bringing Forth the Body: An Introduction', in M. J. Casper and P. Currah (eds), *Corpus: An Interdisciplinary Reader on Bodies and Knowledge*, 1–20, New York: Palgrave Macmillan.

Davis, J. (2016), 'A smattering of Crumbs and Two Milligrams of Bone'. Literary Archaeology' project website. http://www.bristol.ac. uk/arts/research/literary-archaeology/blog/2016/-a-smattering-of-crumbs-and-two-milligrams-of-bone.html (accessed 4 September 2020).

González-Ruibal, A. (2013), 'Reclaiming Archaeology', in A. González-Ruibal (ed.), *Reclaiming Archaeology beyond the Tropes of Modernity*, 1–29, Oxon: Routledge.

Hartman, S. (2007), *Lose Your Mother: A Journey along the Atlantic Slave Route*, New York: Farrar, Straus and Giroux.

Hines, J. (2004), *Voices in the Past: English Literature and Archaeology*, Cambridge: D. S. Brewer.

Ingold, T. (2016), 'From Science to Art and Back Again: The Pendulum of an Anthropologist', *Anuac*, 5 (1): 5–23.

Jackson, V. (2016), 'How I Feel', 'Literary Archaeology' project website. Available online http://www.bristol.ac.uk/media-library/sites/arts/research/documents/how-i-feel-valda-jackson.pdf (accessed 4 September 2020).

Jones, S., and L. Russell (2012), 'Archaeology, Memory and Oral Tradition: An Introduction', *International Journal of Historical Archaeology*, 16 (2): 267–83.

Kisuule, V. (2016), 'The Slave, The Sea, The Static, The Silence', 'Literary Archaeology' project website. Available online http://www.bristol.ac.uk/media-library/sites/arts/research/documents/the-slave-the-sea-the-static-the-silence-vanessa-kisuule.pdf. (accessed 4 September 2020).

Levy, A. (2010), 'I Started to Realise What Fiction Could Be. And I Thought, Wow! You Can Take on the World', *The Guardian*, 30 January. Available online http://www.theguardian.com/books/2010/jan/30/andrea-levy-long-song-interview (accessed 30 January 2017).

Marshall, Y., and B. Alberti (2014) 'A Matter of Difference: Karen Barad, Ontology and Archaeological Bodies', *Cambridge Archaeological Journal*, 24 (1): 19–36.

Monteith, C. (2016), '"A Haunting."' 'Literary Archaeology' project website. http://www.bristol.ac. uk/arts/research/literary-archaeology/blog/2016/a-haunting.html (accessed 4 September 2020).

Morrison, T. ([1987] 2008), 'The Site of Memory', in C. C. Denard (ed.), *Toni Morrison What Moves at the Margin: Selected Nonfiction*, 65–80, Jackson: University Press of Mississippi.

Nelson, A. (2013), 'DNA Ethnicity as Black Social Action', *Cultural Anthropology*, 28 (3): 527–36.

The New York African Burial Ground Unearthing the African Presence in Colonial New York (2009), Washington, DC: Howard University Press. Available online https://www.gsa.gov/largedocs/Vol5_GenAud_NYABG_2.pdf. (accessed 30 January 2017).

Puig de la Bellacasa, M. (2012), '"Nothing Comes without Its World": Thinking with Care', *Sociological Review*, 60 (2): 197–216.

Rogers, J., and T. Waldron (1995), *A Field Guide to Joint Disease in Archaeology*, Chichester: John Wiley and Sons.

Santana, J. R. Fregel, E. Lightfoot, J. Morales, M. Alamon, J. Guillen, M. Moreno and A. Rodrıguez (2015), 'The Early Colonial Atlantic World: New Insights on the African Diaspora from Isotopic and Ancient DNA Analyses of a Multiethnic 15th–17th Century Burial Population from the Canary Islands, Spain', *American Journal of Physical Anthropology*, 159 (2): 300–12.

Schroeder, H., T. C. O'Connell, J. A. Evans, K. A. Shuler and R. E. M. Hedges (2009), 'Trans-Atlantic Slavery: Isotopic Evidence for Forced Migration to Barbados', *American Journal of Physical Anthropology*, 139 (4): 547–57.

Schwyzer, P. (2007), *Archaeologies of English Renaissance Literature*, Oxford: Oxford University Press.

Shanks, M. (2012), *The Archaeological Imagination*, California: Left Coast Press.

Singleton, T. A. (1999), 'An Introduction to African-American Archaeology', in T. A. Singleton (ed.), *'I, too, am America': Archaeological Studies of African-American Life*, 1–17, Charlottesville: University of Virginia Press.

Sofaer, J. R. (2006), *The Body as Material Culture: A Theoretical Osteoarchaeology*, Cambridge: Cambridge University Press.

Tilley, L. (2015), *Theory and Practice in the Bioarchaeology of Care*, Switzerland: Springer International Publishing AG.

Van Dyke, R. M., and R. Bernbeck (2015), 'Alternative Narratives and the Ethics of Representation', in R. M. Van Dyke and R. Bernbeck (eds), *Subjects and Narratives in Archaeology*, 1–26, Colorado: University of Colorado Press.

Wallace, J. (2004), *Digging the Dirt: The Archaeological Imagination*, London: Bloomsbury.

4

Creative facticity and 'hyper-archaeology': The spatial and performative textualities of psychogeography

Spencer Jordan

In today's age of 'post-truth', Oxford Dictionaries' word of 2016, scepticism and denial have become the new normal. Traditional battlegrounds such as climate change have broadened to embrace a far wider, more visceral, declamation of scientific opinion and 'fact'. In this maelstrom no certainties are left unscathed. The very assertion of 'truth' has become a political act, the aim not to embrace clear and unequivocal 'fact' but rather to commit to a wider ideology in which the primary purpose is the disruption of the neo-liberal consensus. In our 'post-truth' world, truth has been replaced by belief (D'Ancona 2017; Sim 2019). The focus of this new paradigm is not simply present or future time; it is also very much engaged with the past (McIntyre 2018). Denial of climate change and the wider implications of what has been termed the 'Anthropocene', for example, involves not only a careful rebuking of scientific projections but also a systematic denial of the historical and archaeological record. In announcing the withdrawal of the United States from the Paris Agreement on climate change in 2019, for example, President Trump not only dismissed belief in an environmental crisis; he also rejected both the data and the academic communities on which an understanding of the crisis stands. If you believe the Earth is only 6,000 years old, it is also very possible to deny the vast array of scientific data that underlines mankind's negative impact on the Earth's climate, including the landscape degradation and species extinction associated with the more extreme definitions of the Anthropocene (Hamilton, Bonneuil and Gemenne 2015: 1–3).

Although this may seem an extreme example, beneath it lies a growing distrust of expert opinion. Scientific data and academic research are dismissed as either misinformed or, at worst, neo-liberal propaganda (D'Ancona 2017). The root causes of this situation are many and varied, but Fukuyama's 'vetocracy' surely touches on something deeply profound (Fukuyama 2015), namely the perception of disempowerment among individuals and communities created by dysfunctional political and social systems. The lesson for academics is that facts are no longer enough to win the argument; instead, as much attention needs to be given to the means by which those facts are disseminated, validated and comprehended. In the case of archaeology, archaeologists need to see themselves more as 'participants in conversations' with the public, as envisaged by Pluciennik (2015: 65). One way this can be taken forward is by thinking of academic and scientific discourse as a set of powerful narratives, a move already underway through what has been termed the 'linguistic turn' in archaeology (e.g. see Clark 2004). Davies notes the importance of understanding the Anthropocene, for example, more as 'a way of seeing' than an explicit manifesto (2016: 193). Yet this intersection between narrative theory and science-based disciplines is still in its infancy in many areas, including archaeology (Dyke and Bernbeck 2015: 1). Much remains to be done, not only in terms of the mechanics of how these interdisciplinary approaches will develop but also, and perhaps more crucially, with regard to the wider ethical and moral issues that such approaches bring into view. Put simply, doesn't creative experimentation merely run the risk of adding to the issues and complexities already generated by our post-truth age?

This chapter directly engages with these concerns by offering an account of the outcomes of the research project *Walkways and Waterways*. At the chapter's heart is the use of psychogeography as a methodology by which an interdisciplinary synthesis between archaeology and creative practice can be investigated. Drawing upon Alexandra Warwick's concept of 'artefactual fictions' (2012), where archaeological artefacts are primarily understood as discursive entities, the chapter extends this concept in three important ways: first, by engaging with non-textual 'fictions', specifically ideas of 'presence' within the performative dimension of psychogeography (Giannachi, Kaye and Shanks 2012); second, by examining how technological developments such as mobile technology and Wi-Fi constitute a radical transformation of our media landscape, fundamentally impacting on the production and consumption of narratives (Jordan 2019); and third, by considering the intertwined notions of 'performative presence' and 'artefactual fictions' from the perspective of the digitally mediated interplay between textual and spatial practice. If at the heart of the linguistic turn is an understanding of knowledge construction as a kind of dialogue, politically and socially situated, then this chapter also invites consideration of the notion that such a conversation also has spatial, or physical, bounds. In this sense, psychogeography offers a way of perceiving our stories as physical journeys in and of themselves, a methodology that can help explore ways by which archaeologists might reconnect not only with the process of storytelling itself but also the physical remains of our archaeological legacy. The chapter begins by offering an overview of representations of archaeology in contemporary fiction and non-fiction and their relationship to storytelling within archaeology. It then explores how psychogeographical methods might be used to comprehend and to create new archaeological stories, stories which are not simply textual but spatial, performative and technologically enabled.

The new archaeological imperative

Like all the stories in Jon McGregor's 2012 collection *This Isn't The Sort of Thing That Happens to Someone Like You*, 'The Remains' has the subtitle of a town or village in the East of England, in this case, Friskney, a Fenland village midway between Boston and Skegness (Lea 2017: 238). The story is delivered through a terse, declarative syntax, in which 'The Remains' are the unwritten first two words of each sentence, as in the story's opening sentences: 'Are believed to still be intact. Are understood to be within an area of approximately seventeen square miles. Are believed to have been concealed' (McGregor 2012b: 188). At this point the story appears to be relating the details of a murder in which the remains of an unidentified victim have been found buried in the fenland peat. However, it quickly becomes something else: 'May be wrapped in a silken winding sheet and buried with jewellery and other possessions pressed neatly into the folded hands' (McGregor 2012b: 189). 'The Remains' are made deliberately ambiguous, existing as both the consequence of contemporary murder and ancient sacrificial or ritualistic death, revealed through an unsettling passive narratorial voice. Neither period takes precedence, forming instead a shifting narrative that finally dissolves into the endless repetition of a single sentence, 'Have yet to be found' (McGregor 2012b: 192), across the story's entire final page. This meditation on landscape as both a contemporary and also archaeological construct runs throughout McGregor's collection of short stories. In 'We Wave and Call', the narrator comes across an old fort while on holiday abroad; the story 'Supplementary Notes to the Testimony of Appellants B & E' purposely locates the narrative within an archaeological context, close to 'the remains of what is believed to be a former manor or grange, with a series of raised earthworks' (McGregor 2012c: 148–9); 'In Winter the Sky', a story told through prose and poetry, refers to 'No dramatic finds of Saxon villages/No burial mounds or hidden treasure' (McGregor 2012a: 31). This overt sensitivity to the archaeological record is also found in Sarah Hall's short story collection, *The Beautiful Indifference* (2012a), where the historical heritage of the Cumbrian landscape is never far away: in 'Butcher's Perfume', 'there were two main roads from town – the old toll road, and the Roman' (2012: 22); in 'She Murdered Mortal He', the unnamed central character manages a company that arranges ghost tours; and in 'Vuotjärvi', the central setting is the brooding waters of an ancient lake.

While ancient landscapes and ruined buildings have been the mainstay of folk tales and the Gothic for hundreds of years, what is new about contemporary literary representations of the archaeological such as these is their use of the 'realist' tradition of the short story (March-Russell 2009: 235–45). Although this tradition is most clearly associated with writers such as Anton Chekhov, Ernest Hemingway and Raymond Carver, its influence is evident in contemporary short story writing such as that of McGregor and Hall. Their stories are set in real places, are about ordinary events (although often with tragic or extraordinary outcomes) and are told in an economical style. The 'realism' then, is as much an affect of the story's subject, as it is of form (May 2002: 83–106). In both McGregor's and Hall's stories, the archaeological is represented in a realistic manner, with little of the romanticization or exaggeration of Gothic fiction. As this chapter will show, if this archaeological imperative has a function, I would suggest that, at least in part, it is to encourage us to look at the world in new ways. Yet the archaeological also has a deep connectivity to the very form of the realist short story, with its buried subtext, poking through the placid surface of the story's quotidian detail. Hemingway called this 'the iceberg effect', where much of the story remains off the page, and yet whose presence is nevertheless felt by the reader (Scofield 2006: 140). To make this work, the realist writer has to use external detail to infer the hidden psychological complexity of the characters (May 2002: 94). The representation of landscape within McGregor's and Hall's stories then, with its historical and archaeological layering, mirrors that of the very form they are deploying. The archaeological not only operates metaphorically as a key part of the setting but is also a playful synecdoche for the entire narrative structure of the story itself. In Hall's short story 'Voutjärvi' (2012d), for example, the dark depths of the eponymous lake, timeless in its 'benthic silence' (172), foreshadows the tragedy about to unfurl as well as acting as a powerful metaphor for the ancient Finnish landscape in which the story is set (Lea 2017: 187–8). Like most of Hall's stories in the collection, 'Voutjärvi' relies on subtextual meaning and implication. Yet place as a historicized concept is also important for Hall; indeed, as Lea notes, '[Hall's] vocabulary is firmly rooted in the quiddity of turf, water, and Cumbrian rock, emerging from it as smooth or jagged as if found' (2017: 155). The archaeological is therefore never just metaphorical for Hall; it is both implicit and explicit in the landscape, language and people of her stories.

This renewed interest in the archaeological is also evident in contemporary creative non-fiction. A good example is Charlotte Higgins's *Under Another Sky: Journeys in Roman Britain* (2014) in which the author sets out to explore how 'the idea of Roman Britain has resonated in British culture and still forms part of the texture of its landscape' (2014: xx). Although posing as an objective account of a journey, Higgins constructs a story using creative techniques that would be familiar to any writer of fiction, including characterization, setting and emplotment. In fact, a growing number of non-fiction writers continue to demonstrate an interest in the textual representation of contemporary journeys across an historicized British landscape, including John Higgs's *Watling Street: Travels through Britain and Its Ever-Present Past* (2017), Tom Chesshyre's *From Source to Sea: Notes from a 215-Mile Walk along the River Thames* (2017) and James Canton's *Ancient Wonderings: Journeys into Prehistoric Britain* (2017). Ian Sansom suggests that 'it now seems to be a rite of passage for the middle-class, middle-aged Englishman to go off on a long walk and then to write a book about it' (2017: 32). Yet he overstates the gendered bias. Lauren Elkin's *Flâneuse: Women Walk the City in Paris, New York, Tokyo, Venice and London* (2016) and Rebecca Solnit's *Wanderlust: A History of Walking* (1999) remind us that women have also engaged in these long, topographical walks. As Solnit contends, walking creates 'an odd consonance between internal and external passage, one that suggests that the mind is also a landscape of sorts and that walking it is one way to traverse it' (Solnit 1999: 6). For Solnit, then, walking creates a symbiotic relationship between the physical and emotional. Indeed, for Solnit, it is the emotional and subjective that is the real arena of exploration, the physical passage providing the means by which the internal landscape is traversed.

This encroachment of creative and performative practice into the domain of archaeology has not been a one-way process. It is not so much that creative writing has had to break down the ramparts of archaeological research, as reach out to a discipline already highly attuned to literary and creative potential. The archaeologist Gavin Lucas, for example, has emphasized the importance of creative engagement within archaeological study and the rootedness of any interpretation in the present: 'archaeology is a materialising activity – it does not simply work with material things, it materializes. It brings new things into the world; it reconfigures the world' (Lucas 2004: 117). Michael Shanks is even more emphatic, stating the need for archaeologists to 'look beyond the academic discipline of archaeology through memory practices, tradition and innovation to a (modern) human condition' (2012: 149). Crucially, storytelling, as both Lucas and Shanks confirm, is at the heart of this.

Psychogeography 2.0

This chapter argues that psychogeographical literature, with its emphasis on a physical journey across what I term an 'hyper-archaeologicalized' landscape, provides an effective analytical focus through which the literary–archaeological nexus can be examined. Critically, it expands the corpus of contemporary texts usually considered to be psychogeographical, to argue for an approach in which the interpenetration of psychogeographical ideas across textual forms and genres is amorphous and fluid. Traditionally, psychogeography is often viewed as something of an enigma with no agreed definition about what the term actually means. Perhaps Robert Macfarlane has come closest to describing the strange playfulness that lies at its heart:

> Unfold a street map of London, place a glass, rim down, anywhere on the map, and draw round its edge. Pick up the map, go out into the city, and walk the circle, keeping as close as you can to the curve. Record the experience as you go, in whatever medium you favour: film, photograph, manuscript, tape. Catch the textual run-off of the streets: the graffiti, the branded litter, the snatches of conversation. Cut for sign. Log the data-stream. (2005: 3)

Coverley calls psychogeography a 'meeting point' of concepts and ideas, each with separate, though interconnected, histories and traditions (2010: 11). Yet despite this undoubted fuzziness, there still remains a central methodological core to psychogeography that can be traced back to its beginnings in post-war Paris and the Lettrist Group, a forerunner of what would become the Situationist International. For the Situationists, led by Guy Debord, psychogeography was 'the study of the specific effects of the geographical environment, consciously organized or not, on the emotion and behaviour of individuals' (1955: 8). In broad terms, then, psychogeography started life as the study of the interplay between psychology and geography. Central to its development was Debord's notion of the *dérive*, 'a technique of rapid passage through varied ambiences', an open, aimless drift through the city (1958: 62). In the 1950s, this activity was an end in itself and the idea that written accounts of the dérive might be the principal output was not seriously considered by the Situationists. They tended to avoid making connections with other disciplines that might have extended or deepened their work (Sadler 1999: 160), and by the early 1960s the movement imploded under the weight of its own internal rivalries. Psychogeography and the concept of the dérive were quietly forgotten.

However, things began to change in the 1990s, which witnessed a resurgence of interest in psychogeographical concerns. Stewart Home's *Neoism, Plagiarism and Praxis* (1995), Iain Sinclair's *Lights Out for the Territory* (1997) and Rebecca Solnit's *Wanderlust: A History of Walking* (1999) are just three examples from a much longer list of autobiographical works of non-fiction with psychogeographical influences. Iain Sinclair opens *Lights Out for the Territory* (1997) with preparations for a journey in what becomes a sardonic take on the classic adventure tale: 'The notion was to cut a crude V into the sprawl of the city, to vandalize dormant energies by an act of ambulant signmaking (I had developed this curious conceit while working on my novel *Radon Daughters*: that the physical movements of the characters ... might spell out the letters of a secret alphabet)' (1997: 1). Alongside these works, a parallel corpus of fiction emerged which also drew on psychogeographical ideas. Such fiction includes Peter Ackroyd's *Hawksmoor* (1985), Geoff Nicholson's *Bleeding London* (1997), W. G. Sebald's *Rings of Saturn* (1998) and, more recently, Zadie Smith's *NW* (2013). The latter novel is set mainly in Willesden and is experimental both in its chronological and also spatial structuring. Indeed, Knepper goes as far to say that *NW* deploys an 'interactive experience of worldly/textual navigation and re-routing ... to prompt its readers to remap known relations to place and explore the contested production of localities in a globalising world' (2013: 116). The characters spend the novel journeying across their locality, metaphorically beating the bounds of the spatial limits of their lives. In the centre of Willesden, one of the characters sets off to find an old shrine in a church: 'Another twenty yards and the full improbability of the scene is revealed. A little country church, a medieval country church, stranded on this half-acre, in the middle of a roundabout' (Smith 2013: 69). Chapter nine even parodies the instructions offered by Google Maps, finally ending with, 'These directions are for planning purposes only. You may find that construction projects, traffic, weather, or other events may cause conditions to differ from the map results' (Smith 2013: 38). Willesden is at the confluence of a number of Roman roads and was famous as a site of pilgrimage to the Shrine of Our Lady (Knepper 2013: 120). The titles of the novel's four sections, 'Visitation', 'Guest', 'Host' and 'Crossing', play with this idea of a revelatory journey. *NW* embraces some of the classic tropes of the psychogeographical novel but deploys them in innovative and unexpected forms. Smith offers the reader a multicultural interpretation of locality, space and place. There is very little nostalgia here; indeed, the usual story arc of psychogeography, with the narrator finally reaching some kind of insight or emotional harmony, is subverted at every stage in *NW*. The past, when it exists at all, such as the Black Madonna in the shrine of Our Lady of Willesden, is indifferent and unspeaking. Characters wander aimlessly and unbidden across this small patch of London. In the section 'Crossing', chapter titles chart the drifting progress of one of the central characters, traumatized, incapable of navigation and yet drawn back into the physical spaces of her past: 'Willesden Lane to Kilburn High Road', 'Shoot Up Hill to Fortune Green' and so on. The effect is neither comforting nor nostalgic: rather, it is deliberately unsettling, an experimental remapping of locality in a world transformed by globalization and transcultural immigration (Loh 2013: 171).

While this is very much in keeping with the general philosophy of psychogeography, in particular the acute sensitivity to the relationships between physical and subjective journeys, it is also clear from works such as *NW* that psychogeography has undergone significant changes from its inception by Debord, creating what I term a psychogeography 2.0. Where the Situationists were concerned with the overt politicization of the dérive and, with it, its focus on the industrial cities of Western capitalism, by the 1990s writers had developed a much stronger interest in the forgotten and overlooked historical legacies of place, that contrasted 'a horizontal movement across the topography of the city with a vertical descent through its past' (Coverley 2010: 14). In psychogeography 2.0, the landscape becomes 'hyper-archaeologicalized', permeated by undiscovered artefacts and historical latency. In Smith's 'immersive' recreation of Willesden, Sinclair's excavations into London's 'secret history' and Sebald's haunting journey along East Anglia's coastal path, time is compressed through a slow collapsing between past and present, a move which is also echoed in the short fictions of writers such as McGregor and Hall.

In thinking more critically about these characteristics, it is insightful to draw on Warwick's typology of nineteenth-century literature which separates archaeological fiction into two categories – the 'stratigraphic' and the 'artefactual' (Warwick 2012). The former attempts to take the reader back in time, to render the past whole again in a simplistic, straightforward way that emphasizes authenticity. It is stratigraphic in the sense that this vision of the archaeological draws on the notion of the past as layered and distant, as something remote that can be pulled back into the light and revealed (Warwick 2012: 85). Conversely, what Warwick terms *artefactual fiction* examines the process by which archaeological artefacts can be understood as discursive entities first and foremost. As Warwick notes, in artefactual fictions, 'the object is not part of a stratum, at home with others in its period, but out of the context of its first existence' (2012: 88). Such artefactual fictions are necessarily disruptive and transgressive, as the archaeological object becomes a discursive construct of the present rather than an authentic fragment from the 'past'. I contend that this concept of artefactual fiction provides an effective way of theorizing not only nineteenth-century literature but also psychogeographical literature, particularly in its representation of archaeological traces. I suggest that three important aspects of psychogeography are specifically illuminated by this application. First, that psychogeography, as with artefactual fiction, is fundamentally 'situated', in the sense that the experience occurs within a particular socio-economic context, both spatially and temporally. Second, that the artefact is conceived as a disturbance, a spatial and temporal anomaly. Third, such archaeological traces say nothing of the past. Instead, they act as signifiers to our entrapment within the 'present'. As Warwick notes in her analysis of artefactual fiction, '[t]he disturbance produced by archaeological objects is not the horror of the past, but of the recognition of the conditions of the present' (2012: 94).

Yet an engagement with artefactual disturbances may not be simply textual. As already discussed, psychogeography, in its original incarnation, was a *performative* experience, woven around Debord's concept of the dérive. This performative aspect of psychogeography is very much under-researched, which is curious given the growing synergy between archaeology and performance theory (Parker Pearson 2010; Parker Pearson and Shanks 2001). As Giannachi, Kaye and Shanks (2012) point out, theories of 'presence' within performance studies have strong connections with wider archaeological questions of 'the performance and construction of the past in memory, narrative … in the experience of place' (2012: 2). Giannachi in particular notes the opportunity offered by what she calls 'ubiquitous computing' for performative works created through improvisation, in real time and in situ (Giannachi 2012: 60). This digitally enhanced landscape is still a relatively unexplored terrain, especially in regard to performative exploration. Yet it is clear that there exists both exciting potential and pitfalls when it comes to utilizing augmented and immersive technologies within more traditional performative practices, such as psychogeography. It is towards a consideration of these issues that this chapter now turns.

Digital storytelling

Digital technology is transforming every facet of our lives. Even the dusty domain of archaeology has experienced a technological revolution through the use of geophysical imagery, laser scanners, 3D modelling, augmented reality systems and, most recently, 3D printing. As Rose Ferraby (2017: 6) notes, technologies such as geophysics have not only impacted the working practices of archaeologists but have fundamentally reconfigured what she calls 'the archaeological imagination'. More widely, technological advances such as the mobile phone and pervasive broadband connectivity have introduced nothing short of a revolution in how individuals engage with each other and their environment. According to Ofcom, in 2016, 93 per cent of adults in the UK owned a mobile phone, 71 per cent of UK adults had a smartphone and 73 per cent of UK adults were users of social media sites, percentages which are likely to keep on rising (Ofcom 2017). There now exists a new kind of 'space', what Scott McQuire calls *relational space*, generated by technological speed and instantaneous connectivity, breaking down previous restraints of place and time, 'in which the global is inextricably imbricated with the face-to-face' (McQuire 2008: 23).

These social and technological changes necessitate a radical overhaul of the theoretical and practical assumptions of psychogeography. At the very least, there now exists the very real opportunity to explore psychogeography as both a spatial and performative experience, collapsing the divide between writer and reader (Jordan 2019). The use of 'technology' within the field of psychogeography is not entirely without precedent. It was the Situationists themselves who described the use of walkie-talkies in a hypothetical dérive across Amsterdam (Anon. 1960). Yet the use of mobile technology in particular as a means of transforming spatial encounters is still very much in its early stages. *Ghosts in the Garden* (2012), *City Strata* (2012) and *I Tweet Dead People* (2012), all funded through *REACT* (Research and Enterprise in Arts and Creative Technology, an AHRC-funded Knowledge Exchange Hub), are just three examples of creative projects that have examined the interplay between digital technology, place and storytelling. Such projects have tended to fall into discrete areas, such as digital heritage including *Linking the Chain: A Network for Digital Heritage in Wales* (2010); narrative and storytelling such as *These*

Pages Fall Like Ash (2013) by Tom Abba and Duncan Speakman, in which readers are invited to visit certain areas of Bristol, locating digital fragments and uploading their own responses; and historical and spatial exploration such as *Hackney Hear* (2012), Bristol's *Hello Lamp Post* (2013) and *Shadowing* (2014). Koehler (2013) analyses how Twitter stories such as Rick Moody's 'Some contemporary characters' (2010) and Jennifer Egan's 'Black box' (2012) explore what he calls 'new ways of understanding craft as a synthesis of readers' affect and participation in an unfolding narrative' (Koehler 2013: 387). In their exploration of location-based interactive narratives, Paay and Kjeldskov note the immersive nature of 'augmented reality' when played out across a city (2011: 271). They end their essay with a call for further work to be done on the use of 'user-generated story content that enable … urban citizens to participate in the media content creation side' (2011: 271).

This chapter reports on a digital project that takes up this challenge. *Walkways and Waterways* (2013), funded by Creative Exchange Wales Network (CEWN), was a collaborative project involving Cardiff Metropolitan University, the University of South Wales and the digital media start-up, Fresh Content Creation. The purpose of the project was to lead a technologically enabled psychogeographical walk through the Welsh capital, Cardiff. Previous projects, such as Chris Speed's 'Walking through Time', showed what could be done in terms of the real-time tracking of individuals across historical maps (Speed 2015). As Speed states, 'being "in" the map and being located on a street that no longer exists offers new methods of understanding our surroundings' (Speed 2015: 177). *Walkways and Waterways* wanted to extend this approach by using Twitter to capture the creative responses of participants as they progressed across the city. *Walkways and Waterways* was therefore much more focused on the relationship between narrative, place and walking. More crucially, it sought to explore this interaction in real time.

The event itself consisted of a digitally mediated journey, retracing the last two miles of the Glamorganshire Canal, from Cardiff Castle to the Bay (previously known as Tiger Bay). The Canal itself fell into ruin soon after the Second World War and has long since been built over. Only memories and topographical scars remain. Retracing it through the centre of the city involved traversing a variety of terrains, including a large modern shopping centre, before finishing at the location of the canal's old sea lock, beneath the A4232 flyover.

The event was advertised through social media. Twenty participants attended, ranging from young children to the retired. While the physical journey was led by project members, exploration was digitally augmented by Twitter through which further guidance and information was given in real time. The smartphone allowed each participant to upload photographs and commentary to #GlamCan, providing a shareable forum through which every individual itinerary could be recorded. Embedded within the walk were twelve 'treasures', forming, what was described as, a 'treasure trail'. In this way, the project employed real-time gaming and 'play' as a way of enhancing participation and engagement. Tweets sent by the project team such as 'What do you want to learn about the Glamorganshire canal today?' prompted participants to both find and then record the next 'treasure'. Sometimes, as in the case of a marooned paddle post in the subway beneath the A470, participants were invited to discuss its function, 'What do you think made the marks to the left of jack head/paddle post?' Participants then uploaded their responses to Twitter. Sometimes team members responded to particular replies; occasionally participants themselves would engage in a fleeting online discussion, 'A crane / Yes, but what for?'

Specific directions sent through Twitter guided the participants across the city: 'Walk through the old tunnel, follow the guides. Turn to your right at Hilton and look up / Go into the arcade opposite, take stairs on the left, walk down & follow guides; this is tricky water to navigate!' Old photographs were tweeted to the participants at key locations, asking them to compare the existing topography with what was recorded in the photograph: 'Can you see a building in this image that is still there now?'; 'See if you can spot what is missing from the picture we just sent? What is still the same?' Participants were encouraged to respond through their own tweets which were then shared in real time across the group. Sometimes these responses were simple factual responses to the questions: 'old tunnel'; 'custom house unchanged'; 'rope'. At other times a more abstract, creative response was forthcoming that captured the participant's fleeting emotional responses: 'Dark, cold, wet. Voices echo in tunnel / swimming along the canal through tides of shoppers'. And just occasionally, memories suddenly surfaced: 'Remember canal as a child. Memories of swimming in it / Met my husband here – 40 years ago!'

In other situations, the limitations of a tweet (short textual responses of up to 140 characters, including spaces) might be considered unnecessarily restrictive. Yet, out on the street, this imposed concision became a strength. Each tweet offered the opportunity to add up to four photographs taken on the smartphone. The tweets therefore gave participants the opportunity to explore the interplay between text and image as they progressed along the path of the canal, a simple yet powerful augmentation of their creative output. Each tweet became part of a single, collective narrative, a real-time amalgamation of over twenty stories that each participant could access alongside their own individual record. In the written feedback, one participant called this 'cataloguing the joint experience via social media'. It was this 'joint experience' that seemed to be a key part of the event's popularity. When asked what they enjoyed about the event, over half stressed its communality: 'companionship of other walkers'; 'meeting new people'; and 'enjoyable group experience'. For almost all the participants, the event's success had also been the way it had encouraged them to see the city in a new way: 'looking at Cardiff in a different light'; 'seeing things that I've passed every day but not noticed'; and, perhaps more interestingly, 'going back in time'. Yet the group experience also threw up issues. When asked about how the event could be improved, a third suggested the pace of the walk. There were certainly moments when the group had to wait for everyone to arrive and engage with an activity. Some of the older participants also highlighted the need for more support for those who weren't so confident with social media. Overall, however, the feedback was positive.

The smartphone was able to support the event in a number of ways that a more traditional non-digital format could not. First, the technology allowed real-time mapping across the city using the phone's global positioning system (GPS). GPS ensured that the position of each participant was always known in relation to the surrounding city space, thereby providing a physical mapping of each individual journey. Second, it provided a means of geographically triggering audio, video and images, augmenting the physical experience of the contemporary city with historical photographs, records and testimony. *Are you standing under the dual carriageway? You made it! Tweet a selfie of you in front of the graffiti.* The smartphones were able to digitally map stories to the historical legacies of specific sites. Third, the phones allowed each participant to record and post their own creative responses through Twitter and then to read one another's, as the journey progressed. Neuhaus (2014) notes how his own mapping of Twitter activity across a number of smart cities, including New York City and London, produced parallel virtual landscapes, created through the narrative activity of the cities' populations. In *Waterways and Walkways* stories emerged on Twitter but they were also generated verbally as the participants moved along the route. At one point, beside the extant post of a crane on what would have been the Sea Lock Pound, one of the participants began to sing a sea shanty, evoking the life of the stevedores and bargemen who had worked on the canal. By the end of the journey the participants had engaged with each other both physically and digitally, remapping their relationship to the spaces of the city and its citizens.

Conclusion

In 2012 Shanks declared that 'we are all archaeologists now' (2012: 21). By this he didn't mean that we are all digging away with our trowels but rather that what he termed the 'archaeological imagination' had become a fundamental means of engaging with who we are. I would certainly concur with this, but would also suggest that if we are all archaeologists, then we are also all psychogeographers, active participants in what has come to be known as 'placemaking' (Thomas 2016). The intimate relationship between writing and physical journeying is nothing new; Robert Macfarlane reminds us that the verb 'to write' derives from the Old English *writan*, meaning 'to incise runic letters in stone', in other words 'drawing a sharp point over and into a surface – by harrowing a track' (Macfarlane 2013: 105). In this sense, the underpinnings of psychogeography 2.0 are as much indebted to a 'hyper-archaeologicized' past as they are to the present.

However, the affordance offered by ubiquitous mobile technology has the potential to dramatically extend how we might understand Warwick's concept of 'artefactual fictions' (2012). Online, real-time engagement with both text and image, utilizing augmented and virtual realities, has the potential to radically democratize our engagement with place. No longer is the psychogeographic journey something one reads vicariously in a book; and no longer does it have to be an avant-garde dérive in the manner of the Situationists' early forays across Paris. Instead, the smartphone offers the opportunity for anyone, at any time, to undertake a physical exploration. This idea of performance is central to psychogeography; indeed, like psychogeography, theories of site-specific performance stress a particular focus on the very 'absences of place' and the constructedness of meaning (Parker Pearson 2010; Giannachi 2012). In this sense then, both psychogeography and contemporary theatre practice have significant overlap. Giannachi defines presence as the medium through which an individual actively engages with their environment (Giannachi 2012: 52). Importantly, this concept of presence is not uncontested; as Giannachi, Kaye and Shanks say, it is not 'a function of unity and synthesis' (2012: 11), but rather the 'traversal of difference' between 'self' and 'other' (2012: 10). This notion of 'traversal of difference' seems especially apt for psychogeography too, embracing as it does the central idea of a transgressive journey, leading to some kind of transformative encounter with absences and gaps, as in the case of *Walkways and Waterways*.

The application of digital technology only strengthens these ideas. As Zubrow reminds us, although archaeology has always been concerned with 'telling stories about the past' (2006: 10), such 'archaeological imagination' is increasingly mediated through digital technology (Zubrow 2006; Ferraby 2017). *Walkways and Waterways* has indicated how even a simple smartphone can transform spatial exploration, radically overhauling concepts such as the dérive and placemaking. In effect this amounts to a transformation in the relationship between the reader and the writer, foregrounding the role of the former in the creation of knowledge in what Tringham terms 'recombinant histories' (Tringham 2015). Pluciennik takes this further, suggesting that archaeologists should act as 'mediators and facilitators of meaningful conversations' (2015: 67). The role that digital technology can play in these conversations and recombinations should be apparent from projects such as *Walkways and Waterways*. Yet it is also clear that digital technology goes much further in terms of its impact. The very notion of 'absence' and 'presence', for example, takes on new and radical meanings within McQuire's relational space (2008), where the digitally mediated divide between the local and the global, the self and the other is reconfigured. Yet, as Graham, Zook and Boulton remind us, the notion of a single, all-encompassing augmented reality is itself a fiction. Rather, there are a plurality of augmented realities that are 'enacted and practiced in contingent and relational ways' (2012: 470). In other words, recourse to the digital still does not alter the fundamental fact that at the heart of any experience is a situated human being.

Shanks is equally keen to stress the importance of human experience. He describes how the Greek concept of chora (Khôra) is central to any understanding of the archaeological imagination. Drawing on Heidegger, Shanks describes chora as 'people's inhabitation of a place' (2012: 146; Heidegger 1983). In other words, chora is not simply empty space, but rather space that gives place for being. Central to this idea is what Shanks calls 'engagement with the remains of the past' (2012: 146). Yet chora also captures what Derrida saw as the notion of difference and radical transgression, wavering 'between the logic of exclusion and that of participation' (1995: 89). It is clear that these ideas resonate strongly with the performative dimension of psychogeography, particularly the concepts of 'presence' and 'traversal of difference'. Locative media, rather than threatening these approaches, offers an exciting enhancement of these more transformative and transgressive elements.

In their discussion of the archaeological imagination, Warwick and Willis note how the rational and the creative have always been irrevocably intertwined in narrative explorations of the past (2012: 1). Yet they sound a note of warning: 'the archaeological imagination is plural and constitutive of new knowledge but equally has the capacity to elide or disguise such knowledge: enhancing fact with fancy, but also relieving fact of its discomfort' (2012: 4). This sense of threat is acknowledged by Shanks when he notes that the archaeological imagination should not be trusted out of hand (2012: 149). Issues remain around whose voice is being heard and the interrelationship between fact and fiction. Digital technology, especially social media, has been identified as one of the main culprits behind the post-truth phenomenon, the *Economist* noting that two-thirds of Americans get their news through news filtering platforms such as *Facebook* (2016: 21). In this context, Pollock's recommendation that writers should never present fiction disguised as fact makes sense (2015: 283). Yet one of the things psychogeography 2.0 has also shown is that we do not necessarily see or understand the world in such a polarized way. The archaeological imagination is at its very root the stories we tell ourselves and the pathways we choose to take across our landscape. The misinformation behind 'post-truth' assertions is to be deplored, but at the same time social media is part of what Carson calls 'polyvocal' forms of news that support 'alternative ways of establishing authority' through enhanced participation and 'subjective voice' (Carlson 2017: 194). Making sure that we are able to utilize stories to help in the understanding of difference and the 'discomfort' of fact, to use Warwick and Willis's term, remains a vital goal for the years ahead.

In his book, *Underland: A Deep Time Journey* (2019), Macfarlane notes the narrative power of viewing the Earth across the endless eons of geological time: 'When viewed in deep time, things come alive that seemed inert … A conviviality of being leaps to mind and eye. The world becomes eerily various and vibrant again' (2019: 15–16). If, as I would argue, the notion of 'conviviality of being' is also at the heart of storytelling, then projects such as *Walkways and Waterways* suggest ways in which new entanglements of embodied exploration and digital technology open up innovative and affective forms of narrative that offer a similar kind of revelatory experience to Macfarlane's temporal reframing. In this transmedial landscape, the archaeological object becomes part of a transformative encounter that is both situated and embodied, and in which physical and emotional interconnectedness, Shanks's notion of chora (2012), become overt parts of the story.

References

Ackroyd, P. (1985), *Hawksmoor*, London: Hamish Hamilton.
Anon. (1960), 'Die Welt als Labyrinth', *Internationale Situationniste*, 4 (June): 5–7.
Bonneuil, C. (2015), 'The Geological Turn: Narratives of the Anthropocene', in C. Hamilton, C. Bonneuil and F. Gemenne (eds), *The Anthropocene and the Global Environmental Crisis*, 17–31, London: Routledge.
Canton, J. (2017), *Ancient Wonderings: Journeys into Prehistoric Britain*, London: William Collins.
Carlson, M. (2017), *Journalistic Authority: Legitimating News in the Digital Era*, New York: British Columbia Press.

Chesshyre, T. (2017), *From Source to Sea: Notes from a 215-Mile Walk along the River Thames*, Chichester: Summersdale.

Clark, E. A. (2004), *History, Theory, Text: Historians and the Linguistic Turn*, Cambridge, MA: Harvard University Press.

Coverley, M. (2010), *Psychogeography*, Harpenden, Hertfordshire: Pocket Essentials.

D'Ancona, M. (2017), *Post-Truth: The New War on Truth and How to Fight Back*, London: Ebury Press.

Davies, J. (2016), *The Birth of the Anthropocene*, Oakland: University of California Press.

Debord, G. (1955), 'Introduction to a Critique of Urban Geography', in K. Knabb (ed.), *Situationist International Anthology*, 8–11, Berkeley, CA: Bureau of Public Secrets, 1981.

Debord, G. (1958), 'Theory of the Dérive', in K. Knabb (ed.), *Situationist International Anthology*, 62–6, Berkeley, CA: Bureau of Public Secrets, 1981.

Derrida, J. (1995), *On the Name*, Stanford, CA: Stanford University Press.

van Dyke, R. M., and R. Bernbeck (2015), 'Alternative Narratives and the Ethics of Representation: An Introduction', in R. M. van Dyke and R. Bernbeck (eds), *Subjects and Narratives in Archaeology*, 1–26, Boulder: University Press of Colorado.

Elkin, L. (2016), *Flâneuse: Women Walk the City in Paris, New York, Tokyo, Venice and London*, London: Vintage.

Ferraby, R. (2017), 'Geophysics: Creativity and the Archaeological Imagination', *Internet Archaeology* 44. Available online https://doi.org/10.11141/ia.44.4.

Fukuyama, F. (2015), *Political Order and Political Decay: From the Industrial Revolution to the Globalisation of Democracy*, London: Profile Books.

Giannachi, G. (2012), 'Environmental Presence', in G. Giannachi, N. Kaye and M. Shanks (eds), *Archaeologies of Presence: Art, Performance and the Persistence of Being*, 50–63, London: Routledge.

Giannachi, G., N. Kaye and M. Shanks (2012), 'Introduction: Archaeologies of Presence', in G. Giannachi, N. Kaye and M. Shanks (eds), *Archaeologies of Presence: Art, Performance and the Persistence of Being*, 1–25, London: Routledge.

Graham, M., M. Zook and A. Boulton (2012), 'Augmented Reality in Urban Places: Contested Content and the Duplicity of Code', *Transactions of the Institute of British Geographers*, 38 (3): 464–79.

Hall, S. (2012a), *The Beautiful Indifference*, London: Faber and Faber.

Hall, S. (2012b), 'Butcher's Perfume', in S. Hall (ed.), *The Beautiful Indifference*, 3–39, London: Faber and Faber.

Hall, S. (2012c), 'She Murdered Mortal He', in S. Hall, *The Beautiful Indifference*, 117–47, London: Faber and Faber.

Hall, S. (2012d), '"Vuotjärvi"', in S. Hall (ed.), *The Beautiful Indifference*, 169–85, London: Faber and Faber.

Hamilton, C., C. Bonneuil and F. Gemenne (2015), 'Thinking the Anthropocene', in C. Hamilton, C. Bonneuil and F. Gemenne (eds), *The Anthropocene and the Global Environmental Crisis*, 1–13, London: Routledge.

Heidegger, M. (1983), *Einführung in die Metaphysik, Gesamtausgabe Band 40*, Frankfurt am Main: Klostermann.

Higgins, C. (2014), *Under Another Sky: Journeys in Roman Britain*, London: Vintage.

Higgs, J. (2017), *Watling Street: Travels through Britain and Its Ever-Present Past*, London: Weidenfeld & Nicolson.

Home, S. (1995), *Neoism, Plagiarism and Praxis*, Chico, CA: AK Press.

Jordan, S. (2019), *Postdigital Storytelling: Poetics, Praxis, Research*, London: Routledge.

Knepper, W. (2013), 'Revisionary Modernism and Postmillennial Experimentation in Zadie Smith's *NW*', in P. Tew (ed.), *Reading Zadie Smith: The First Decade and Beyond*, 111–26, London: Bloomsbury.

Koehler, A. (2013), 'Digitizing Craft: Creative Writing Studies and New Media: A Proposal', *College English*, 75 (4): 379–97.

Lea, D. (2017), *Twenty-First Century Fiction: Contemporary British Voices*, Manchester: Manchester University Press.

Loh, L. (2013), 'Zadie Smith's Short Stories: Englishness in a Globalised World', in P. Tew (ed.), *Reading Zadie Smith: The First Decade and Beyond*, 169–85, London: Bloomsbury.

Lucas, G. (2004), 'Modern Disturbances: On the Ambiguities of Archaeology', *Modernism/Modernity*, 11 (1): 109–20.

Macfarlane, R. (2005), 'A Road of One's Own', *Times Literary Supplement*, 7 October: 3–4.

Macfarlane, R. (2013), *The Old Ways: A Journey on Foot*, London: Penguin.

Macfarlane, R. (2019), *Underland: A Deep Time Journey*, London: Hamish Hamilton.

McGregor, J. (2012a), 'In Winter the Sky', in J. McGregor (ed.), *This Isn't the Sort of Thing That Happens to Someone Like You*, 5–35, London: Bloomsbury.

McGregor, J. (2012b), 'The Remains', in J. McGregor (ed.), *This Isn't the Sort of Thing That Happens to Someone Like You*, 188–92, London: Bloomsbury.

McGregor, J. (2012c), 'Supplementary Notes to the Testimony of Appellants B & E', in J. McGregor (ed.), *This Isn't the Sort of Thing That Happens to Someone Like You*, 147–56, London: Bloomsbury.

McGregor, J. (2012d), 'We Wave and Call', in J. McGregor (ed.), *This Isn't the Sort of Thing That Happens to Someone Like You*, 130–43, London: Bloomsbury.

McIntyre, L. (2018), *Post-Truth*, Cambridge, MA: MIT Press.

McQuire, S. (2008), *The Media City: Media, Architecture and Urban Space*, London: Sage.

March-Russell, P. (2009), *The Short Story: An Introduction*, Edinburgh: Edinburgh University Press.

May, C. E. (2002), *The Short Story: The Reality of Artifice*, London: Routledge.

Mitchell, D. (2015), *Slade House*, London: Sceptre.

Neuhaus, F. (2014) 'The Use of Social Media for Urban Planning: Virtual Urban Landscapes Created Using Twitter Data', in N. N. Pinto, J. A. Tenedório and A. P. Antunes (eds), *Technologies for Urban and Spatial Planning: Virtual Cities and Territories*, 113–34, Hershey, PA: Information Science Reference.

Nicholson, G. (1997), *Bleeding London*, London: Gollancz.

Ofcom. (2017), *The Communications Market Report*, London: Ofcom.

Paay, J., and J. Kjeldskov (2011), 'Bjørnetjeneste: Using the City as a Backdrop for Location-Based Interactive Narratives', in M. Foth, L. Forlano, C. Satchell and M. Gibbs (eds), *From Society Butterfly to Engaged Citizen: Urban Informatics, Social Media, Ubiquitous Computing and Mobile Technology to Support Citizen Engagement*, 253–73, Cambridge, MA: MIT.

Parker Pearson, M. (2010), *Site-Specific Performance*, Basingstoke: Palgrave MacMillan.

Parker Pearson, M., and M. Shanks (2001), *Theatre/Archaeology*, London: Routledge.

Pluciennik, M. (2015), 'Authoritative and Ethical Voices: From Diktat to the Demotic', in R. M. van Dyke and R. Bernbeck (eds), *Subjects and Narratives in Archaeology*, 55–81, Boulder: University Press of Colorado.

Pollock, S. (2015), 'Wrestling with the Truth: Possibilities and Peril in Alternative Narrative Forms', in R. M. van Dyke and R. Bernbeck (eds), *Subjects and Narratives in Archaeology*, 277–86, Boulder: University Press of Colorado.

'The Post-truth World' (2016), *The Economist*, 10 September: 21.

Sadler, S. (1999), *The Situationist City*, Cambridge, MA: MIT Press.

Sansom, I. (2017), 'Whither England? Psychogeography, Walking and Brexit', *Times Literary Supplement*, 7 July: 32.

Scofield, M. (2006), *The Cambridge Introduction to the American Short Story*, Cambridge: Cambridge University Press.

Sebald, W. G. (1998), *Rings of Saturn*, trans. M. Hulse, London: Harvill.

Shanks, M. (2012), *The Archaeological Imagination*, Walnut Creek, CA: Left Coast Press.

Sim, S. (2019), *Post-Truth, Scepticism & Power*, London: Palgrave Macmillan.
Sinclair, I. (1997) *Lights Out for the Territory: 9 Excursions in the Secret History of London*, London: Granta.
Smith, Z. (2013), *NW*, London: Penguin.
Solnit, R. (1999), *Wanderlust: A History of Walking*, London: Viking.
Speed, C. (2015), 'Walking through Time: Use of Locative Media to Explore Historical Maps', in L. Roberts (ed.), *Mapping Cultures: Place, Practice, Performance*, 160–80, London: Palgrave Macmillan.
Thomas, D. (2016), *Placemaking: An Urban Design Methodology*, London: Routledge.
Tringham, R. (2015), 'Creating Narratives of the Past as Recombinant Histories' in R. M. van Dyke and R. Bernbeck (eds), *Subjects and Narratives in Archaeology*, 27–54, Boulder: University Press of Colorado.
Warwick, A. (2012), 'The Dreams of Archaeology', *Journal of Literature and Science*, 5 (1): 83–97.
Warwick, A., and M. Willis (2012), 'Introduction: The Archaeological Imagination', *Journal of Literature and Science*, 5 (1): 1–5.
Zubrow, E. B. W. (2006), 'Digital Archaeology: A Historical Context' in T. L. Evans and P. T. Daly (eds), *Digital Archaeology: Bridging Method and Theory*, 10–31, Abingdon, Oxon: Routledge.

Part III

Literature, archaeology and layering the past

5

Deciphering the city: Ancient Egypt in Victorian London and psychogeographical archaeology

Eleanor Dobson

A year prior to the appearance of Jean-François Champollion's landmark work on the decipherment of ancient Egyptian hieroglyphs, *Lettre à M. Dacier* (1822), Thomas de Quincey published his 1821 *Confessions of an English Opium-Eater*, which includes an account of nightmare visions of 'Isis and Osiris', 'stone coffins, … mummies and sphynxes', 'crocodiles' and 'unutterable slimy things, amongst reeds and Nilotic mud' (de Quincey 1823: 171–2). De Quincey's experiments with opium, conducted in London but which, in this moment, evoke a Gothicized Egypt, reveal how the ancient and the 'eastern' resided just below the surface both of the city and of the individual psyche. Opium, in his case, is the catalyst that grants access to this deeper stratum. As the century progressed, however, ancient Egypt became increasingly visible without the need for psychoactive agents, through both the influx of genuine historical artefacts into the city and the proliferation of monuments and entertainments which drew upon Egypt's myriad mythologies. The Egyptian Hall, built in 1812 and located on 170–1 Piccadilly, brought ancient Egyptian motifs into the heart of the metropolis, designed to appeal to diverse audiences with an appetite for ancient Egypt as spectacle. The Egyptian Court, which opened in 1854 in the Crystal Palace at Sydenham, was the most immersive ancient Egyptian-themed space in the city, one of a series of courts designed to illustrate the history of art across a geographical span from Europe to the Middle East and from antiquity to the Renaissance. The obelisk known as Cleopatra's Needle was erected on the Victoria Embankment in 1878. As the century progressed, the Egyptianate landmarks of London proliferated, contributing to an ever-growing ancient Egyptian presence at the very heart of the British Empire.

The translation of ancient Egyptian writing by scholars such as Champollion and Thomas Young in the early nineteenth century had created a long-standing association between Egypt and the idea of secrets to be deciphered. By the later nineteenth century, however, hieroglyphic script no longer represented the impenetrable and unknowable; rather, hieroglyphs were, more and more, emblematic of a riddle that might be solved, an active invitation to decode, as scholars building upon Champollion's and Young's foundations continued to decipher the ancient Egyptian language. Chris Elliott notes, for instance, that 'four original texts in Ancient Egyptian hieroglyphs were composed for inscription on buildings in England' between the years 1840 and 1860 (2013: 171), heralding a shift in perceptions of hieroglyphs as component of an ancient and elusive script to modern tools of inscription. As ever more Egyptian monuments appeared in London, the act of decipherment extended beyond language to include architecture and the archaeological symbols and relics from antiquity that permeated the modern metropolis.

This chapter explores how the symbolism of ancient Egypt and its presence across various London spaces is evoked in Bram Stoker's *The Jewel of Seven Stars* (1903; reissued with an alternate ending in 1912) and Guy Boothby's *Pharos the Egyptian* (1898; 1899), both prime examples of what I term 'hieroglyphic' texts, which invite their readers to decode them. The routes that these novels chart and the locations their characters pass offer particular symbolism ripe for 'decipherment', the kind of movement and iconography which is a key focus of psychogeographical methodologies (Pleßke 2014: 312). I argue that individual journeys in such works have considerable symbolic implications and explore how Stoker and Boothby – who corresponded, at least, between 1893 and 1904,[1] a period in which both their novels were first published – recognized certain iconographic details in various monuments. Armed with a modicum of Egyptological knowledge and a focus on the city's geography, a reader of these novels can participate in a kind of 'psychogeographical archaeology', bringing to light hidden meanings lying just beneath the surfaces of these texts. Stoker and Boothby encourage such engagements with their novels, rewarding knowledge of the city in which they both lived, as well as symbolic detective-work that mimics the processes of the amateur Egyptologist.

Drawing upon Michel Foucault's notion of the 'heterotopia' (2008) – a place in which various time periods coexist – I suggest that a psychogeographically and Egyptologically informed reading of these texts can be a particularly productive means of understanding how ancient Egypt in the Victorian imagination came to be a point of collision between archaeological 'fact' and imaginative fantasy. Literary scholars have analysed how the emergence of Egyptian iconography, in London in particular, made a distinct and supernaturally charged impression on literature of the nineteenth century and beyond (Luckhurst 2012: 90), encouraging texts where fantasy and reality collide (Stauffer 2007) and stimulating the emergence of an 'Egyptian gothic' (Luckhurst 2012: 158). Julian Wolfreys argues in his analysis of Richard Marsh's *The Beetle* (1897) that Marsh's novel, set in the 'middle-class districts of West London' (2007: 22) participates in a 'textual mapping' of the city (ibid.: 15), where the eponymous antagonist 'is only ever encountered secreted away, largely unobserved, in an unassuming "villa" in a West London suburb' (ibid.). From the supposedly safe and familiar streets of West London, the Beetle exerts remarkable psychological power over the city and its inhabitants, creating a new geographically distinct locus of threatening power beyond 'the East End of London … commonly the stereotypical setting for late Victorian Gothic' (ibid.: 22). This chapter builds upon Wolfreys's methodology to show the encoded 'hieroglyphic' significances of the cityscape in the work of Stoker and Boothby.

Paying attention to the 'exotic zones' (Luckhurst 2012: 90) which encourage a geographic merging of London with ancient Egypt identified in Luckhurst's (2012), Stauffer's (2007) and Wolfreys's (2007) analyses, this study proposes a methodology that unites recent literary and archaeological concerns. Brenda J. Bowser has established the 'emergence of an "archaeology of place", around the turn of the millennium, 'more attendant to understanding the ways in which people impart meaning to their cultural and physical surroundings' (2004: 1). This privileging of 'subjective' (ibid.) and 'phenomenological experience' (ibid.: 2) and the discipline of archaeology's own 'draw[ing upon] method and theory from … cultural geography, oral history, and architecture' (ibid.) has, as David Gange notes, made a significant impact on contemporary historical methodologies: 'historians are looking increasingly to archaeologists, geographers and anthropologists rather than literary scholars for their method and conceptual frameworks' (2017: 252). Gange contends that 'A host of historians in the present practice their discipline with a renewed confidence in the archive of the feet, the importance of place' (ibid.), akin to Spencer Jordan's conception of 'stories as physical journeys' in Chapter 4. Foucault's heterotopias themselves rely on the 'archive' (2008: 20) that a particular place itself offers up, inviting us to read a place as 'simultaneously mythic and real' (ibid.: 17). Fiction, of course, is one way in which the city space manifests on a 'mythic' level, and scrutinizing this cultural form in particular alongside these places suggests a way in which literary studies might also benefit from the archaeology of place.

I argue that Stoker and Boothby – as authors attuned to the presence of ancient Egypt in the modern metropolis – create disturbing spatial and temporal ruptures that can not only be identified by readers 'hieroglyphically' but that invoke imperial anxieties of 'reverse colonization' (Arata 1990). Their heterotopic city spaces imagine the reintroduction of ancient power into the modern world, the threat that Egyptological traces pose lurking on the peripheries of the real at the height of Empire. As the powerhouse at the centre of the British Empire, with which the history of Egyptology is inextricably entwined, London is a logical site for such archaeological fantasy and the novels draw attention to the colonial plundering of ancient sites and the mass movement of Egyptian artefacts to the imperial centre. Opening with an analysis of Stoker whose geographies, of the two writers, have attracted more critical attention, I turn next to Boothby, demonstrating how in both novels we witness the merging of the familiar spaces and streets of upper- and middle-class London with ancient Egyptian presences. Allowing fictional and real spaces to collide, the novels demonstrate that the sites of London's West End might be understood as arcane allegories of Empire that both haunt and enchant the modern city of London for its inhabitants.

The Jewel of Seven Stars

The role of geography in Stoker's novels, particularly in his more famous *Dracula* (1897), has long been examined by critics (Mighall 1999; Davies 2004). As in *Dracula*, London is a major setting in *The Jewel of Seven Stars*, and this novel too sees the capital city invaded by a sexually threatening, ancient aristocrat – in this case, the mummy of the fictional Egyptian queen Tera. The novel's protagonist, Malcolm Ross, receives a summons in the night from Margaret Trelawny, the woman he loves. Margaret's father, an Egyptologist, is in a state of unconsciousness; experts are called, but no one can explain Trelawny's condition, and when they keep watch in his room, they themselves fall into trance-like states. Trelawny's ancient Egyptian artefacts are blamed for these narcotic effects, in particular the mummy of the ancient Egyptian queen. Eventually, Trelawny recovers, revealing that he intends to carry out the queen's plan to be resurrected in the modern world. Trelawny – with Ross, Margaret, his colleague (Corbeck) and doctor (Winchester) in tow – takes Tera's body to his secluded Cornwall laboratory, where the ancient relics necessary for the process are arranged. Upon unwrapping the queen, however, the group realize that she is the double of Trelawny's daughter. It transpires that Trelawny had discovered the queen's mummy at precisely the moment at which his wife gave birth to Margaret and that the concurrence of these events established a psychic and physical connection between the two. In the novel's original ending published in 1903, the experiment goes horribly wrong. The queen's body vanishes, and all the characters but Ross are left dead. In the revised ending of 1912 – likely the work of Stoker's publishers rather than Stoker himself – the experiment fails and Tera's body remains inert. The narrative concludes with the marriage of Margaret and Ross, though colouring this moment is the implication that Tera's spirit might have entered Margaret's body.

Stoker often encoded his work with hidden meanings, and critics have examined how this manifests in *The Jewel of Seven Stars*. Glennis Byron offers the most thorough decoding of Stoker's choice of name for Tera and her English doppelgänger, Margaret Trelawny, for example. Margaret's full name 'contains two anagrams of Tera, most notably the last four letters of her first name reverse the name of Tera' (I would add that one can actually spell the word 'anagram' using the letters of 'Margaret Trelawny', ending with the first five letters of 'Margaret' spelled backwards); Byron further observes that 'Tera has its roots in the Greek *teras* or monster' (2007: 61). The encryption of Tera's name within Margaret's, both in her first name and surname, links the two characters textually so that one appears as the mirror image of the other, while the name's etymology (along with its homonym, 'terror') hints at Tera's dangerous nature before it has been fully revealed through narrative events. Through leaving such textual clues, Stoker encouraged his readers to dig beneath the surface of his text to bring into view the full meanings of his novel. Beyond the linguistic symbolism identified by Byron, however, Stoker's encoding extends to a manipulation of geographic symbolism. Semi-autobiographical information, including Stoker's own experiences of London, exacts a powerful influence on *The Jewel of Seven Stars*. Indeed, David Glover suggests that Stoker 'constantly invites a biographical reading' because of his use of 'topical references and allusions', as well as basing his characters on himself and those he knew (1996: 3), encouraging the critical detective work inherent to the psychogeographical and Egyptological readings I employ here. At the most basic level, the protagonist of *The Jewel of Seven Stars*, Ross, is a barrister. Stoker himself trained as a barrister, although he never worked in law. Perhaps more significant, and more geographically striking, is the fact that several of Stoker's close friends were members of the Hermetic Order of the Golden Dawn, a secret society whose main temple and meeting places were close to Stoker's house (Hebblethwaite 2008: xxxiii).[2] The Golden Dawn dedicated much of its energy to the learning of sorcery and the procurement of purportedly substantial magical abilities, including those associated with ancient Egypt. Over the course of Stoker's novel, Margaret comes to exhibit the kinds of magical power that Golden Dawn members claimed to have harnessed. Stoker's vision of ancient Egyptian magic in the modern world was likely informed by his associates in the Golden Dawn, and there is evidence to suggest that *The Jewel of Seven Stars* was approved of by its initiates. The Scottish writer J. W. Brodie-Innes – a member of the group's Edinburgh temple – wrote to Stoker stating that he had read the novel aloud to his family, praising the way in which the text shed 'a clearer light on some problems which some of us have been fumbling in the dark after for long enough'.[3] The rituals of groups such as the Golden Dawn were themselves heavily imbued with ancient and esoteric symbolism, a counterpoint to the Egyptian symbolism of London's landmarks, which Stoker infuses with supernatural and emblematic potency.

Stoker never travelled to Egypt. His alternative geographies (including *Dracula*'s Transylvania) were instead informed through research at the British Museum, an institution to which he sends his characters in both *Dracula* and *The Jewel of Seven Stars* when information on foreign lands is required, and which Golden Dawn members frequented for their own purposes. Stoker regularly visited the Reading Room at the British Museum to conduct research for his novels (Cowie and Johnson 2002: 157) and as such was frequently in close proximity to one of the most significant global collections of ancient Egyptian artefacts. The museum is, according to Foucault, a noteworthy example of 'heterotopias that are characteristic of Western culture in the nineteenth century' in that they seek to accumulate 'all times' (2008: 20) and, I would add, all places, if we consider their imperialist role in Victorian knowledge creation. The British Museum was an important social hub for those with Egyptological interests. Stoker was acquainted with the director of Egyptian Antiquities at the museum, E. A. Wallis Budge, whose popular works on ancient Egypt were among Stoker's personal collection of books on the subject. Stoker was also familiar with the pioneering archaeologist Flinders Petrie and was a close friend of the artist Lawrence Alma-Tadema (Murray 2004: 119), who increased the historical authenticity of his paintings by including artefacts on display at the British Museum under Budge's curatorship (Curl 1982: 192). Evidently, then, Stoker was involved in Egyptology's social networks – both the professional and amateur – and its heterotopias, based around this group in London's West End.

The Jewel of Seven Stars can be closely mapped onto the London geography with which Stoker was personally familiar. At the beginning of the novel, Stoker provides the reader with an exact route that Ross takes from his rooms on 'Jermyn Street' to Trelawny's house: his cab turned onto 'Piccadilly', 'bowled swiftly along Knightsbridge … turned up the Kensington Palace Road and presently stopped opposite a great house on the left-hand side, nearer … the Notting Hill than the Kensington end of the avenue' (Stoker 2008: 8, 10).[4] Kensington Palace Road does not – and did not – exist, but Stoker later refers to the location as 'Kensington Palace Gardens', a real road on which he imagines the Egyptologist's house. Jermyn Street, close to the central cluster of the West End's gentlemanly institutions, associations and clubs, is a fitting home for Ross and is situated between the British Museum and Trelawny's collection, which is itself at one point light-heartedly described as indistinguishable from the former (ibid.: 33). Thus, from the outset, Ross is located centrally in a heterotopic area surrounded by – and saturated with – ancient Egyptian artefacts, among which rests the dormant mummy of Tera (Figure 5.1).

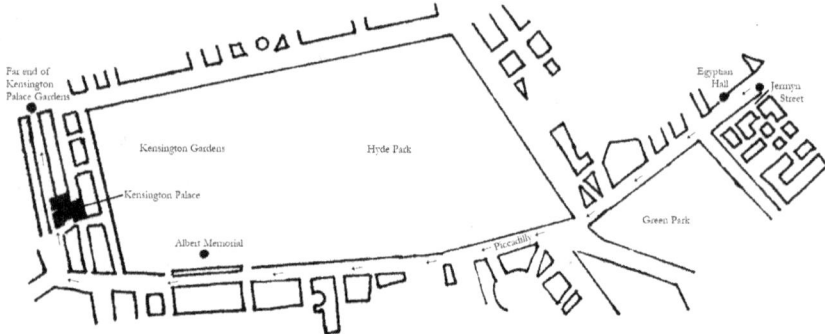

Figure 5.1 Ross's route from Jermyn Street to Kensington Palace Gardens, passing the Egyptian Hall and the Albert Memorial. Author's own.

That Stoker provides such a detailed list of directions from Ross's to Trelawny's address is peculiar, especially as this level of real geographical detail does not occur elsewhere in the novel. Stoker leaves out details about the novel's Cornish location, for example, inventing the locale of 'Kyllion' (perhaps combining the real locations of Kynance and Mullion coves, and likely with symbolic emphasis in the first syllable; read 'kill'). Likewise, the Egyptian setting is invented: the Valley of the Sorcerer is evidently based on (but distinct from) the Valley of the Kings, the valley opposite Thebes where New Kingdom ancient Egyptian royalty and nobility were often entombed. As Shelley Trower notes, Stoker's description of Cornwall is deliberately hazy, 'becoming part of Egypt', simultaneously 'part of yet different and separable from England' (2012: 200). The indistinctness of geographical location in both cases means that they blur into fantastical spaces, on the peripheries of the known world, somewhere 'other' in comparison to the defined – and real – geography of London.

In contrast, Stoker's early reference to London's real streets seems deliberate and considered. Gill Davies observes of *Dracula* that 'the detailed geography of London is deployed to highlight a number of imperial and national anxieties' and highlights the significance of 'the geography of London … [in] the representation of Dracula's growing power' (2004). Dracula follows a potential victim up Piccadilly, and, as Davies notes, one of Dracula's properties is located 'significantly at the west end of Piccadilly, near to Buckingham Palace Gardens' (ibid.). Dracula's proximity to Buckingham Palace places him as a threat to the highest echelons of British society and to

Britain's imperial mission. In *The Jewel of Seven Stars*, another journey along Piccadilly is recorded, and the destination of Kensington Palace Gardens again highlights the vicinity of a royal residence as a key location in Tera's struggle to assume power. The journey along Piccadilly reveals places and monuments in the vicinity whose symbolism Stoker draws attention to through this geographic detail. Although Ross does not mention these features in his narration, his route would have taken him past both the Egyptian Hall, with its distinctive ancient Egyptian-style façade, and the Albert Memorial in Kensington Gardens. The Egyptian Hall was England's first major public building with a neo-Egyptian façade. The distinctive frontage was inspired by the temple of Hathor at Dendera and featured many archetypal elements of ancient Egyptian architecture, including sphinxes, pseudo-hieroglyphs, a distinctive tapering pylon shape and lotus columns (Richards 2009: 18). Above the entrance were statues of the Egyptian deities Isis and Osiris, the mythology of which is evoked in Stoker's text. From 1819, the Egyptian Hall was a museum and subsequently housed art exhibitions, panoramas, anti-Spiritualist demonstrations, and illusion and moving picture shows until its demolition in 1905 (Parramore 2008: 26). David Gange states that strongman-turned-antiquarian Giovanni Belzoni's celebrated recreation of the tomb of Seti I at the Hall in 1820 'brought ... Egypt ... to life in London, confusing lines between the museum and the city, the spiritually-charged primeval world and the immanent, material present' (2013: 77–8). An understanding of such confusion is vital to a psychogeographical appreciation of London's heterotopic potential to harbour ancient Egyptian encounters.

This idea of immersive exhibits breaking down concepts of time and space is important, not just in the context of the Egyptian Hall but in the wider contemporaneous cultural engagement with ancient Egypt. As a modern 'western' place masquerading as the ancient and the 'eastern', frequently housing ancient Egyptian artefacts discovered by the era's most distinguished Egyptologists, the Egyptian Hall provided an unusual home for its relics. With its galleries and great hall decorated in an ancient Egyptian style to match the exterior, it was not simply a remarkable piece of neo-pharaonic architecture but a theatrical experience in its own right (Luckhurst 2012: 96). Visually, artefacts were transported back to a fantastical reimagination of their original context, beheld as part of a simulation of the time and geography that produced them.

The experience of the viewer, therefore, would have been quite different to an encounter with a typical museum exhibit (the British Museum being the closest institution with a substantial Egyptian collection), with its emphasis on classification. Instead, categories of artefact and artifice, authenticity and pretence, ancient and modern, would have seemed far more fluid, the experience much more explicitly heterotopic.

This fluidity is harnessed by Stoker whose novel, like the Egyptian Hall itself, complicates notions of time and space. In ancient Egyptian myth, the god Osiris (one of the gods of the Egyptian Hall's façade's statues) was murdered and dismembered by his brother Set. After his murder, his wife (and sister) Isis found the pieces of his corpse and, with the aid of other gods, restored his life by a process that involved mummification followed by sexual revival. It is the subsequent magical production of an heir that allows Osiris to live again. The plot of Stoker's novel gestures towards this narrative in several ways. The dead body of Tera has been, through the severing of her hand, partially dismembered, and the Egyptologist who acquires her body as an artefact with the intention of reviving it is not impervious to its sexual allure. It is symbolic that, unlike his other mummies, Trelawny keeps Tera's body in his bedroom. Tera's revival, however, does not come about through the production of a genetic heir, but rather a psychic one. Trelawny's daughter, Margaret, is Tera's physical double, increasingly channelling the queen as the novel progresses. The incestuous nature of Isis and Osiris's union is paralleled in Trelawny's attraction to a woman with an uncanny resemblance to his own daughter. In this sense, the Egyptian Hall and its statues appear to be directly linked to Stoker's plot, as Stoker draws on the ancient Egyptian mythology associated with the deities depicted. Yet instead of spelling these associations out for his readership, Stoker encourages a ludic engagement with his text where the individual reader is rewarded for both their knowledge of London and their knowledge of Egyptology (Figure 5.2).

The other site that Ross's cab would have passed on the detailed route that Stoker sets out – the Albert Memorial – has even stronger symbolic links to the details of *The Jewel of Seven Stars*. Installed in Kensington Gardens in 1872, the monument features several surrounding statues each with a different theme (Asia, Africa, America and Europe; Agriculture, Commerce, Engineering and Manufactures). The Africa group is dominated by the figure of a pharaonic

Figure 5.2 'Africa' group of Albert Memorial, September 2017. Author's own.

queen. Ancient Egyptian civilization is also commemorated on the Frieze of Parnassus which surrounds the base of the central part of the monument. The pharaohs Cheops (also known as Khufu, generally held to have commissioned the construction of the Great Pyramid of Giza) and Nitocris (a female pharaoh whose actual existence is debated, to whom the smallest of the three main pyramids of Giza is attributed by Manetho and, incidentally, the only woman on the frieze) are immortalized among the architects, while an unnamed Egyptian symbolizes the civilization's contributions to sculpture. Nitocris, hovering tantalizingly out of reach in the historical record, and perhaps not a real historical figure at all but rather legendary, is of particular interest. Credited with the mass execution of her brother's killers by Herodotus, she might be seen to symbolize the kind of merciless, mass violence that Tera herself comes to embody.

It is the ancient Egyptian queen of the memorial's Africa group that is, however, most closely linked to Stoker's novel, featuring an intriguing combination of historically accurate and inaccurate details. The design of this sculpture changed dramatically from its conception to its creation. William Theed, the sculptor behind the design, stated that

> my endeavour has been ... to lead back the mind of the beholder to the period when the oldest state of antiquity gave an impetus to science and nourished the infancy of that art ... . The female figure seated on the lion and listening to the teachings of Britannia, is allegorical of modern Egypt, for whose progress in civilization, the world is so much indebted to British enterprise. The half buried and rudely sculptured Sphynx, the emblem of her enigmatical past. (Theed, quoted in Bremner 2007: 97)

Evidently several fundamental changes to the design took place subsequent to this moment. The lion – deemed too closely linked to iconography associated with Britain – was substituted for a camel (a historically inaccurate steed for an ancient Egyptian queen). The queen herself certainly appears to hail from ancient rather than modern Egypt, and instead of being instructed by Britannia, who appears elsewhere in this grouping (tellingly, instructing a black African subject), rests a guiding hand on a figure that looks to be an ancient Egyptian servant leaning upon a sphinx. The change in the design glorifies ancient Egyptian power, making the central figure a representative of ancient rather than modern Egypt. Furthermore, the removal of Britannia to the back of the grouping changes the emphasis of the statue as a monument representing British power over Egypt to one representing ancient Egyptian might in its own right (though, of course, not without a gesture to Britain's 'civilizing' mission in modern Africa). Echoes can be deciphered in Stoker's novel, in which modern British characters (Trelawny at the forefront) attempt and fail to control ancient Egyptian magic. It is Egypt which is magically and scientifically advanced in Stoker's novel, needing no instruction from Britannia's representatives.

In keeping with the tradition of powerful females – either goddesses or queens – being depicted wearing the vulture headdress in ancient Egyptian art and sculpture, the statue represents authoritative femininity. Simultaneously, however, the figure holds the *heqa* sceptre, similar to a shepherd's crook, which was usually depicted in the hands of a male god or monarch (more customary for queens or goddesses were the papyrus or lotus sceptres). Although this is almost certainly either an unintentional error in design or else a deliberate choice made for aesthetic reasons rather than historical accuracy, the result sees the power of a king reassigned to the figure of a queen. This links explicitly to Tera, who dons all of the male pharaonic regalia as a physical symbol of her claim to 'all the privileges of kingship and masculinity' (Stoker 2008: 129). Indeed, Tera's willingness to have herself depicted in male clothing makes her similar to the female pharaoh Hatshepsut (Dobson 2019: 41–7). The sphinx that forms part of the Africa group sports the cartouche of Thutmose III, meant, as Benedict Read points out, to suggest 'Egypt's pre-eminent conqueror' (1982: 100). Yet, others, including Stoker, may instead have seen the female pharaoh next to the sphinx with this cartouche, and thought instead of Hatshepsut, Thutmose's stepmother, aunt and co-regent.

London was evidently saturated in Egyptian symbolism, and in the novel it is seemingly due to the density of these powerful Egyptian presences – many of them coded feminine in the goddess Isis, the pharaoh Nitocris and the female pharaoh suggestive of Hatshepsut – that Tera herself can wield such dangerous power so far away from her country of origin. Remembering his second meeting with Margaret, Ross recalls a boat trip that strongly evokes Enobarbus's description of the titular Egyptian queen in Shakespeare's *Antony and Cleopatra* (1623). The scene is depicted as sumptuous, the water 'golden-brown under the canopy of translucent green' (Stoker 2008: 7), suggestive of the colouring of Shakespeare's Cleopatra's 'burnish'd' barge (2.2.230), with its 'beaten gold' deck (2.2.231). Stoker's oars are less ostentatious – not 'silver' like Shakespeare's queen's (2.2.233) – though they still 'flashed and dripped' with water (Stoker 2008: 7), giving them a similar luminous quality. The intense heat suggested by Shakespeare's use of the adjective 'Burn'd' to describe polished, sun-warmed metal (2.2.231) finds a parallel in Stoker's 'fierce July sunlight' (Stoker 2008: 7); both Margaret and Cleopatra find relief from scorching temperatures, in the 'cool shade'– underneath a canopy of trees in Stoker's text and in 'divers-colour'd fans, whose wind did seem / To glow the delicate cheeks which they did cool' in Shakespeare's (2.2.242–3). Margaret, assuming the role of the queen, reclines in the boat while Ross – evidently the successor of Shakespeare's 'pretty dimpled boys' who guide Cleopatra's barge (2.2.241) – stands and rows. The reader later learns that the river is the Thames between Cookham and Windsor, though the section of the river does not need to be that of central London for Stoker's association to be understood. The Thames is equated with the Nile; modern Britain and ancient Egypt cease to be geographically and temporally distinct. Here the English woman and the figure of the Egyptian queen begin to coalesce, symbolic – at this early stage – of the very real and frightening possibility of the fusion of ancient and modern women at the end of the novel.

The lethargic sumptuousness of the novel's opening is thus disrupted by Stoker's narrative of a murderous queen who seeks revival in the modern world, specifically 'in a more northern land' than her native Egypt (Stoker 2008: 130). If Tera seeks to colonize Britain from the tactical position of central London, the city is already one primed to receive her. Stoker imagines the queen situated amidst a hub of Egyptological traces, close to the collections of the British Museum, statues of female pharaohs and the goddess Isis. His Gothic narrative centres on the threat of reverse colonization – in Tera's tomb, 'In every picture where hope, or aim, of resurrection was expressed there was the added symbol of the North' (ibid.: 129) – and these imposing figures representative of immortality and queenship already populating the landscape suggest (to the reader in the know) that this will be but a small leap for Tera. In Stoker's original ending, after having noted their ignorance as to the queen's motivations to be resurrected in modern times, how she had 'waded … through blood' (ibid.: 209) to pursue these ends and evidently fearing that Tera intended to employ her powers for 'the conquering of unknown worlds' (ibid.: 214), most of the characters are left dead and the queen's body disappears, the implication being that she has reawakened and is at large. In the revised version we are left with the chilling implication that while the experiment to revive her appears to have failed she has in fact possessed Margaret's body. In both scenarios the logical next step for the queen is to return to the heterotopia provided by London, where she might reign both as a modern and an ancient monarch.

Pharos the Egyptian

Boothby's *Pharos the Egyptian* was serialized in *The Windsor Magazine* in 1898 before it was published as a novel the following year. The narrative follows

Cyril Forrester, an artist living in London, as he meets the mysterious Pharos, an old man with a beautiful young ward, Valerie de Vocxqal. It transpires that Pharos is the ancient Egyptian Ptahmes, who seeks revenge on Forrester as his mummified body is kept in the artist's studio, having been brought back to Britain by Forrester's late father earlier in the century. Pharos's vengeance is far from straightforward, however. He leads Forrester on a perilous journey to Egypt and back; Forrester, meanwhile, is unaware that Pharos has injected him with a pathogen, and as he travels he unwittingly spreads a plague that decimates Europe. At the novel's close, Pharos's threat is eradicated; the ancient Egyptian deities annihilate him as punishment for his crimes. While the protagonists – Forrester and de Vocxqal – survive, London's population is devastated.

Cleopatra's Needle features early on in the novel, and the Thames was associated with Egypt in central London most powerfully in the instalment of this obelisk. The Needle inspired a host of connotations when it was erected and was directly associated with issues of monarchy, not just as an artefact connected (erroneously) to the Egyptian queen Cleopatra VII through its moniker but as an artefact inscribed with royal cartouches. The British royal family were also linked to this obelisk; Cleopatra's Needle had 'personal associations' with Prince Albert, who suggested that the obelisk might be erected in Hyde Park to mark the site of the Crystal Palace before it was moved to Sydenham (Bremner 2009: 226, 228). As a result, after Albert's death it was proposed that the Needle, if brought to London, might make a fitting memorial, and proposals for an obelisk to be erected when early ideas for the Albert Memorial were circulating furthered this association (ibid.: 234, 236). Notions of British and ancient Egyptian royalty were intimately entwined in such monuments, and the antagonists in the fictions bound to such places often threaten an entire nation, the reigning monarch – in the case of Boothby's and Stoker's novels, Victoria and Edward VII, respectively – effaced from the text. These rulers are, in both narratives, conspicuous by their absence (Figure 5.3).

Cleopatra's Needle is a unique landmark, psychogeographically speaking. This obelisk, dating back to around 1450 BCE, became simultaneously, upon its erection on the Embankment, London's oldest and newest monument. The Needle remains to this day one of the most striking examples of the intrusion of the remnants of Egypt's ancient civilization into the modern

Figure 5.3 Cleopatra's Needle, August 2017. Author's own.

city, reconstructing the metropolis as a Foucauldian heterotopia, a place in which 'time ... accumulates indefinitely' (Foucault 2008: 20). As a 'heterotopia of time' the city 'enclose[s] in one place all times, all epochs, all forms, all tastes' (ibid.). Foucault's main example of the typical heterotopia of time, the nineteenth-century museum, can be extended outwards into the Victorian city.

Museum-like in its acquisition and display of artefacts and iconography, the city's open spaces were, through such installations as the Needle, transformed into ones of exhibition, where traces of different times collided and combined.

The Thames provided a fitting backdrop for this monument, not merely as the city's most ancient natural landmark but also in its associations with the goddess Isis. The section of the Thames flowing through Oxford bears the goddess' name, also immortalized at the end of the Thames's Celtic name, *Tamesis*. Although the exact etymological origins are disputed, the river had, by this point, been associated with Isis for hundreds of years (Ackroyd 2008: 26–7). The keystones of Henley Bridge even feature masks of the river deities – the male Thames and the female Isis – suggesting that the river brings together the complementary ancient British and the ancient Egyptian in a harmonious pairing that unites 'western' with 'eastern', male with female. While de Quincey had already made the connection between the Thames and the Nile in his drug-induced visions far earlier in the century, the instalment of the Needle only cemented the Thames's Egyptian connections.

The Needle brings together ancient Egyptian and nineteenth-century engineering and design; guardian sphinxes and benches were made up to complement its imagery (the sphinxes bearing, like the sphinx in the Albert Memorial's 'Africa' group, the cartouche of Thutmose III). The Victoria Embankment proved an ambiguous location for the Needle, which was, for many years, the subject of extended debate. Having been completed eight years before the Needle's arrival, the Embankment provided the city with a modern sewerage system and, less than three months after the obelisk's installation, became the first British street to feature permanent electric lighting (though gas lighting was restored in 1884 for financial reasons). Thus, the Needle was a symbol of supreme antiquity within an area of London closely associated with cutting-edge modernity.

Tellingly, Forrester, the protagonist and narrator of *Pharos the Egyptian*, describes the Embankment in modern terms, emphasizing its 'myriad lights' and the distant sound of a train (Boothby 1899: 25). Forrester, who has been drawn to the Needle as he wanders flâneur-like through the streets of London's West End, is struck by the extraordinary age of the monument and, having acknowledged the modernity of his surroundings, ponders 'the changes the world had seen since the giant monolith first saw the light of day' (ibid.). With an almost supernatural allure, the Needle draws Forrester to the riverside where, in a scene that evokes the real tragedy that occurred during its transit from Egypt, he witnesses a man drowning:

> I remember distinctly standing beneath a gas-lamp at the corner of Villiers Street, as the clocks were striking midnight, … I … strolled down towards the river … then, crossing the road, made my way along the Embankment towards Cleopatra's Needle. … The myriad lights of the Embankment were reflected in the river like lines of dancing fire, and … behind me a train was rolling across the bridge from Charing Cross with a noise like distant thunder. … I must have been thinking of my picture, and of the land and period which had given me the idea. … I know that on this occasion the ancient monument, in front of which I soon found myself, affected me as it had never done before. I thought of the centuries that had passed since those hieroglyphics were carved upon the stone, of the changes the world had seen since that giant monolith first saw the light of day. … I was so absorbed … that when a sudden cry of 'Help, help!' rang out from the river it was with a sensible shock that I returned to the commonplace and found myself standing where I was. … The cry had come from the other side of the Needle. I accordingly hastened to the steps … shouting … that a man was drowning. It might have all been part of some evil dream: the long line of silent Embankment on either side, the swiftly-flowing river, and that despairing appeal for help coming so suddenly out of the black darkness. Then I became aware that I was not alone on the steps. There was another man there, and he stood motionless, peering out into the dark stream, scarcely a dozen paces from me. (Boothby 1899: 24–6)

Forrester's sojourn is one which is charted with precise geographical detail (from Villiers Street to the Embankment, with reference to Charing Cross), but we are alerted to the fact that while this is the real London of Boothby and his original readership, we are also in a space of supernatural possibilities. The witching hour begins with the chiming of the clocks at midnight. Like Ross's night-time summons, this journey takes place while most of the city sleeps; Forrester has access to a city at once the same and perceptibly different from its daytime counterpart, an 'evil dream' version of the metropolis. While the trappings of modernity are ever-present they are described in such a way as to connect them to the natural world, evocative of pathetic fallacy and hinting at the dangers to come: the 'lights of the Embankment' are 'like lines of dancing fire', the noise of the train 'like distant thunder'. These naturalistic similes also serve to undercut the modernity of the sights and sounds of the metropolis, making them seem instead timeless. As Forrester slips into daydream the heterotopic nature of the Needle's environs are emphasized; Forrester exists in a space in which multiple time periods collide, where the ancient and the modern are both present and the lines between them blurred.

That Cleopatra's Needle should be used as a location for drowning suggests something of the dark magic of Pharos – the figure who stands motionless as the unfortunate man drowns – and that of the Needle itself. The Needle's history encompassed tragedy and disaster: when en route from Alexandria to London the obelisk broke free from the ship which was towing it and six volunteers went out to retrieve it and drowned in the effort. This story is recorded on a bronze plaque which was attached to the south side of the Needle's mounting stone in 1882. The Needle, therefore, not only stood as a symbol of the British imperial relationship with Egypt but also as a memorial to those who died endeavouring to make its installation possible. Boothby instils his literary version of the obelisk with a strong sense of the uncanny – the Needle functions as a cursed object, heralding the imminent doom of those around it, linking directly to its true history: the fast-moving water and the man's futile cries for help suggest the horror of the drownings that the plaque on the Needle leaves untold. Not only does the Needle call forth musings on the ancient world – the time when 'that giant monolith first saw the light of day' – or indeed on Forrester's present with its trappings of modernity, it also serves as an anchor to a particular event: the tragic drownings of 1877. Multiple layers of time exist in this unique space. Echoing the growing trend of depicting real museums in fiction towards the end of the nineteenth century (Hoberman 2011: 10), the city's real Egyptian monuments – Cleopatra's Needle in this case – are seen to exist in reality and in literary counterparts. Functioning as a kind of alternate reality, the artificial (Boothby's fantastical plot) is made more believable or, rather, Boothby facilitates the reader's suspension of disbelief, by allusions to the authentic. Simultaneously, this real space is enchanted, reimagined in a Gothicized account that privileges the darker moments in the Needle's history to provide a sinister tone early on in Boothby's text.

Boothby's novel, far more than Stoker's, hinges upon plausible journeys and real details of these places. Many road and place names are given throughout, with a particular density of these in the portions of the novel set in Britain's capital and to a lesser extent in the section in Egypt. Forrester travels from London to Naples (visiting the Teatro di San Carol), to Pompeii (with excursions to the Temple of Mercury and Temple of Isis), to Cairo (major plot developments occurring at the Sphinx and the Great Pyramid of Giza), to Luxor (with reference to the Temple of Ammon at Karnak, the Necropolis of Thebes and the Temple of Luxor), to Constantinople via Port Said, and then back to London via Vienna, Prague, Berlin and Wittenberge. Forrester and Pharos chart a course that encloses much of the Mediterranean Sea and traverses several countries famed for their fallen empires (Roman, Byzantine and Egyptian). Beginning and ending in London, this loop starts and finishes at the centre of the British Empire: Pharos seeks to decimate London through the introduction of a plague into the city, a disease which Forrester has unwittingly spread from eastern to western Europe as they travelled.

As with Stoker's Tera, Pharos is quick to invade the fashionable West End. Indeed, Piccadilly, the road along which Ross travels to Trelawny's house, also features in *Pharos the Egyptian*, in this case as a road which Forrester and Pharos both use. We learn early in the novel that Forrester's studio is a short distance from Piccadilly along which he 'stroll[s] … in the direction of my studio' (Boothby 1899: 38). Piccadilly, representing Forrester's home and London more broadly, might be read as symbolic for that which Pharos seeks to destroy: Forrester, in particular, not only as an individual to whom he is opposed but also, as Stoker's Dracula earlier identified, the 'teeming millions' of potential victims who traverse the city's major thoroughfares (Stoker 1897: 49). Pharos not only wreaks his revenge on the closest living relative to the man who removed his body from its original resting place but also implicates Europe more generally, intentionally infecting the working classes as well as the upper echelons of society. In so doing, Boothby suggests that all are implicated in the imperial mission, concentrated as it is in the city space: in Pharos's eyes, all must be punished indiscriminately. It is, however, the Needle that functions as the point of origin for his widescale revenge, located a short distance upriver from the Houses of Parliament, the seat of political power, which had been yet another proposed location for the Needle before its instalment on the Embankment.

Boothby thus draws upon the symbolism of London's ancient Egyptian traces to instil his text with the weight of historical events including the tragic loss of life in the transportation of Cleopatra's Needle; he suggests, like Stoker, that his antagonist's thriving within this city space – indeed, Pharos's first appearance being in the Needle's shadow – is due in part to the already-established Egyptian presence. It is noteworthy that neither Tera nor Pharos arrives in London of their own accord; their objectified bodies are purchased or plundered and installed in homes as, at best, artefacts of scientific interest and, at worst, curiosities. Both make a bid to resist their status as imperial loot, taking advantage of their position at the heart of Empire. Boothby's and Stoker's attention to geographical detail supports an interpretation of their texts as warnings about the repercussions of colonialism through possibilities of Egyptian resistance in a city already permeated by its symbolism. Images of and icons associated with Egyptian gods and monarchs had flooded London's West End as Britain's imperial mission progressed. Stoker and Boothby turn this on its head, transforming these buildings, statues and monuments from statements of Britain's imperial hold over Egypt to eerie presences that suggest the reverse: the glamour of ancient Egypt, the obsession with collection, has instead resulted in the colonization of the city itself, the construction of a heterotopia in which ancient Egypt has, in a sense, invaded London, breaking down a linear sense of time and rendering the city prime for exploitation at the hands of the once-inert bodies of the ancient Egyptian dead.

Conclusion

Both Stoker and Boothby depicted a London space that was at once fantastic and authentic, based upon the real city that had allowed them – and their readers – access to the world of ancient Egypt. Just as ancient Egypt seeped into the make-up of London, London influenced fictional texts dealing with ancient Egyptian themes. Stoker and Boothby made references to London's real locations and symbolism, drawing inspiration from its artefacts, institutions and architecture to instil their texts with an authoritative air produced by allusions to the real. *The Jewel of Seven Stars* and *Pharos the Egyptian* can be read as narratives about the Egyptianized cityscape, their authors actively drawing on the stories and significances behind notable landmarks such as the vengeance of Nitocris, the myth of Isis and Osiris, and the tragic loss of life in the transportation of Cleopatra's Needle, in order to provide their writing with a kind of mystical significance. The employment of the cryptic in order to blur fantasy and reality enchants the city space, bringing the modern and ancient worlds into a close synchrony. The effect is Gothic, as ancient Egyptian antagonists infiltrate a space at once real and unreal, ancient and modern; both Stoker and Boothby exploit ancient Egyptian presences in London to underline the imperial anxieties at the heart of their texts.

What these texts invite us to do is to continue to decipher symbolism via twin psychogeographical and Egyptological modes, extending beyond these works to a wealth of literary material that might be scrutinized in similar ways, from the early nineteenth century through to the present day. The perceptive reader will have observed that the photographs of the Albert Memorial's 'Africa' group and Cleopatra's Needle in this chapter are my own; it is possible to walk these routes as part of my methodology, to harness the 'archive of the feet' (Gange 2017: 252) in order to psychogeographically experience place as these writers might have done. The city has, of course, changed dramatically in the interim, with sites such as the Egyptian Hall having been demolished, requiring the consultation of maps and the paper archive in order for us as modern psychogeographers, historians and archaeologists to access as close to an approximation of these places as they existed as we can, 'to achieve', in Bowser's words, 'an understanding of the meanings of archaeological places', 'to reconstruct senses of place' (2004: 2). Literature has a significant part to play in this piecing together, crucial as it is to a sense of place's mythology; at this 'new frontier of exciting and innovative approaches to understanding the past' (ibid.), the imaginative uses of each place contribute to its multifaceted existence as heterotopia. As the significances of many such monuments are known only by a fraction of those who encounter them, it is up to the reader to crack the codes and piece together the fragments that such authors have left. Waiting for us are not only vestiges of authorial playfulness, imagination and fantasy but also the more ominous remnants of Empire and the Gothic 'antagonists' who sought to resist its bonds.

Notes

1. The Brotherton Collection, Leeds University Library, contains five letters from Boothby to Stoker dated between 26 May 1893 and 12 November 1904.
2. Stoker first moved to London in 1878, incidentally the year in which Cleopatra's Needle was erected. In 1884 the Stokers moved to 17 St Leonard's Terrace in Chelsea where they stayed for twelve years before their address is recorded as having changed to number 18 in 1896. They remained registered at this address for another 10 years, during which time Stoker wrote *The Jewel of Seven Stars*, situating the opening events just a short distance north of his own home. The Golden Dawn's Isis-Urania Temple congregated at 17 Fitzroy Street, with meetings also held at Mark Mason's Hall, both destinations being a short cab ride from Stoker's address.
3. Brotherton Collection, Leeds University Library, Letter from J. Brodie-Innes to Bram Stoker, 29 November 1903, quoted in Murray (2004: 229).
4. Due to the rarity of the 1903 and 1912 editions of *The Jewel of Seven Stars*, I quote from the 2008 Penguin edition.

References

Ackroyd, P. (2008), *Thames: Sacred River*, London: Vintage.

Arata, S. D. (1990), 'The Occidental Tourist: *Dracula* and the Anxiety of Reverse Colonization', *Victorian Studies*, 33 (4): 621–45.

Boothby, G. (1899), *Pharos the Egyptian*, London: Ward, Lock.

Bowser, B. J. (2004), 'Prologue: Toward an Archaeology of Place', *Journal of Archaeological Method and Theory*, 11 (1): 1–3.

Bremner, G. A. (2007), 'Between Civilization and Barbarity: Conflicting Perceptions of the Non-European World in William Theed's *Africa*, 1864–69', *Sculpture Journal*, 16 (1): 94–102.

Bremner, G. A. (2009), 'The "Great Obelisk" and Other Schemes: The Origins and Limits of Nationalist Sentiment in the Making of the Albert Memorial', *Nineteenth-Century Contexts*, 31 (3): 225–49.

Byron, G. (2007), 'Bram Stoker's Gothic and the Resources of Science', *Critical Survey*, 19 (2): 48–62.

Champollion, J. F. (1822), *Lettre à M. Dacier relative à l'alphabet des hiéroglyphes phonétiques*, Paris: Firmin Didot.

Cowie, S. D., and T. Johnson (2002), *The Mummy in Fact, Fiction and Film*, Jefferson, NC: McFarland.

Curl, J. S. (1982), *The Egyptian Revival: An Introductory Study of a Recurring Theme in the History of Taste*, London: Allen & Unwin.

Davies, G. (2004), 'London in *Dracula*; *Dracula* in London', *Literary London: Interdisciplinary Studies in the Representation of London*, 2 (1). Available online http://www.literarylondon.org/london-journal/march2004/davies.html (accessed 7 April 2017).

De Quincey, T. (1823), *Confessions of an English Opium-Eater*, 2nd edn, London: Taylor and Hessey.

Dobson, E. (2019), 'Cross-Dressing Scholars and Mummies in Drag: Egyptology and Queer Identity', *Aegyptiaca: Journal of the History of Reception of Ancient Egypt*, 4: 33–54. Available online https://journals.ub.uni-heidelberg.de/index.php/aegyp/article/view/66092/58907 (accessed 28 August 2019).

Dobson, E. (2020), 'Perfume, Cigarettes and Gilded Boards: *Pharos the Egyptian* and Consumer Culture', in E. Dobson (ed.), *Victorian Literary Culture and Ancient Egypt*, 162–84. Manchester: Manchester University Press.

Elliott, C. (2013), 'Compositions in Egyptian Hieroglyphs in Nineteenth Century England', *Journal of Egyptian Archaeology*, 99: 171–89.

Foucault, M. (2008), 'Of Other Spaces (1967)', trans. Lieven De Cauter and Michiel Dehaene, in M. Dehaene and L. De Cauter (eds), *Heterotopia and the City: Public Space in a Postcivil Society*, 13–29, London: Routledge.

Gange, D. (2013), *Dialogues with the Dead: Egyptology in British Culture and Religion 1822–1922*, Oxford: Oxford University Press.

Gange, D. (2017), 'Retracing Trevelyan? Historical Practice and the Archive of the Feet', *Green Letters: Studies in Ecocriticism*, 21 (3): 246–61.

Glover, D. (1996), *Vampires, Mummies and Liberals*, Durham, NC: Duke University Press.

Hebblethwaite, K. (2008), 'Introduction', in B. Stoker, *The Jewel of Seven Stars*, K. Hebblethwaite (ed.), xi–xxxviii, London: Penguin.

Hoberman, R. (2011), *Museum Trouble: Edwardian Fiction and the Emergence of Modernism*, Charlottesville: University of Virginia Press.

Luckhurst, R. (2012), *The Mummy's Curse: A True History of a Dark Fantasy*, Oxford: Oxford University Press.

Marsh, R. (1897), *The Beetle: A Mystery*, London: Skeffington.

Mighall, R. (1999), *A Geography of Victorian Gothic Fiction: Mapping History's Nightmares*, Oxford: Oxford University Press.

Murray, P. (2004), *From the Shadow of Dracula: A Life of Bram Stoker*, London: Jonathan Cape.

Parramore, L. (2008), *Reading the Sphinx: Ancient Egypt in Nineteenth-Century Literary Culture*, Basingstoke: Palgrave Macmillan.

Pleßke, N. (2014), *The Intelligible Metropolis: Urban Mentality in Contemporary London Novels*, Bielefeld: Transcript.

Read, B. (1982), *Victorian Sculpture*, New Haven: Yale University Press.

Richards, J. (2009), *The Ancient World on the Victorian and Edwardian Stage*, Basingstoke: Palgrave Macmillan.

Shakespeare, W. (1623), *Antony and Cleopatra*. Available online http://shakespeare.mit.edu/cleopatra/full.html (accessed 29 January 2020).

Stauffer, A. M. (2007), 'Ruins of Paper: Dickens and the Necropolitan Library', *Romanticism and Victorianism on the Net*, 47. Available online http://www.erudit.org/revue/ravon/2007/v/n47/016700ar.html (accessed 9 September 2017).

Stoker, B. (1897), *Dracula*, New York: Grosset and Dunlap.

Stoker, B. (1903), *The Jewel of Seven Stars*, London: Heinemann.

Stoker, B. (1912), *The Jewel of Seven Stars*, London: William Rider.

Stoker, B. (2008), *The Jewel of Seven Stars*, ed. K. Hebblethwaite, London: Penguin.

Theed, W. 'Description of "Africa" ', The Royal Archives Vic/Add. H 2/914, quoted in G. A. Bremner (2007), 'Between Civilization and Barbarity: Conflicting Perceptions of the Non-European World in William Theed's *Africa*, 1864–69', *Sculpture Journal*, 16 (1): 94–102.

Trower, S. (2012), 'On the Cliff Edge of England: Tourism and Imperial Gothic in Cornwall', *Victorian Literature and Culture*, 40: 199–214.

Wolfreys, J. (2007), *Writing London Volume 3: Inventions of the City*, Basingstoke: Palgrave Macmillan.

6

From the Great Castle of the Hill to the Great Mound on the river: Imperialism and transatlantic archaeology in Thomas Hardy's 'Ancient Earthworks'

Anna West

If you have been to Dorset, you may have seen Maiden Castle, an Iron Age earthwork fortress sometimes considered the finest example of a hillfort in England. First a Neolithic settlement in 600 BC, it was taken over by the Roman army in AD 43, with its inhabitants moving slightly north to settle in a town now known as Dorchester. If you have not been to Dorset, you may have encountered this well-preserved site through Thomas Hardy's *The Mayor of Casterbridge* (1886), where it serves as a meeting point for midnight trysts.

If you are from the US Midwest, the sight of Maiden Castle may remind you of the mounds and earthworks strewn across Wisconsin, Ohio, Missouri and other Midwestern states – cultural sites of indigenous peoples, sometimes having served as burial mounds for tribes local to the region. If you have been to Detroit's historic Fort Wayne – an army fort established in 1843 along the Detroit River near an area known as Springwells and the site of the last peace treaty signed in Michigan between the US government and indigenous tribes – you may have seen a small hill enclosed on all sides by a chain-link fence labelled 'Indian Mound'. You will not have seen, however, what was known to nineteenth-century Detroiters as the Great Mound, once standing at the junction of the Detroit and Rouge Rivers, or any of the other numerous indigenous mounds that existed in Detroit – because they have been destroyed.

This chapter looks at the diverging narratives of two archaeological sites linked by the 1885 publication of Hardy's short story 'Ancient Earthworks' in the *Detroit Post*. Picturing these two sites – in Dorchester and Detroit – raises questions of preservation and archaeological practice and, inextricably bound up with them, questions of empire, racism and economics. In its original publication context in Detroit, 'Ancient Earthworks' can be read as a satire of the destruction wrought by archaeological digging in the Victorian era and of the economic and imperialistic values that drove it.

'Ancient Earthworks' in context

In this brief short story – which covered less than three columns of a broadsheet page in the 15 March 1885 *Detroit Sunday Post* – Hardy opens with an emotive description of an ancient earthwork on a stormy night. The description continues for three paragraphs before identifying the ruin, which the narrator introduces using the older form of its name, 'Mai-Dun – The Great Castle of the Hill' (Hardy 1885: 13). Not until the fourth paragraph does the human first-person narrator make a physical entrance on the scene, and the following paragraphs that make up the middle of the story relay his journey from a cottage to the earthwork through the squalls of the storm to meet a friend, placing emphasis on the experience of climbing the three escarpments of the earthwork and reflecting on the life – past and present – of the fortress itself (Figure 6.1).

The plot of the story takes place entirely at the end: at the bottom of the second column in the *Post*, the narrator finally meets his friend. His friend's motive for meeting turns out not to be a 'meditative ramble' as supposed; rather, the friend begins an illegal night-time dig upon the site in the name of the 'unmolested pursuit of science' (13). They uncover a skeleton and several artefacts – including a gold statuette of Mercury, which the narrator later wonders if his friend had pocketed instead of replacing. The narrator views his friend uneasily as one of those 'men who, in their enthusiasm for some special science, art or hobby, have quite lost the moral sense which would restrain them from indulging it illegitimately' (13), although the friend promises to do nothing more than dig for knowledge's sake, 'to verify a theory or displace it, and ... to take away nothing – not a grain of sand', claiming such action is 'no sin' (13). The story ends with a postscript labelled 'Five years later', in which

Figure 6.1 The escarpments of Maiden Castle. Author's own.

the narrator has his suspicion confirmed when the statuette is found among the effects of his friend who has since passed away, and the statuette is then placed in the local museum (13).

Critics have not always known what to make of 'Ancient Earthworks'. In his study of Hardy's short stories, Martin Ray writes that it is:

> one of Hardy's least successful short stories. One feels that he wanted to write a moody, evocative sketch about Maiden Castle, but then felt obliged to tack on some narrative stage business at the end to justify it. In its earliest publication in America, [the story] has a plot and characterization which are more perfunctory even than in the version which we read now. (1997: 291)

Like many of Hardy's writings, 'Ancient Earthworks' evolved through subsequent revisions and publications; the 'definitive' version of the short story read today is titled 'A Tryst at an Ancient Earthwork'. Ray traces the revisions made as the story was published in 1893 in the *English Illustrated Magazine* and then in its UK and US releases in Hardy's short story collection *A Changed Man and Other Tales* (1913), which was updated again the following year for the special 1914 'Wessex Edition' publication of Hardy's oeuvre (1997: 290). While the variants between the versions of the story once it was published in book form are minor, Hardy made significant revisions between the 1885 'Ancient Earthworks' and the 1893 'Ancient Earthworks at Casterbridge' (Ray 1997: 290–301). The most significant change between the first two versions, Ray notes, is the addition of about fifty lines towards the end, which increases the focus on its human characters and shifts the story from 'a rather static sketch' into 'more of a dramatized work of fiction' (1997: 294).

More sympathetic criticism of the story tends towards the stance expressed by F. B. Pinion in his notes to the *Collected Stories*: 'The narrative is slight, but the description of Maiden Castle … is impressive and indicative of Hardy's interests as a member of the Dorset Natural History and Antiquarian Field Club' (Hardy 1988: 925). As Harold Orel and Martin Davies have noted, the story fits in with Hardy's other archaeological writings of the mid-1880s, including a paper given in 1884 at a meeting of the Dorset Antiquarian Club titled 'Some Romano-British Relics Found at Max Gate, Dorchester' and his descriptions of Maiden Castle and Maumbury Rings in *The Mayor of Casterbridge*, which he had nearly finished at the time of his composition of 'Ancient Earthworks' (Orel [1986] 2000: 10–11; Davies 2011: 52–6).[1]

In his biography of Hardy, Michael Millgate notes that the story's covert excavation on Maiden Castle has its origins in real life. Hardy was an active member of the Dorset Antiquarian Club, but he was at odds with 'a prominent local antiquary named Edward Cunnington, who had made a number of significant archaeological "finds" near Dorchester in the early 1880s – including … "an amber cup, allegedly complete till Cunnington trod on it"' (Millgate 2004: 227; Newman and Pevsner 1972: 485, as quoted in Millgate). According to Millgate, a dig Cunnington carried out on one end of Maiden Castle served as inspiration for the story. Hardy avoided publishing the story in England for eight years after its first printing, and when it finally was published in the UK in the *English Illustrated Magazine*, he complained to his friend Florence Henniker that the editor had identified the location of the story against his wishes, writing that 'it is just possible that a character who appears in the narrative may be said to be drawn from a local man, still living, though it is really meant for nobody in particular' (Hardy 1980: 43). Despite Hardy's protest, it seems clear that Cunnington – whom he somewhat ironically referred to as 'our local Schliemann' in his paper for the club – served as an inspiration for the character (Millgate 2004: 228).

The story's first place of publication, however, serves as the link between our two opening forts. The circumstances surrounding the composition of this piece and the arrangement of its publication in the *Detroit Post* are not exactly certain: Hardy sent a postcard in early February 1885 to T. H. S. Escott, the editor of the *Fortnightly Review*, to confirm that the manuscript was in preparation and would be sent in the following days. Millgate speculates Escott likely acted as an agent in placing the story with the *Detroit Post*, as Hardy received payment through Escott (Hardy 1978: 130). Hardy's interest in archaeology and his desire to publish the piece (with its caricature of Cunnington) at a distance would perhaps suffice to explain the motive for the story and its placement. But did Hardy know about Detroit's ancient earthworks when he composed his story or when he placed it? I have yet to find definitive proof of whether or not he was aware of the possible impact of his story. While the *English Illustrated Magazine* manuscript of the story is held at the Harry Ransom Center, the original *Detroit Post* manuscript has not been located, nor has any correspondence that might explain the placement of the story, beyond the postcard to Escott.

In general, Hardy was aware of and concerned by the methods and approaches of archaeologists whose work sometimes destroyed rather than documented the cultural artefacts and sites they sought to investigate. As Orel notes, 'more often than any other popular creative writer of his time Hardy … spoke of how recklessly earlier generations had dug into barrows and destroyed the archaeological evidence, discarded anything that could not be converted to pounds and pence, and triumphantly claimed that their wanton and sometimes piratical behaviour advanced (rather than betrayed) the cause of knowledge' ([1986] 2000: 11). In his later life, Hardy was friends with the archaeologist Augustus Pitt-Rivers and admired his work to systematize the act and documentation of the archaeological dig (Orel [1986] 2000: 11). Due to his interest in and knowledge of archaeology – and his moving depictions of English sites such as Stonehenge in his novels – Hardy was asked to write pieces arguing for the preservation of historical sites for the periodical press.[2] Despite its Dorset specifics, Hardy's story of Maiden Castle resonates on a broader scale, and its appearance in the *Detroit Post* is significant in this regard.

The existence and destruction of North American mounds was a topic frequently written about in the American periodical press, as well as in scientific papers on both sides of the Atlantic. A 1883 *Science* article by F. W. Putnam, the curator of the Peabody Museum of Archaeology and Ethnology at Harvard University, outlines the central question inspired by the immense earthworks – 'Who made the mounds?' (1883: 168). With the science of archaeology nascent in the United States, it was widely believed that the mounds were created by an ancient race of no relation to indigenous populations of the day. In the article, Putnam argued that:

> There are so many kinds of mounds in this country, that it shows a limited experience in their investigation when a writer here and there asserts that they are all the work of the present Indians, or their immediate ancestors; and an equal disregard of known facts, when another confidently asserts that they were all made by a people unlike and superior to the Indian races and of great antiquity. Each earthwork, mound, and burial-place should be investigated and studied by itself. (1883: 168)

He concluded, 'by a proper study of the mounds and earthworks of North America, facts will at last be accumulated by which an approximate determination of their chronology and relation to existing peoples will be made possible' (1883: 168). While Putnam was responsible for helping develop the scientific methods used in archaeology in the United States, the mounds themselves were quickly disappearing, levelled to make way for urban development, diminished in size in rural areas by ploughing and agricultural activity and plundered by 'pot hunters' (Milner 2004: 18). One newspaper article covering the levelling of what was once the largest mound in St. Louis (known as Mound City for the prevalence of earthworks) reported that 'curiosity hunters flock there daily by the hundred, hoping to secure and carry off some relic of the past ages' (Milner 2004: 18). By the time the study Putnam suggested was carried out, many of the sites had already been destroyed.

Whether arbitrarily or at the hand of an editor, the story of Dorset's ancient earthwork could be transposed across the Atlantic and read as a local story, a story perhaps of the Great Mound on the Rouge River in Detroit. The initial lack of an identifier for the earthwork in 'Ancient Earthworks' lends the opening description a sense of universality: the mound depicted could easily be one of Detroit's ancient earthworks. In contemporaneous texts, including Detroit naturalist Bela Hubbard's *Memorials of a Half-Century* (1887) published two years later, a sketch of the Great Mound on the Rouge River is labelled, 'Diagram of Ancient Earthwork, Springwells, Near Detroit' (Hubbard 1887: 221). In his manuscript submitted to the *English Illustrated Magazine*, Hardy offers the title 'An Ancient Earthwork' along with pictures of Mai-Dun itself (Ray 1997: 293). The plural in Hardy's *Detroit Post* title – 'Ancient Earthworks' – creates a space to read the story unbound from its local details.

From historical accounts, Detroit may have had its own 'local Schliemann' in the form of Michigan ethnologist and amateur archaeologist Henry Gillman. His reports of excavations on various mounds in Michigan are strewn with references to artefacts accidentally destroyed in the process, and his methods seemed to parallel that of the friend in Hardy's story. In his 1873 report to the Smithsonian, for example, he admitted that 'in the rude method pursued in opening this mound many choice relics were destroyed; a large number also were carried away, scattered, and lost' (Gillman [1873] 1877: 367). When sites he excavated were later visited in 1925 by the archaeologist W. B. Hinsdale, Hinsdale lamented the state's lack of a systematic and comprehensive approach to the collection of data and methods of excavation, urging for steps to be taken to preserve what remained 'from further damage and destruction' (1925: vii). In a passage of *Memorials of a Half-Century*, Hubbard describes accompanying Gillman on an excavation of the Great Mound. Like the characters of Hardy's story, they uncover an altar as well as a skeleton early on, then proceed to uncover an array of artefacts and skeletons (Hubbard 1887: 234–7). The purpose of their dig – like that of the friend in 'Ancient Earthworks' – is to ascertain the true nature of the mound.

The Great Mound, as Hubbard records, was an ancient mound that had been in continued use until the late eighteenth century as a central burial ground for regional tribes, who brought the bones of their dead for internment at the site. He urged, 'We must regard this great mound – now being so ruthlessly destroyed – as a vast necropolis, containing the dead of many centuries, belonging both to the prehistoric past and to our modern era' (Hubbard 1887: 237). Like Hardy's narrator, who imagines the early inhabitants of Maiden Castle in repose on the mounds 'yawn[ing] and stretch[ing] their arms in the sun', Hubbard imagined how the scene at the Great Mound had both changed and remained the same (Hardy 1885: 13). The canoe had given way to the 'winged barks of commerce, the barge and the steamer', and the forests were 'superseded by cultivated farms and village streets, and smoking factories' (Hubbard 1887: 238–9). 'Still, as of old', he wrote, 'the warm sunshine rests upon this spot', but

> the beings these cheered in the olden time have all perished from the land; … and the proud pile which they created to immortalize their memory has nearly disappeared, and will soon have vanished altogether, in the progress of an unheeding and remorseless civilization. (238–9)

Hubbard's comment on the 'progress of an unheeding and remorseless civilization' mirrors contemporaneous rhetoric in relation to indigenous tribes. In the United States in particular, the destruction of the burial mounds paralleled the displacement and obliteration of indigenous peoples.

The rhetoric of 'civilization' and the destruction of indigenous culture

In order to understand the possible implications of Hardy's story in its Detroit context and the significance of its defence of preserving earthworks, it is necessary to examine the history of the rhetoric of 'civilization' in North American settler-indigenous relations, a term that recurs throughout documentation of the relationship between the US government and indigenous tribes. In the years following the formation of the United States in 1776 and the end of the American Revolution in 1783, President George Washington and the early US government recognized individual tribes as independent nations and continued the process of making treaties to provide for the expansion of white settlers on indigenous-held lands (Hirsch 2014). From the 1790s well into the twentieth century, however, the US government formulated a policy of 'civilization', with the stated goal of assimilating indigenous peoples to the practices of white settlers and with the implicit target of forcing tribes to cede their lands (Ethridge 2007).

In his book *Stamped from the Beginning: The Definitive History of Racist Ideas in America* (2016), Ibram Kendi argues that throughout history, racist ideas have been formulated to justify economically motivated racist policies and 'to redirect the blame for their era's racial disparities away from these policies and onto [people of color]' (2016: 9). He explains that 'Racially discriminatory policies have usually sprung from economic, political, and cultural self-interests', with 'the principal function' being 'the suppression of resistance to racial discrimination' (9–10). Instead of critiquing the policies themselves, 'Consumers of these racist ideas have been led to believe there is something wrong with [the people they target]' (10). This goes back to Aristotle's (and Plato's, and possibly Socrates's) notion of the Ladder of Being, or the Great Chain of Being, which by the Enlightenment period placed the white European male at the pinnacle of civilization. Aristotle's writings on human hierarchy shaped notions of the superiority of some groups over others; for example, Kendi writes, Aristotle invented the idea of 'climate theory to justify Greek superiority, saying that extreme hot or cold climates produced intellectually, physically, and morally inferior people who were ugly and lacked the capacity for freedom and self government' in order to support the 'normalizing of Greek slaveholding practices and Greece's rule over the western Mediterranean' (17). While *Stamped from the Beginning* traces the history of racist ideas against black people in the United States over the course of US history, Kendi's argument is also supported by the timeline of US–indigenous relations over the course of the nineteenth century, with the Eurocentric conceptualization of 'civilization' justifying racist policies against indigenous peoples.

This rhetoric of 'civilization' focused on agriculture and education with the goal of assimilating indigenous peoples to Eurocentric practices in order to gain control of indigenous lands. The 1790 Treaty of New York between the US government and the Creek nation, for example, proposed in Article XII that the Creeks 'may be lead to a greater degree of civilization, and to become herdsmen and cultivators, instead of remaining in a state of hunters' (Kappler 1904: 28). The public-facing goal of this plan, as historian Robbie Ethridge explains, was for indigenous peoples to become 'self-sufficient farmers' (ignoring the fact 'many … had been agriculturists for millennia'), but the true aim 'was to settle [them] on small farms and thus force them to give up hunting on their vast territories' (2007: 1). By suggesting that 'remaining in a state of hunters' indicated a lesser degree of 'civilization', the policy reinforced racist notions of white superiority and paved the way for future appropriation of indigenous lands.

The second aim of 'civilization' policies targeted education. In 1818, the House Committee on Indian Affairs proposed 'the establishment of schools' in order 'to produce this desirable object [civilization]' (Fletcher 1888: 162, brackets original). The committee explained the rationale behind this education initiative with the following: 'In the present state of our country one of two things seems to be necessary. Either that those sons of the forest should be *moralized* or *exterminated*' (162, italics mine). This led to the passing of the Civilization Fund Act in March 1819, which stated:

> For the purpose of providing against the further decline and final extinction of the Indian tribes adjoining the frontier settlements of the United States, and for introducing among them the habits and arts of civilization, the President of the United States shall be ... authorized ... to employ capable persons of good moral character to instruct them in the mode of agriculture suited to their situation; and for teaching their children in reading, writing, and arithmetic, and performing ... other duties. (163)

Under the guise of concern for the extinction of tribes, the Act was meant to assimilate indigenous youths into Euro-American culture, thus opening native lands to white settlers and resolving the ongoing conflicts and battles between the US and indigenous tribes.

In *Stamped from the Beginning*, Kendi details 'two kinds of racist ideas: segregationist and assimilationist' (2016: 2). These can both be seen in the US government's policy reports concerning indigenous tribes, as they alternate between an appeal to the assimilationist ('civilize') and the segregationist (remove or 'exterminate'). In 1824, the Bureau of Indian Affairs was established as part of the War Department, with the purpose of carrying out the 'civilization' plan. When Andrew Jackson was elected president, one of his first pieces of legislation was the Indian Removal Act of 1830, which forced all eastern tribes to move west of the Mississippi River (Peters 1846: 411–12; Thornton 1987: 114). From the 1840s to the 1860s, four key ideological and economic factors influenced the spread of racist ideas about indigenous peoples and shifted US policy in relation to them: (1) the 1845 invention of the term 'Manifest Destiny' and the following widespread belief that white

Euro-American settlers had been ordained by Providence to continue their westward expansion (Pratt 1927: 798); (2) the 1849 Californian Gold Rush that exponentially increased emigration to the Pacific coast and fuelled the genocide of California-based tribes (Thornton 1987: 107); (3) the 1859 publication of *On the Origin of Species*, with the theory of natural selection unwittingly fuelling Herbert Spencer's development of 'social Darwinism' and Francis Galton's study of eugenics (Kendi 2016: 210); and (4) the 1861–5 American Civil War with the increased nationalism that resulted, which led to the dismantling of tribal sovereignty (Hirsch 2014). This all culminated in the outlawing of treaties in 1871 with the Indian Appropriations Bill (where it was tacked on as an addendum), shifting indigenous peoples from members of sovereign nations to 'dependent wards' of the state (Prucha 1976: 79).

During this period, the message of 'civilize' or 'exterminate' is repeated in the annual reports of the Commissioners of Indian Affairs as well as state and federal legislation, with economic considerations as the driver. In the *Annual Report of the Commissioner of Indian Affairs* for 1868, for example, the commissioner discusses the conflicts emerging along emigration routes to the West, suggesting

> If it be said that the savages are unreasonable, we answer, that if civilized they might be reasonable. ... If it be said that because they are savages they should be exterminated, we answer that, aside from the humanity of the suggestion, it will prove exceedingly difficult, and if money considerations are permitted to weigh, *it costs less to civilize than to kill*. (1868: 42, italics mine)

Repeatedly, the blame for conflicts is placed on the 'savage' nature of indigenous peoples, with the supposition that such conflicts might be prevented if these tribes were as 'civilized' as their Euro-American displacers.

By 1868, the indigenous population in the United States had fallen to an estimated 300,000 according to the *Annual Report of the Commissioner of Indian Affairs* (1868: 1). While original indigenous population numbers before the arrival of European settlers are unknown, scholars estimate there were over 5 million indigenous people living in the conterminous United States (Thornton 1987: 32). In his study *American Indian Holocaust and Survival: A Population History since 1492*, Russell Thornton attributes the decrease in population to 'disease; warfare and genocide; removal and relocations; and destruction of ways of life' (1987: 91). The government's 'civilization' policies were a targeted effort for the destruction of tribal ways of life. This becomes clear in the solutions to the so-called 'Indian problem' proposed in the 1868 commissioner's report, which suggested gathering 'all tribes east of the Rocky Mountains' on 'one or two territories' (*Annual Report 1868*: 44–5). In this district, the writer urged, 'agriculture and manufactures should be introduced ...; schools should be established ...; their barbarous dialects should be blotted out and the English language substituted', all with the aim to 'blot out the boundary lines which divide them into distinct nations, and fuse them into one homogeneous mass' (44). The author concluded, 'Aside from extermination, this is the only alternative now left us' (44). With the end of tribal treaties in 1871 and the subsequent formation of reservations, agents of the Department of Indian Affairs were issued the *Regulations of the Indian Department* in 1884, which laid out the regulations for 'civilization' including: the restriction of indigenous peoples to their reservation (*Regulations* 1884: 85); the abolition of traditional dances (89); and the removal of medicine men (89). Such regulations aimed to undermine tribal culture and dismantle tribal identity, lumping diverse tribal nations into 'one homogenous mass' that could be set up as a 'savage' other (*Annual Report 1868*: 44).

In the same March 1885 issue of the *Detroit Post* that holds Hardy's story 'Ancient Earthworks', several articles on indigenous peoples demonstrate the underlying rhetoric reiterating racist ideas used to support discriminatory US policies. In the 'Children's Corner' section of the paper, an unnamed writer informs its young audience that 'Indian boys are exceedingly deficient in moral qualities' and admonishes, 'Savage life has no charms unless it is seen from a distance, say from the deck of a Lake Superior steamboat, or in the pages of a Leather Stocking novel' ('Indian Boys' 1885: 11). Three pages before Hardy's story, an article by an anonymous 'special correspondent' entitled 'A Savage Display | The New Orleans Exhibit of Ethnology' describes an exhibition of indigenous artefacts in Louisiana (1885: 10). It opens with the declaration: 'The savage and semi-savage races now populating portions of our territory are, in obedience to inexorable law, passing away' (10). The article marvels at the built landscapes created by indigenous peoples, declaring them as approaching a sophisticated civilization, but it attributes these landscapes to ancient 'mound-builders' whose culture – 'the myths, the traditions, the government, the household customs' – has been 'utterly lost' (10). In this sense, the article attempts to see indigenous earthworks in a similar way to that in which Maiden Castle was viewed by Hardy's contemporaries: as sites of an ancient 'great people', not of tribes very much still alive (10). To recognize the earthworks as feats of engineering by the 'savage' tribes with whom the US government was continually fighting over territory would be to admit that these tribes were, in fact, civilized – with their own systems of society, culture and morality.

The distancing and dehumanization of indigenous peoples were central to the question of the mounds' construction. As Michael Schiffer explains:

> Instead of attributing the construction of these mounds to Indians, Americans invented the myth of lost races. It was believed that Indians lacked the organizational and technical skills to build such mounds, and so Americans looked to groups such as the Phoenicians or Lost Tribes of Israel. At a time when the United States was waging wars against Indian tribes, taking their lands and forcing them onto reservations, the myth helped to justify racist practices. (2017: 3)

By the end of the century, Cyrus Thomas – appointed by John Wesley Powell, the first director of the Bureau of Ethnology in the Smithsonian Institution – led a survey of mounds to finally settle the question of their creation. In 1894, he submitted a report to the Smithsonian that definitively overturned the 'lost-races myth', proving that the still-extant indigenous tribes and their ancestors were responsible for the ongoing construction of the mounds (Schiffer 2017: 3–9). The destruction of the mounds was part of the destruction of indigenous culture, supported by the belief that indigenous peoples were becoming extinct and so the genocide of tribes across the North American continent could be justified.

This belief, to return to Kendi, was developed and distributed through public rhetoric and government policy based on *economic* drivers, primarily the seizure of land and resources by white settlers. In Detroit, little by little the mounds were carted away for their sand (sold for local construction) and to clear space for new structures. Hubbard cites a local who recalls the Great Mound when it was '700 or 800 feet long, 400 feet wide, and not less than forty feet high', noting that by the late 1880s, 'not only [had the mound] been reduced more than half the entire length, but more than half also of its width on the river side … and the present extreme height nowhere exceeds thirty feet above the stream' (1887: 228–9). At the time of the publication of Hardy's story, Detroit's Great Mound was in danger of being lost.

Reading 'Ancient Earthworks' as satire and allegory

In this broader context, Hardy's short story 'Ancient Earthworks' engages with contemporaneous questions of not only archaeology and preservation but also the rhetoric underlying the economics of an expanding empire. The story functions on multiple levels through Hardy's use of generic mode for the purpose of social commentary on a topic or practice. Hardy is known for his utilization of multiple generic modes in his writing: as Richard Nemesvari argues, 'Hardy's willingness to mix apparently disparate genres within his fiction comes close to being his most distinctive novelistic device' (2011: 6). Peter Widdowson outlines 'the crucial problematic of Hardy's fiction' as 'his attempts to find a form to "render visible" abstract and analytic "essences" of contemporary social relations' (1989: 178). As Andrew Radford has noted, Hardy was adept at 'manipulat[ing] a popular genre only to draw ironic attention' (Nemesvari 2011: 153). Moving between and concurrently within multiple literary modes offered Hardy the chance to explore the way form 'disrupts the reading experience of its audience in order to help disrupt its class and cultural complacency' (159). 'Ancient Earthworks' does exactly this. First, it disrupts the complacency at the loss of indigenous earthworks, serving as a plea for the preservation of ancient earthworks for their own sake. Second, through its satirical mode, the story highlights the imperialistic attitudes often hidden in archaeological agendas and the irony of the public rhetoric of bystander effect (e.g. the sense that as an observer and not an actor, there is nothing one can do). Finally, 'Ancient Earthworks' might be read as an allegory for imperialism itself. The result of these readings reveals Hardy's wider engagement with empire through his focus on the local.

In its *Detroit Post* context, the style of 'Ancient Earthworks' – with its lengthy descriptions and 'perfunctory' plot – suggests the appearance of a newspaper article rather than a short story. Even its *Post* title, as Davies has also noted, sounds more like a headline of a news story: 'Ancient Earthworks | and What Two Enthusiastic Scientists Found Therein | Thomas Hardy's Graphic Description of Maiden Castle | The Stupendous Ruin Found in Dorsetshire, England' (Davies 2011: 48). The use of subtitles (whether editorially added or Hardy's own) adds to this effect and allows the story visually to match the format of the paper:

> Its Outlines | As Viewed by Night | Its Impressiveness Increases | On the Second Defence | Echoes of Departed Valor | The Product of Fancy | The Third Escarpment | The Pleasure of Solitude | Unmolested Pursuit of Science | What the Shovel Disclosed | A Relic of Ancient Worship | Homeward Meditations. (Hardy 1885: 13)

The subheadings permit a quicker read of the story, with the reader capable of skimming through the headings as one might through an article. If the newspaper served as the forum for the dissemination of public rhetoric – as seen in the previous section with the inclusion of racist rhetoric in relation to indigenous peoples – then Hardy's story usurps this forum for its own polemic. On a surface reading, his story argues for the preservation of ancient earthworks, with the majority of the story focusing on a description of and sense of marvel at the structure of the earthwork itself.

Dig one layer deeper, and 'Ancient Earthworks' satirizes the imperialistic agendas often hidden in contemporaneous archaeological discourse. In tone and content, the story matches archaeological reports like Henry Gillman's 1873 report to the Smithsonian 'The Moundbuilders in Michigan'. Like most reports on a particular site, it starts with a description of the site itself and its location, then moves into the specifics of the dig and the artefacts uncovered. The language used to describe Maiden Castle in 'Ancient Earthworks' mirrors the language used by Gillman to describe the Great Mound. Maiden Castle 'rises against the sky with a Titanic personality that compels the senses to regard it and consider. The eyes may bend in another direction, but never without the consciousness of its towering presence behind' (Hardy 1885: 13); Detroit's Great Mound is depicted as possessing such 'size, shape, and well-defined outlines' that it 'could hardly fail to attract the attention of even the superficial observer' (Gillman [1873] 1877: 366). Hardy had practice writing in this mode, as seen in his archaeological paper presented to the Dorset Natural History and Antiquarian Field Club, 'Some Romano-British Relics Found at Max Gate, Dorchester'. In his early days as a writer of novels by serial installation, Hardy sometimes would create 'an extremely specific literary satire aimed at the kind of stories published by the very magazine that serialized Hardy's novel' (Nemesvari 2011: 154). Here, the shift into a pseudoscientific tone sets the stage for the satirical depiction of the antiquarian conducting the dig and the 'scientific' nature of the dig itself.

Perhaps the most notable satirical element in the story is the caricature of the scientist-friend, who is depicted as acting illegally and using unscientific methods to satisfy personal interest. The friend's motive mirrors that of the North American mounds inquiry, as he seeks to verify who built Maiden Castle. This is foreshadowed by the narrator's thoughts as he climbs the escarpments, 'Who was the man that said: "Let it be built here" – … on this best spot of all? Whether he were some great one of the Belgae, or of the Durotriges, or of the Anglo-Romans, must ever remain Time's secret' (Hardy 1885: 13). In the 1885 version, upon discovering an altar covered with an intricate mosaic, the friend shouts 'that he knew it always – it is a Roman fort and not British at all' (13). In a single-line paragraph, the narrator responds, 'what if it is Roman?', and the implications of the question hang. Does the value of what might be uncovered – and of the structure itself – shift with the identity of its originators? The friend's response – that it means 'a great deal … . That it proves all the world to be wrong, and himself right alone' – reveals ironically that ego, and not scientific inquiry, is at stake in this case.

In the 1893 version, Hardy expands the friend's exclamation: 'that he knew it always – that it is not a Celtic stronghold exclusively, but also a Roman; the former people have probably contributed little more than the original framework which the latter took and adapted till it became the present imposing structure' (Hardy 1988: 701). Davies notes that this was 'a view tending in exactly the opposite direction to modern knowledge' (2011: 50). By putting this theory into the mouth of the friend, Hardy satirizes the notion that the 'savage' Celtics were not capable of engineering such a structure and only a 'progressive' civilization like the Roman Empire could be responsible. This notion echoes transatlantic archaeological attitudes, specifically the theory promoted by the supporters of the lost-races myth in the United States: that some other ancient civilization must have constructed the mounds, and not the 'savage' tribes who used and 'modified' them in the present day.

In contrast to his pronouncement of acting in the name of science, the friend's methodology for cleaning artefacts is depicted as primitive and unscientific. When the friend uncovers the altar mosaic, 'he pulls handfuls of grass, and mops the surface clean, finally rubbing it with his handkerchief' (Hardy 1885: 13). As he digs on, 'sometimes he falls on his knees, burrowing with his hands in the manner of a hare', and with every object uncovered, the two men 'wash it in the same primitive way by rubbing it with the wet grass', including the gold 'figure of Mercury' (13). He makes no record of his findings, and when the statuette is later found among his effects, its label misleadingly reads 'Debased Roman' (13).

While the satire focuses on the friend's attitude and actions, the narrator is not exempt. The possibly editorial subtitle to 'Ancient Earthworks' in the *Post* – 'And What Two Enthusiastic Scientists Found Therein' – is satirical, transforming the narrator into an 'enthusiastic scientist' like his friend, but the story implicates the narrator in his friend's actions, complicating the idea of an innocent bystander in an era of rampant destruction of indigenous cultures and peoples. Upon meeting his tool-bearing friend, he agrees to 'take the lantern and accompany him' (Hardy 1885: 13). When he realizes the purpose of their meeting, the narrator protests that he 'had no idea, in keeping the whimsical tryst, that he was going to do more at such an unusual hour than meet ... for a meditative ramble through the ruin' (13). Yet he does not leave. The narrator asks 'what authority he has for [cutting up the sod], remembering a certain gaunt sign-post and inscription without, forbidding this very operation, under stringent penalties' but is satisfied by his friend's response that 'forbidden or not forbidden, honest men or marauders, it is certain we shall not be disturbed at our work till after dawn' (13). The satirically subtitled sections – the 'Unmolested Pursuit of Science' and 'What the Shovel Disclosed' – show the narrator eliding moral responsibility for the act, excusing it in the name of science and transferring agency from the human actors onto their tools. His 'contribution to the labor' is solely that of 'directing light constantly upon the hole', a statement that functions literally as he holds the lantern as well as metaphorically in his later documentation of the dig (Hardy 1885: 13). However, his contribution evolves to full participation when artefacts are uncovered, as indicated by the shift to the first-person plural 'we': 'He draws out an object; we wash it in the same primitive way by rubbing it with the wet grass,' and later, 'we clean it as before' (13). He becomes so absorbed in the process that even a sudden squall does not stop him from 'still directing light across the hole' (13). Despite what the subheading suggests, the displacement of agency onto the shovel does not extricate the narrator from the act being carried out. When at last his friend is exhausted, he concludes, 'We dig no further' (13). In this last statement, the narrator becomes fully complicit in the dig.

However, the narrator remains unaware of his involvement in the act. In the final section before the 'Five Years Later' postscript where the statuette is found, the narrator offers his 'Homeward Meditations':

> As I walk on I muse upon my friend and cannot help asking myself this question: Did he really replace the gold image of the god Mercurius with the rest of the treasures? He seemed to do so, and yet I cannot testify to the act. Probably, however, he was as good as his word. (Hardy 1885: 13)

His focus remains on his friend's moral compass, and not his own, and the irony is not only that his friend was *not* 'as good as his word', but that his own actions assisted this theft (13). If, as Nemesvari suggests, 'the goal of satire is to push readers toward an understanding of their own complicity in the structures being exposed', then 'Ancient Earthworks' might be read as pushing its contemporaneous readers to realize their own complicity in the loss of local ancient earthworks, and by extension in the rhetoric underlying their destruction (2011: 176).

In this light, 'Ancient Earthworks' might function also as an allegory for empire. It opens with a long journey to an exotic location in the midst of a storm, alluding along the way to John Bunyan's *Pilgrim's Progress* (1678), a popular allegory in nineteenth-century North America in particular due to its parallels to the settler experience of a long and difficult journey to a promised paradise (Smith 1966: 6). The journey is followed by the explicit appropriation of that site for personal gain through the act of the dig. Furthermore, the story documents the passive response of the 'colonizer-at-home' (the narrator), who hopes that the 'colonizer-abroad' (his friend) is 'probably … as good as his word' (and when it turns out he is not, the Museum benefits) (Hardy 1885: 13).

Hardy is not known for engaging with topics related to empire in his fiction; he believed that 'a writer of fiction (unlike other people) is more likely to exercise an influence for humanity in any given direction by belonging to no Committee pledged to a course, as he then escapes the charge of exaggerating for a purpose' (Hardy 1980: 135–6). As Jane Bownas and Rena Jackson explain, most of Hardy's writing in relation to empire focuses on 'the links between class and empire, as Hardy knew them in life, … reflected in the population distribution of migrants throughout Hardy's empire' of rural Wessex (2013: 410). With the start of the Second Boer War, two letters to his friend Florence Henniker give a glimpse of Hardy's personal thoughts on empire, disparaging the idea of '"civilised" nations' as any more civilized than supposedly 'old and barbarous ones' and expressing trepidation that 'this Imperial idea is, I fear, leading us into strange waters' (Hardy 1980: 232, 241). While these thoughts are vague, in his shift with the turn of the century from fiction to poetry, Hardy began to feel that he could 'express more fully in verse ideas and emotions that run counter to the inert crystallized opinion – hard as a rock – which the vast body of men have vested interests in supporting' (Millgate 2004: 302).[3] As a poet, works like his epic verse-drama *The Dynasts* (1904–8) and poems like 'My Country' and 'The Man He Killed' addressed the dangers of nationalism and empire, promoting the idea of a global kinship. However, in the midst of his fiction career in 1885, the form of the allegory might have allowed Hardy to write about empire in a veiled manner.

In the story's composition, Hardy undercuts the value placed on traditional Eurocentric tropes of plot, character, agency and place. While he satirizes the plot and caricatures his human characters, the majority of the story is focused on the earthwork itself, which takes the place of a traditional human character. Like the heath in the opening of *The Return of the Native* (1878), the non-human earthwork is introduced as the central character. It is described in anthropomorphic (or animalistic) terms as having 'protuberances' with 'the aspect of warts, wens, knuckles and hips' and is compared to 'an enormous many-limbed organism of an antediluvian time – partaking of the cephalopod in shape – lying lifeless, and covered with a thin green cloth which hides its substance while revealing its general contour' (13). In this sense, the earthwork takes on a life (or at least a past life). The use of the passive voice throughout – removing a human subject from lines like 'that the summit of the second defense has been gained is suddenly made known by a contrasting wind from a new quarter' and 'a glimpse is obtained of the actual entrance some way ahead' – reinforces this attention on the earthwork and removes agency from human actors (Hardy 1885: 13). It concurrently satirizes the displacement of agency, opening gaps in the text for the reader to insert questions. For example, the story is passive in its description of the gold statuette's discovery among the deceased friend's effects (it simply 'has been found') as well as its placement in the museum: the story concludes 'The figure is bequeathed to the – Museum', but it does not specify who did the bequeathing (13). In the *Detroit Post* version Hardy does not include a name for the museum, in line with his wish for the story to be separated from its geographical inspiration. While he expressed dismay at the location being identified in the *English Illustrated Magazine* version, he sent along photographs of Maiden Castle (Hardy 1980: 43, 35; Ray 1997: 293), and when he published the story in *A Changed Man*, he chose a photograph of Maiden Castle for the frontispiece (Hardy 1984: 302–4). This insistence on the visual representation of Maiden Castle, however, again focuses attention on the physicality of the earthwork itself, and not necessarily on its setting in a specific place.

Instead, Hardy seems to locate the story in a feeling brought about by the experience of the earthwork as a subject in its own right and as an embodiment of its past peoples, their identities and daily lives. The narrator must climb three escarpments to reach the top of the earthwork. Each escarpment is more difficult to mount than the prior and in turn, causes the narrator to exert more effort to realize his destination: 'The first was a surface to walk up, the second to stagger up, the third one can only be ascended on hands and toes' (Hardy 1885: 13). This line is an allusion to *Pilgrim's Progress*, in which Christian, on his path up the Hill Difficulty, 'fell from running to going, and from going to clambering upon his hands and knees, because of the steepness of the place' (Bunyan [1678] 2008: 46). Notably, this reference to the allegory popular among European settlers in North America at the time does not point towards a promised paradise (or a plot resolution) but rather leads the narrator further and further into reflection on the people who once stood where he now stands. These mediations on the people who once inhabited Maiden Castle are inextricably bound up with his experience of the landform itself – with the wind moving through plant life and the curves of the fortress to become the voices of the past peoples. In this way, the story drives towards a relationship with the land while documenting through satire its exploitation as a site.

If the story itself functions as an extended metaphor for empire, the climb up the earthwork might be considered a metaphor for the difficult questions embedded in archaeological study in relation to empire. Like Hardy's short story, this chapter ends with the question of the museum. The relationship between empire and archaeology is clear to anyone who walks the halls of the British Museum (or the Metropolitan Museum in the United States), where the question of preservation versus appropriation becomes an uncomfortable aspect of the museum visit. This 'third escarpment' of Hardy's story is perhaps the most difficult one for the modern reader, who must encounter the traces of Victorian progressivism not only in the museum but in the daily aftermath of centuries of Eurocentrism that designated a diverse range of non-Anglo-European cultures and peoples as a singular exotic 'Other' – and, in economic and racial terms, as being of less value and as having a lesser voice than their Anglo-European colonizers (see Order 2012: 737–55). As Hardy's narrator notes of his climb of the second escarpment, 'to turn aside, as did Christian's companion, from such a Hill Difficulty, is the more natural tendency' (Hardy 1885: 13). This allusion to *Pilgrim's Progress* refers to the moment when Christian and his companions encounter a hill with three paths: Danger, Destruction and Difficulty. Christian chooses the path difficulty, deciding, 'Better, tho' difficult, the right way to go' (Bunyan [1678] 2008: 46).

Museums today are grappling with the difficult question of how to decolonize. This requires a rethinking of curatorial narratives to remove a historically imbedded Eurocentric lens as well as a consideration of what form amends 'for centuries of exploitation and corruption at the hands of European colonizers' should take (Kwateng-Clark 2019: 1). A November 2018 report put together for the French government provides an example of the latter: French historian Bénédicte Savoy and Senegalese economist and writer Felwine Sarr created recommendations on the return of African art and artefacts to their countries of origin, urging the immediate return of two dozen items obtained through war and suggesting the provision of 'an inventory of all works originating from their territory' to each country once colonized by the French to determine which pieces to return (Noce 2018: 1). While museums like the Musée du Quai Branly in Paris hold over 90,000 objects from formerly colonized African territories, Savoy notes that in contrast, '"we are dealing with the case of a continent which has almost nothing left of its history when we have it all. The aim is not to empty Western museums to fill up the African ones, but to invent a new relationship based on ethics and equity"' (Noce 2018: 1). In response to this report, the director of the Victoria & Albert Museum in London, Tristram Hunt, called for a more 'nuanced' approach, one that acknowledges the impact of empire on culture. He quotes Edward Said to explain that '"partly because of empire, all cultures are involved in one another; none is single and pure, all are hybrid, heterogenous, extraordinarily differentiated, and unmonolithic"' (Hunt 2019: 1). He suggests that decisions must be made 'based on the history of each object' and its 'complex, layered meaning' (Hunt 2019: 1).

In the United States, the passing of the Native American Graves Protection and Repatriation Act in 1990 required federally funded museums to return indigenous cultural items – including human remains – to their respective indigenous communities (Kwateng-Clark 2019: 1). Yet the question of what reparations can look like for indigenous peoples – who are continuing to battle for the rights to land deemed as theirs – remains.[4] Even the term 'reparations' is problematic: it implies an economic solution, which, as indigenous studies scholar Daniel Wildcat points out, is a very American approach. In his *Washington Post* article 'Why Native Americans don't want reparations', Wildcat writes that 'The prevailing culture of the United States is a money culture. America's ceremonies, habits and dominant institutions are all shaped by money' (2014: 1). In contrast, 'For many Native Americans, our land ... is a natural relative, not a natural resource. And our justice traditions require the restoration of our land relationship, not monetary reparations' (Wildcat 2014: 1). He explains, 'Reparations are ill-suited to address the harm and damage experienced by people who understand themselves, in a very practical and moral sense, as members of communities that include nonhuman life' (2014: 1). Monetary reparations appear as an assimilationist approach, continuing to view land through the Eurocentric lens of real estate, a commodity that can be exchanged for currency.[5] Instead, indigenous leaders look towards land and water rights, inclusion of indigenous genocide in US history curriculum and criminal justice for the disproportionate number of unsolved crimes perpetrated against indigenous people, especially women (Levin 2019: 1).

For Hardy, the act of preservation was bound up with the local, but he too grappled with the exact steps that should be taken. When consulted on what should be done to save Stonehenge from being purchased by an American for relocation to the United States, Hardy advocated for government purchase of the site for its preservation and a protection of the surrounding Salisbury landscape against modernization so as to safeguard the feeling of the place, but he went on to say, 'What should next be done, or if anything else should be done, is a more difficult question' in relation to 'the condition of the ruins and the best means of preserving them' from the weather and general deterioration (Hardy [1899] 1969: 198). In his paper presented to the Dorset Natural History and Antiquarian Field Club on the relics found during the construction of Max Gate, Hardy reflected:

> In spite of the numerous vestiges that have been discovered from time to time of the Roman city which formerly stood on the site of modern Dorchester, and which are still being unearthed daily by our local Schliemann, one is struck with the fact that little has been done towards piecing together and reconstructing these evidences into an unmitigated whole – ... a whole which should represent Dorchester in particular and not merely the general character of a Roman station in this country. (Hardy [1890] 1969: 194)

He concluded by asking a series of specific questions:

> where stood the large buildings, where the small, how did the roofs group themselves, what were the gardens like, if any, what social character had the streets, what were the customary noises, what sort of exterior was exhibited by these hybrid Romano-British people ... Were the passengers up and down the ways few in number, or did they ever form a busy throng such as we now see on a market day? (194)

In Hardy's eyes, archaeology was an intimate science – a revealing of the particular and not the general, and through these particulars, a tying of the past to the present. This pushes in direct opposition to the work of the imperialistic policies and legislation like the 'Civilization Regulations' that sought to assimilate indigenous peoples and eliminate their sense of cultural identity (or, at least, in the case of the 'Civilization Regulations', to reduce tribal differences to a singular 'Indian' identity) and to erase the sense of a North American history that predates Euro-American settlers, perpetuating instead the idea of the continent as a blank slate.

Hardy's writings resisted the imperialistic drive to homogenize, seeking instead to preserve the particularities of the local – whether it be the dialects of Dorset or the folklore and customs or the rural way of life that was rapidly shifting under the urbanization and industrialization of England. His intense focus on the local suggests an ethos that would have favoured the preservation of artefacts in or near their sites of origin – preserving the historical and cultural human–land relationship as much as possible – to their removal to another location.[6] For his part, Hardy's oeuvre sought to preserve the local cultural heritage of Dorset – while acknowledging its hybridity of ancient and modern cultural sources – through his rendering of the fictional Wessex, documenting a people and place with the care of an archaeologist for future generations.

'Ancient Earthworks' today

If you walk up a small bluff in Fort Wayne – just beyond the last remaining burial mound – you can see a view of the Detroit River joined by the River Rouge from a similar vantage point as it would have been from the top of the Great Mound, except, as with Hubbard's layering of the past onto his present, the present view shows Zug Island with its steel mill to the right and the skyline of downtown Detroit to the left.[7] Standing there, you might ask yourself how the shifts in the landscape in the past century reveal economically motivated decisions. Fort Wayne has been preserved – that is, it still exists, although the Victorian homes of officers are now dilapidated, roofs sunken in and windows boarded up. Standing in Maiden Castle, by contrast, you will see a sign marking it as an English heritage site – a source of income for the community, adding to its draw for tourism.

The Detroit earthworks have been all but forgotten, although recent work by historians and artists seeks to bring them into the public eye. In his series 'The Mound Project', visual artist Scott Hocking photographs the sites of former indigenous mounds and constructs art-installation mounds on the sites of ruined buildings. Outside of Detroit, several protected indigenous earthworks still stand – such as the Effigy Mounds National Monument in Iowa or the Serpent Mound Historical Site in Ohio – but site destruction has continued to the present day. As Schiffer points out, looting still contributes to the problem, with 'avid collectors … willing to pay premium prices' (2017: 169). Although the Antiquities Act passed in the United States in 1988 prohibits the sale of artefacts, Schiffer notes that 'Carved catlinite pipes, for example, are offered on the Internet for $1,500 to $2,500' (169). Consequently, 'the looters who feed the voracious collector market have damaged … sites and reduced any potential to yield new information about the lives of these peoples' (169). Beyond the earthworks, questions of preservation of tribal sites and of reparations remain ongoing battles.

Through these readings of 'Ancient Earthworks' in its original publication context, one can see Hardy's concern for preservation and for ethical methods of archaeology as well as his grappling with imperialism's role in archaeological practices. A story serves as both cultural artefact and a site for excavation, capturing a moment in time as a consumer good but holding within it layers of cultural sediment that shape its form and function. The importance of 'Ancient Earthworks' lies in the unearthing of a story that continues – an unearthing of implicit attitudes and approaches that remain bound up with preservation today.

Notes

1 For an analysis of the archaeological content and reception of Hardy's paper on the relics found during the construction of his home Max Gate, see Davies (2011: 52–6).
2 See, for example, an interview with Hardy entitled 'Shall Stonehenge Go?' published in the *Daily Chronicle* on 24 August 1899 (Hardy [1899] 1969: 196–200).
3 For more on Hardy's emerging public voice as poet, see Kathryn King and William Morgan's 1979 article, 'Hardy and the Boer War: The Public Poet in Spite of Himself'.
4 For a recent example, see 2016 media coverage of the Dakota Access Pipeline protests, which sought to prevent the construction of an oil pipeline through

Standing Rock Indian Reservation impacting ancient burial grounds and local water sources.
5 See also Ella Shohat and Robert Stam's chapter 'The Imperial Imaginary' in *Unthinking Eurocentrism* (1994).
6 See also Davies (2011: 171) for his reading of Hardy's poem 'Christmas in the Elgin Room'; he argues that Hardy 'anticipates ... the late twentieth-century policy of keeping artefacts as far as possible in their original context'.
7 Hubbard's map places the Great Mound directly across the River Rouge from the site of Zug Island at the junction of the Detroit and Rouge rivers. Converted into an island by the construction of a shipping canal in 1888, Zug was sold in 1891 as a site for industrial waste; by 1902 the first blast furnaces on the island were constructed. For its environmental and health impact in the form of EPA violations and a 'hum' perceived by Ontario residents across the Detroit River, see local media coverage.

References

Annual Report of the Commissioner of Indian Affairs: For the Year 1868 (1868), Washington: Government Printing Office. Available online https://archive.org/details/usindianaffairs68usdorich/page/44 (accessed 29 September 2019).

Bownas, J., and R. Jackson (2013), 'Empire', in P. Mallett (ed.), *Thomas Hardy in Context*, 406–14, Cambridge: Cambridge University Press.

Bunyan, J. ([1678] 2008), *The Pilgrim's Progress: From This World, to That Which Is to Come*, London: Penguin.

Davies, M. J. P. (2011), *A Distant Prospect of Wessex: Archaeology and the Past in the Life and Works of Thomas Hardy*, Oxford: Archaeopress.

Ethridge, R. (2007), 'Plan of Civilization', *Encyclopedia of Alabama*, 21 March. Available online https://encyclopediaofalabama.org/article/h-1131 (accessed 29 September 2019).

Fletcher, A. (1888), *Indian Education and Civilization: A Report Prepared in Answer to Senate Resolution of February 23, 1885*, Washington: Government Printing Office.

Gillman, H. ([1873] 1877), *The Moundbuilders and Platycnemism in Michigan: Reprinted from Smithsonian Report for 1873*, Washington: Government Printing Office.

Hardy, T. (1885), 'Ancient Earthworks', *Detroit Post*, 15 March: 13.

Hardy, T. ([1890] 1969), 'Some Romano-British Relics Found at Max Gate, Dorchester', in H. Orel (ed.), *Thomas Hardy's Personal Writings*, 191–5, Lawrence: University Press of Kansas.

Hardy, T. ([1899] 1969), 'Shall Stonehenge Go?', in H. Orel (ed.), *Thomas Hardy's Personal Writings*, 196–200, Lawrence: University Press of Kansas.

Hardy, T. (1976), *The Complete Poems of Thomas Hardy*, ed. J. Gibson, London: Macmillan.

Hardy, T. (1978), *The Collected Letters of Thomas Hardy*, vol. 1, ed. R. L. Purdy and M. Millgate, Oxford: Clarendon Press.

Hardy, T. (1980), *The Collected Letters of Thomas Hardy*, vol. 2, ed. R. L. Purdy and M. Millgate, Oxford: Clarendon Press.

Hardy, T. (1984), *The Collected Letters of Thomas Hardy*, vol. 4, ed. R. L. Purdy and M. Millgate, Oxford: Clarendon Press.

Hardy, T. (1988), *Collected Short Stories*, ed. F. B. Pinion, intro. D. Hawkins, London: Macmillan.

Hinsdale, W. B. (1925), *Primitive Man in Michigan*, Ann Arbor: University of Michigan.

Hirsch, M. (2014), '1871: The End of Indian Treaty-Making', *American Indian*, 15 (2). Available online https://www.americanindianmagazine.org/story/1871-end-indian-treaty-making (accessed 19 September 2019).

Hocking, S. (2007), 'The Mound Project'. Available online https://scotthocking.com/mound.html (accessed 14 October 2019).

Hubbard, B. (1887), *Memorials of a Half-Century*, New York: Knickerbocker Press.

Hunt, T. (2019), 'Should Museums Return Their Colonial Artefacts?' *The Guardian*, 29 June. Available online https://www.theguardian.com/culture/2019/jun/29/should-museums-return-their-colonial-artefacts (accessed 13 October 2019).

'Indian Boys' (1885), *Detroit Post*, 15 March: 11.

Kappler, C. J. (1904), *Indian Affairs: Laws and Treaties*, vol. 2, Washington: Government Printing Office.

Kendi, I. (2016), *Stamped from the Beginning: The Definitive History of Racist Ideas in America*, New York: Bold Type Books.

King, K., and W. Morgan (1979), 'Hardy and the Boer War: The Public Poet in Spite of Himself', *Victorian Poetry*, 17 (1/2): 66–83.

Kwateng-Clark, D. (2019), 'Art Museums Need to Address Colonial Theft – Not Diversity', *VICE*, 8 February. Available online https://www.vice.com/en_us/article/nexemx/moma-new-york-closing-inclusion (accessed 13 October 2019).

Levin, S. (2019), '"This Is All Stolen Land": Native Americans Want More Than California's Apology', *The Guardian*, 21 June. Available online https://www.

theguardian.com/us-news/2019/jun/20/california-native-americans-governor-apology-reparations (accessed 23 August 2019).

Millgate, M. (2004), *Thomas Hardy: A Biography Revisited*, Oxford: Oxford University Press.

Milner, G. R. (2004), *The Moundbuilders: Ancient Peoples of Eastern North America*, London: Thames & Hudson.

Nemesvari, R. (2011), *Thomas Hardy, Sensationalism, and the Melodramatic Mode*, New York: Palgrave Macmillan.

Newman, J., and N. Pevsner (1972), *Dorset*, Harmondsworth: Penguin.

Noce, V. (2018), '"Give Africa Its Art Back", Macron's Report Says', *Art Newspaper*, 20 November. Available online https://www.theartnewspaper.com/news/give-africa-its-art-back-macron-s-report-says (accessed 23 August 2019).

Order, C., Jr (2012), 'An Archaeology of Eurocentrism', *American Antiquity*, 77 (4): 737–55.

Orel, H. ([1986] 2000), 'Hardy and the Developing Science of Archaeology', in N. Page (ed.), *Oxford Reader's Companion to Hardy*, 10–12, Oxford: Oxford University Press.

Peters, R. (ed.) (1846), *United States Statutes at Large*, Boston: Little and Brown. Available online http://memory.loc.gov/cgibin/ampage?collId=llsl&fileName=004/llsl004.db&rec Num=458 (accessed 29 September 2019).

Pratt, J. W. (1927), 'The Origin of "Manifest Destiny"', *American Historical Review* 32 (4): 795–8.

Prucha, F. P. (1976), *American Indian Policy in Crisis: Christian Reformers and the Indian, 1865–1900*, Norman: University of Oklahoma Press.

Putnam, F. W. (1883), 'An Indian Burial-Mound', *Science*, 1 (6): 168.

Ray, M. (1997), *Thomas Hardy: A Textual Study of the Short Stories*, Aldershot: Ashgate.

Regulations of the Indian Department (1884), Washington: Government Printing Office.

'A Savage Display: The New Orleans Exhibit of Ethnology' (1885), *Detroit Post*, 15 March: 10.

Schiffer, M. B. (2017), *Archaeology's Footprints in the Modern World*, Salt Lake City: University of Utah Press.

Shohat, E., and R. Stam (1994), 'The Imperial Imaginary', in *Unthinking Eurocentrism: Multiculturalism and the Media*, 100–36, London: Routledge. Available online http://www.asu.edu/courses/fms506mg/total-readings/fms270-L03-reading01.pdf (accessed 30 September 2019).

Smith, D. E. (1966), *John Bunyan in America*, Bloomington: Indiana University Press.

Thornton, R. (1987), *American Indian Holocaust and Survival: A Population History since 1492*, Norman: University of Oklahoma Press.

Widdowson, P. (1989), *Hardy in History: A Study in Literary Sociology*, London: Routledge.

Wildcat, D. R. (2014), 'Why Native Americans Don't Want Reparations', *Washington Post*, 10 June. Available online https://www.washingtonpost.com/posteverything/wp/2014/06/10/why-native-americans-dont-want-reparations/ (accessed 13 October 2019).

Part IV

Narrative archaeology and the narratives of archaeologists

7

Something more than imagination: Archaeology and fiction

Robert E. Witcher and Daniël P. van Helden

In his experimental book on the religious history of the ancient world, Keith Hopkins (1999) deploys a range of fictive techniques to explore the experiences of pagan, Christian and Jewish peoples. Chapters of fiction are interspersed with Hopkins's correspondence (potentially genuine but quite possibly invented) with colleagues, who appraise the scholarly value of his efforts to imagine ancient religious life. One criticism he receives from a correspondent about his use of fictional scenes is labelled as:

> the cream bun syndrome. One story may be amusing; two stories may be tolerable; the third story sticks in the gullet … and any subsequent story makes your satiated audience feel more than slightly sick. (Hopkins 1999: 151)

This critique suggests that it is the excessive use of such stories, rather than their fundamental form, that is problematic. Yet Hopkins's correspondent continues: '[s]tories tyrannise, and infantilise their audience. … when you tell stories, how can I respond, except with a polite smile, or a yawn, a laugh or another story?' (Hopkins 1999: 152). The question raised concerns how the scholarly reader should react to a fictional narrative. The commentator's perspective maintains a sharp distinction between fact and fiction, allowing standard scholarly criteria of objectivity and accuracy to be applied to one set of stories and emotional and aesthetic responses to another. Yet, if the border between fact and fiction is not a line but rather a zone, then the reader can evaluate a narrative story and come to a judgement using a wider range of criteria. In this view, there is no need for fictional stories to tyrannize or infantilize their reader any more than an archaeological site report or a scholarly paper might. Both types of narrative can, and should, be evaluated critically in relation to the evidence, their stated objectives and for their plausibility.

The crafts of archaeology and writing are intimately interwoven in the creation of historical narrative. Having destroyed the material remains of the past through excavation, the archaeologist must recreate the past with words. Yet those words are preceded by other literary and archaeological narratives and, in turn, will themselves be combined into new stories. In this chapter, we explore aspects of the long and close relationship between scholarly archaeological accounts and fictional literature, with particular reference to historical novels. In doing so, we follow in a tradition of writing about archaeological writing (Joyce et al. 2002; Connah 2010; Fagan 2010), but respond in particular to a renewed interest in narrative form and fictive techniques within archaeology (Shanks 2012; Van Dyke and Bernbeck 2015; van Helden and Witcher 2020a). We begin with an outline of the role of narrative and intersections of fact and fiction in archaeology, exploring some of the perils and potential for archaeological researchers engaging with fiction. Arguing for the value of fiction and storytelling, we explore how fiction enables access to an ethical, empathetic view of the past which can highlight the situatedness of all archaeological knowledge and the limits of empathy. We use James Michener's ([1965] 2014) novel *The Source* as a case study through which we argue that fiction's capacity to represent different scales of analysis, human agency, multiple perspectives and historical causation offers a reflection of, and a model for, the archaeological research process and the narratives that archaeologists create from the material remains of the past.

Imagining the archaeological: Challenges and risks

Archaeological writing is more than the communication of scientific observation and facts. Humans apprehend the world – past, present and future – through narratives or stories (Gottschall 2012). Archaeology, as a means of making sense of the past, involves storytelling and the transformation of evidence into meaningful narrative, a process which often draws on deeply ingrained literary structures and tropes (White 1973). A century ago, G. M. Trevelyan distinguished three complementary strands of the broader discipline of history: the scientific, the imaginative and the literary. The historian first accumulates and sifts the evidence, then classifies, makes guesses and generalizations, and

> last but not least comes the literary function ... For this last process I use the word literature, because I wish to lay greater stress than modern historians are willing to do, both on the difficulty and also on the importance of planning and writing a powerful narrative of historical events ... Writing is not, therefore, a secondary but one of the primary tasks of the historian. (Trevelyan 1913: 31)

A century later, recognition of the integral importance of the literary in accounts of the past endures: for example, Lekson (2018: 102) contends, 'Narrative is always an argument, a persuasion. Rhetoric is not as important as fact, but it's pretty important. Style is a key element of conventional history.' Today, across the full spectrum of the discipline of archaeology, from the arts and humanities to the sciences, there is little disagreement about the centrality of narrative within archaeological writing (cf. Shanks 2012: 127–44; Gerbault et al. 2014). However, the case for the role of imagination and, specifically, for the use of fictive writing techniques within archaeology is more contentious, even though it has long figured in archaeological accounts.

Archaeologists often work on sites woven into fictional or mytho-historical accounts. The most obvious of these is Troy, the subject of Homer's *Iliad*. It is a site where the very concepts of fact and fiction have been pushed to their limits (Wallace 2004: 102–3). Hence, while early investigators used Homer's text to guide their exploration of the site, later archaeologists have had to unravel the resulting confusion of reality and rhetoric. The example of Troy, however, is far from unique. Arthurian legend, for instance, has influenced a number of archaeologists. Ralegh Radford's mid-twentieth-century excavations around Southwest England were increasingly shaped by his belief in the veracity of the medieval texts, culminating in his claim, following the account of Giraldus Cambrensis, to have discovered the graves of Arthur and Guinevere at Glastonbury Abbey. As a result, the recent reassessment and publication of Radford's excavation archive has demanded the careful disentanglement of the literary from the material evidence (Green and Gilchrist 2015). Nor are such influences, and potential confusions, limited to the allure of early textual sources; modern novels can be equally powerful. In the preface to his analysis of the Renaissance rediscovery of ancient Rome, for example, Leonard Barkan (1999: xxx) describes his personal awareness of walking in the footsteps, not of the actual Roman emperors but rather their characters as portrayed in the Robert Graves (1934) novel, *I, Claudius*.

One of the dangers of such intersections of fictional narrative and archaeology is that they may be deliberately manipulated for political purposes. Butrint, on the coast of Albania, provides an example of the interweaving of archaeology, politics and literature, specifically Virgil's *Aeneid*. The brief appearance of this small port site in Virgil's text has supported long-term identity- and placemaking activities. Three very different regimes – colonial Italians, Greek nationalists and Albanian communists – have been able to draw on this epic poem to articulate distinct political and ethnic claims for the site and for Albania as a whole (Hodges 2017). The risk here is that archaeology becomes not the 'handmaiden of history' (Noël Hume 1964) but rather the handmaiden of historical fiction (for further examples, see van Helden and Witcher 2020b). As such, works of literature may attract but also confuse the conduct of archaeological research, and the resulting hybrids of fact and fiction may be prone to political manipulation.

Despite the apparent dangers, archaeologists have also engaged in writing their own fictive narratives, for example, incorporating imagined scenes into scholarly accounts. Yet, archaeologists who have made use of such narratives have been accused of sanitizing, or alternatively colonizing, the past. Andrew Fleming (2006: 276), for example, argues that the characters who populate fictive archaeological accounts are often socially, politically and morally neutral in order to avoid offence or caricature:

> We are unlikely to find a contemporary archaeologist in the near future writing a narrative vignette like this: 'as he clubbed the odious bastard to death, he was conscious how well his skull would look in the wall-niche – something to give the wife a thrill when she did the dusting – and how good a few slices of his thigh would taste, accompanied by a dandelion salad'.

Fleming argues that the characters created by archaeologists are 'ciphers' (2006: 276–7). Archaeologists choose to create particular types of people and eschew others, perhaps out of a concern not to colonize or appropriate the past. The effect, however, may be precisely to reduce the otherness of the past, shaping it to the concerns of the present. Reinhard Bernbeck (2015: 261) goes further to argue that the fictionalization of individuals in archaeological accounts, however well intended, demonstrates a disrespect for past people, co-opting their lives and experiences in the service of our own. He advocates a shift away from narratives driven by people towards an emphasis on material culture (Bernbeck 2015: 267–71). In this way, Bernbeck's position reflects wider trends in archaeological theory, which seek to de-centre humans through symmetrical, new materialist and post-humanist approaches (see Harris and Cipolla 2017: 129–69).

Bernbeck's (2004: 114) argument that the present imposes self-serving narrative constructions on the past makes a powerful ethical case against the writing of history in any narrative form, let alone fictional. But, as humans, we impose narrative not only on the past but also on the present and future. Narrative is how humans manage the complexity of reality and how we structure our experience of life, the universe and everything (cf. Gadamer 1994: 31; Gottschall 2012). A comprehensive grasp of reality is beyond human understanding, for however correct or complete our picture of one element, many others must be omitted (Wachterhauser 1994: 4–9). Since we make choices about the aspects of reality we acknowledge, the narratives we construct are inevitably partial and political. We have no other means of experiencing and making sense of the past (Shanks 1992: 130–1) or any other aspect of reality. Thus although Fleming and Bernbeck perceive 'presentism' in the ways in which archaeologists have written both conventional and fictional narratives of the past, there is no non-political standpoint from which to proceed. It is in this light that we should understand the use of fictive techniques to reinsert underrepresented groups such as enslaved people, women and children into archaeological accounts in order to address systemic historical and contemporary injustices (cf. Gill et al. 2019; Hobden 2020). For if archaeologists do not speak for the marginalized people of the past, however inarticulately, who will (cf. Tarlow 2001; Pluciennik 2015)?

Hence, far from being politically and morally neutral, these 'characters' are typically introduced into the narrative with clear and decisive purpose.

The disciplinary integrity and authority of archaeologists have traditionally depended upon the maintenance of a clear distinction between scholarly and fictional writing. While novels invent and entertain, the conventional site report documents, as objectively as possible, observations of tangible material traces excavated from the ground. For the fear is that if archaeologists give credence to invented narratives or, even worse, write their own, they risk losing the respect of their peers and surrendering the ground from which to challenge misinformed or malign uses of the archaeological past (González-Ruibal, González and Criado-Boado 2018). Yet, we contend that the crafts of the historical novelist and the archaeologist are less distinct than the frequently asserted binary opposition of fact versus fiction suggests, both in terms of the creative processes involved and in how we evaluate and reach judgement about these narratives (van Helden and Witcher 2020b). The material remains of the past undeniably exist and serve to constrain what can be said about the past (Wickham-Jones 2020); archaeological narratives, fictional or otherwise, can and should be tested against the material, contextual, scientific or comparative evidence. This testing not only ensures that narratives are empirically sound but also provides archaeology's defence against the outright invention of the past in support of fringe ideas or extreme ideologies. Provided that we are explicit and critical in our practice (Pollock 2015: 284), archaeologists should be able to draw on the methods of historical fiction without fear of ceding ethical ground to alien-hunters or political extremists (Shanks 1992: 132–3). Nonetheless, within these evidential bounds there is still wide scope for the writing of multiple and competing stories, for '[a]rchaeology cannot write narratives that are true beyond reasonable doubt, but it can, perhaps, write narrative histories that are clear and convincing' (Lekson 2018: 101).

We therefore argue that a more thorough examination of the borderlands between fact and fiction is required to evaluate the intersection of archaeology and literature. The following sections explore in further detail how and why fiction and storytelling are valuable for archaeological practice and how they might be employed to address questions of empathy which are central to, yet often overlooked by, archaeologists. We then explore these issues through a case study based on James Michener's novel, *The Source*.

Telling stories: The value of fiction

Given the array of potential problems raised by the integration of fictive techniques into archaeological research, it is understandable that archaeologists might decide to stay well away from the border between fact and fiction. It is easier to refortify the line, sanctioning those who stray across it as 'transgressive' (see Praetzellis 2015: 119–32). Yet we argue that the borderlands between archaeology, the literary and the imaginary, are a creative space where the nature of the archaeological is laid bare and becomes amenable to exploration. Existing uses of fictive techniques in archaeological writing demonstrate a great variety of aims and forms and are deployed without any dominant theoretical affiliation (see van Helden and Witcher 2020b). Probably the most common usage has been to articulate archaeological evidence through short fictional vignettes that aim to 'show' rather than tell. By contextualizing the evidence within the temporal or spatial structure of a literary narrative, the reader can encounter and process the material afresh. Sidebotham (2016), for example, connects disparate archaeological sites and objects from around the western Indian Ocean by narrating a story about a merchant travelling from Roman Egypt to India, and Witcher (2017) uses narrative vignettes to show how specific categories of material culture were used in very different ways in diverse parts of the Roman world. Both imaginative accounts seek to demonstrate economic connections and cultural differences in preparation for subsequent scholarly discussion. Information received narratively is processed differently from non-narrative information (Green and Brock 2000; Green, Garst and Brock 2004), so new awareness, and potentially insight, may result from experiencing even familiar material presented in an alternative format (cf. Kavanagh 2020).

As well as benefits for the reader, fictive techniques also offer great potential for the writer/researcher. Writing fictional scenes, or even just thinking fictionally, demands great rigour as well as creativity and compels the writer to identify and confront the fragmentary nature of most archaeological evidence. Whereas traditional scholarly accounts allow the author to steer around gaps in archaeological knowledge by focusing narrowly on the material at hand, the creation of rounded and plausible fictional narrative demands a new attentiveness to the many evidential lacunae. This may demand additional research to identify evidence from elsewhere or the search for new types of evidence to 'fill' these gaps. These narratives often also require an unequivocal choice to be made between competing alternatives (Elphinstone 2020: 67). Questions cannot be ignored or left open because the evidence is mute or inconclusive. Hence while archaeologists might write in a scholarly report about 'ritual specialists of some sort', in a novel (or other fictional narrative) these specialists need specific roles and fleshed-out characters (Patton 2020: 80). Most importantly, the demands of such narratives require logic and realism. Commenting on the value of her collaboration with the novelist Margaret Elphinstone, archaeologist Caroline Wickham-Jones observes that previously 'I had never tried to make my idea of Mesolithic life actually *work*' (Elphinstone and Wickham-Jones 2012: 536, emphasis added). The use of fictive techniques can reposition the author in relation to the available evidence, sharpening thinking and stimulating insights and questions that would not otherwise have been entertained (Gear and O'Neal Gear 2003; Gibb 2000, 2020). In this way, the techniques of fiction can help to mobilize and recontextualize extant knowledge (Wickham-Jones 2020: 45).

Another powerful motivation for adopting fictive approaches is the potential for humanizing our accounts, reinserting and making central the people who created the archaeological material with which we work. Anthropocentric narrative, relating the archaeological evidence to human actions, provides structure and meaning to descriptive detail (Grethlein and Huitink 2017), and fictional narrative specifically allows the lives of human agents to come to the fore. In turn, the incorporation of these tangible individuals and groups into our narratives opens the possibility of working across, and integrating issues of, scale. Archaeologists are often more comfortable and confident dealing with long-term, broad-scale processes, such as the transition to farming. But such processes are the result of, and also have effect on, aggregated human actions (Robb and Pauketat 2013). Conventional archaeological narratives have often struggled to accommodate these multiple scales. The novel, though a highly varied literary type, offers some potential here. In its long form, the profusion of incidental detail and the ability to present alternative perspectives, for example, the author can relate the lives of individuals to the wider forces that shape them and in turn are shaped by them. In this way, fictional narrative can provide a means to move back and forth between scales and to draw out the inherent connections between them.

A final potential benefit for archaeologists engaging with fictive techniques and, especially, the humanizing of narratives is that it may help us to avoid the dangers of hindsight or teleological thinking. Historians and archaeologists are blessed with the knowledge of how the past transpired and are therefore able to identify the significant developments that brought about these events. Yet, this insight sets historians apart from the people of the past and their own attempts to make sense of their present; in the words of Tolkien's Gandalf the Grey: 'even the very wise cannot see all ends' (1978: 73). Hindsight is therefore a mixed blessing, as we may fail to acknowledge the experience and agency of past actors and we risk writing teleological narratives that simply confirm the status quo. A nuanced understanding of the past, particularly historical causation, instead requires us to consider the possible alternatives that were not chosen as well as those that were (Ferguson 1998: 88; Grethlein 2010: 322–3; 2014). By vicariously experiencing history through fictional characters, confronting historical decisions and causation from their perspectives, fictive narrative can encourage deeper reflection on, and the revision of, established explanations.

Seeing through others' eyes

A key technique often used by novelists to connect the reader to the protagonist is empathy. In recent years, empathy has become a major focus of academic research and public policy. It has been characterized as the default tool with which we understand our fellow humans (Stueber 2006: 26) and is widely, though not universally, viewed as a positive force. In seeking to bring together fictive techniques and archaeological research, it is apparent that archaeological theorists have been generally dismissive or evasive on the subject of empathy (see van Helden and Witcher 2020c). This lack of consideration arguably reflects the broader research context, whereby philosophical and especially psychological studies of empathy have concentrated on emotional connectivity across cultures and space rather than through time; few studies examine empathy with people in the past (or future). Yet, a surprising number of archaeologists hint at or confess their ambition to empathize with past people in order to gain insight into the latter's lives. Indeed, we suggest archaeologists make habitual use of empathetic thinking, consciously or otherwise, and that it is therefore important that this is made explicit in order that the effects can be recognized and appropriately critiqued (see van Helden and Witcher 2020c). Barry Cunliffe (2017: vi), for example, provides a visual example in his book on the archaeology of maritime Europe:

> I have chosen to orient our maps with west at the top, giving prime place to the setting of the sun. I find this offers a more stimulating way of trying to empathize with the people of the Mediterranean, while for people living along the Atlantic facade it conforms to the natural orientation of their world. I hope it may help the reader to see things differently – to be able to take a sea-wise view of the world.

In this example, Cunliffe uses cartographical cues to stimulate empathetic thinking; could fictive techniques be used similarly to arouse empathy with people of the past? And with what specific objectives?

The ultimate aim of empathy is to experience the world as another person would, to see through their eyes and to understand (if not to condone) their perspective and actions. The potential value of such insight for archaeologists is obvious; the ability to experience the past from an insider's perspective would offer enormous insight into the motivations and actions of people whose direct testimony is otherwise lost to us (van Helden and Witcher 2020c). The theoretical and practical considerations are, however, challenging. The historicist position, epitomized by Collingwood's (1937: 143–4) re-enactment doctrine, maintains that it is possible to step from one set of shoes into another. This idealizing scenario, however, has been criticized by, among others, the philosopher of hermeneutics, Hans-Georg Gadamer ([1960] 1990: 177–222). To stand outside of time is impossible, for it is our entanglement with history that enables us to think in the first place. Relinquishing our historical position in order to judge the past on its own terms would be to abandon the very condition of our understanding (Gadamer [1960] 1990: 280–95).

For Gadamer, we approach any task of interpretation with a number of prejudices (*Vorurteilen*). It is through these prejudices that our historicity enables and shapes our understanding. Rather than in the more familiar pejorative sense, Gadamer uses prejudice to mean that which precedes judgement. This includes those concepts we need in order to pass judgement, thereby enabling our thinking. The constellation of prejudices with which we approach an object of interpretation is our horizon (Gadamer [1960] 1990: 270–81). We cannot see beyond the horizon; our view is situated. Initially, when we set out to interpret something (be it another person, a text or an archaeological object) we assume that it will conform to our prejudices, which guide our initial thinking. Only when expectations are not met, when a target object refuses to fit into our horizon and affronts our prejudices, do we pause to consider that object as something in need of interpretation. At that point, we attempt to change our preconceptions in order to accommodate integration within our horizon. This is also the point where we turn to empathy, attempting to understand the discrepancy by looking through the other's eyes. Gadamer, however, argues that it is not in the substitution of horizons but in the fusing of our own horizon and that of the target for interpretation that the moment of understanding lies, since we cannot wholly abandon our own point of view.

If our horizon is the precondition for our thinking, it is clear that we cannot hope for a direct or complete form of empathy, to fully experience reality as another does, for there is always an element of our own horizon in the fusion. Our perspective necessarily starts from a self-oriented perspective (how would *I* feel in such a situation) and, at best, ends up aspiring to an other-oriented perspective, grasped from within the limitations of our own vantage point (see Attridge 2004: 17–34 for a similar perspective). Gadamer's critique makes clear that we cannot achieve 'perfect' empathy, assuming completely the experiences of another person. Yet at the same time, we can recognize that such a total understanding is impossible of any aspect of reality. In this sense, our attempt to move from self-oriented to other-oriented empathy still constitutes a valid effort, for the imperfect information it may yield is no better or worse than could be expected via any other means. As the example of Cunliffe above suggests, our understanding of the past can be enriched by seeking to see the world through the eyes of past people, newly alert to our own situated knowledge and assumptions (that north is always to the top of a map) and glimpsing the alternatives (orienting instead towards the setting sun). Here is a literal fusion of horizons. Archaeologists have struggled to resolve the universalist/constructivist dichotomy; determining the former to be culturally unacceptable and the relativism of the latter to be debilitating, most have chosen to avoid the subject. The insight offered by Gadamer is that, if the universalist position is impossible, the hermeneutic circle offers a way of reconciling our individual positionality with that of others. Because characterization and empathy are central to works of fiction, the techniques of novelists and writers of fiction therefore offer great potential for the exploration of these issues.

James Michener's *The Source*

The varied themes discussed above are well illustrated in a historical novel by the American author James Michener: *The Source* (1965). Michener (1907–1997) authored a series of best-selling novels set in an astonishing variety of periods and regions. Many of his works adopt narratives spanning multiple millennia and which therefore address themes of direct archaeological interest. *The Source* is particularly well known in archaeological circles as the story centres on the excavation of a fictional site in modern Israel called Tell Makor (from the Hebrew for 'mound' and 'source'). Michener narrates the long-term history of this settlement, from the Epipalaeolithic through to the 1960s, intertwining the wider history of the Jewish people with the investigation of the site by a team of archaeologists. In the process he addresses broader themes of religion (e.g. animism vs. monotheism), philosophy (e.g. concepts of self and home), politics (e.g. colonialism and nationhood) and identities (individual and corporate). Michener states at the start of the novel that 'Makor, its site, its history and its excavation are wholly imaginary' (1965: n.p.). Nonetheless, as with his other novels, Michener drew on extensive and detailed personal research into historical ideas and archaeological evidence, weaving these together to create a plausible ancient site and the story of its excavation. Tell Makor and its archaeological investigation thus blend the fictional and the factual.

The novel is structured around the discovery of specific archaeological objects which are linked to key episodes in the history of Makor. The chapters proceed in chronological order from the Epipalaeolithic through to the mid-twentieth century; in parallel, Michener also narrates the story of the excavation of Makor's archaeological strata, which necessarily proceeds in reverse chronological order, from the most topmost, recent layers to the deepest and oldest. Thus, like most archaeological site reports, Michener must reconcile two temporal structures proceeding in opposite directions, narrating from prehistory to the present, while the archaeological evidence revealed through excavation proceeds from the most recent to the oldest (cf. Wallace 2004: 15). This structure requires various plot devices, such as finds made out of stratigraphic context, to bring together the relevant material and themes at the appropriate moment for the overall narrative. As each chapter moves to a new stratigraphic level, a new cast of characters and set of historical circumstances is introduced. Level/Chapter XV (the Epipalaeolithic) focuses on the protagonist Ur and the shift from hunting and gathering to agriculture. The subsequent chapters follow the descendants of Ur across the millennia. Although each new set of characters is largely ignorant of their lineage and the contingencies that have created their specific historical situations, the reader is aware of this genealogical thread, which acts as a counterpoint to the broader narrative themes of identity and destiny. From this vast, sprawling novel, we focus on two chapters: Level/Chapter XV *The Bee Eater* and Level/Chapter XII *Psalm of the Hoopoe Bird*.

The Bee Eater, set in 9831 BC, documents the origins of the settlement of Makor, the dynasty of Ur and the transition to farming. Ur's name symbolizes the importance that this man will play as the founder of the genealogical line that runs through the history of Makor. In German, the prefix 'Ur-' indicates a great time-depth, as well as connoting the root or source of something. The name also references Ur of the Chaldees, the birthplace of Abraham, the Patriarch of Judaism, Christianity and Islam, and the novel examines the intersection of these religions through the perspectives of the three directors of the excavation, one Jewish, one Christian and one Muslim. The relationship between these three characters provides a dialogic format for the expression of different perspectives on the organization of the dig and the interpretation of the finds, and for the wider political and religious themes the novel addresses. It is a format adopted in several archaeological works, both fictional and non-fictional (e.g. Flannery 1976; Ray and Thomas 2018). The chapter narrates the experiences and reflections of Ur and his family as they make the transition from hunting and gathering to agriculture, precipitating a host of changes including new concepts of home, property, gods and gender relations. The catalyst for these developments is Ur's wife, who was captured in a raid by Ur's father on a group of agriculturalists. Determined to demonstrate the superiority of agriculture and to transform the lives of her family, she successfully brings round both their son and daughter, leading Ur reluctantly to acknowledge the advantages of farming. When, near the end of his life, his son-in-law, a great hunter, is killed while on a hunting trip, Ur's lingering hopes of his line returning to earlier ways are permanently put to rest and the trajectory of Makor (and humanity) is set.

Neolithization – the processes by which plants and animals were domesticated, communities settled and new forms of material culture such as pottery developed – has long been an important focus of archaeological research. During the mid-twentieth century, studies of the shift to agriculture were dominated by grand narratives such as V. G. Childe's (1936) 'Neolithic (or urban) revolution', which focused on broad-scale systems and processes rather than human agents. Michener's chapter complements and enhances this generalizing scale of analysis by incorporating individuals and social groups who demonstrate complex motives and emotions and who are caught in a variety of causal relationships. Noticeably, Michener resists the temptation to attribute technological developments to the 'genius' of individuals: the 'invention' of farming or the 'discovery' of metallurgy. Agriculture, for example, is portrayed as a process of conversion rather than invention, emerging from networks of people and ideas. While it is Ur's wife and son who make incremental improvements to the family's wheat-growing practice, it is Ur who articulates the momentousness of these changes (Michener [1965] 2014: 99–100):

> Ur cried suddenly, 'That's it!'
>
> 'What?' his wife asked, looking at him suspiciously.
>
> 'We've been trapped into putting all our energy into wheat.'
>
> 'What do you mean trapped?' she asked, caught by an ugly suspicion that Ur had discovered her own source of fear.
>
> 'When we have all the grain in one place, it can easily be destroyed.'

(…) he had dared to express in words the growing fear that she and her son had experienced.

At moments such as this, Michener works to bridge multiple scales of analysis within a single narrative, combining long-term, large-scale processes with the experience and actions of the individuals that (he imagines) ultimately drove forward these changes. In this way, Michener's narrative demonstrates ways of thinking that were ahead of the archaeological accounts of the 1960s (when he was writing the novel) and that would only become central to archaeological interpretation several decades later. Although not all aspects of his treatment of this period withstand scrutiny today – not least due to the many subsequent discoveries and disciplinary developments – his fictional format offered a productive medium for exploring the extant evidence in relation to the mechanisms and consequences of the change in subsistence base.

Accounts of Michener's working practices give insight into how he researched and developed his narratives. A collaborator on one of his later novels describes how Michener conceptualized his approach to novels as a series of concentric circles, moving inwards from extensive library research through to the actual process of writing (cf. Trevelyan 1913; Kings 1978: 95) (Figure 7.1).

A key step in Michener's approach involved the use of trial and error to bring together into logical and meaningful scenes the disparate evidence that he had collated. This 'thinking through' of the evidence often involved Michener putting himself in the position of a protagonist to understand his or her bodily actions or motivations. In another novel, *Centennial* ([1974] 2007), for example, he narrates a scene around knapping flint tools in prehistoric North America. The account of the creation of this scene (recorded by his collaborator, Kings 1978: 52) demonstrates the extraordinary extent to which Michener not only consulted with specialists on the subject to acquire 'facts' but also sought to learn about the skills involved so that he could deduce his own hypotheses, which were then checked with experts and repeatedly refined (see also Hayes 1984: 184). This process parallels that of the archaeological researcher, working systematically to combine the evidence into plausible narratives. Arguably, however, the ambitious sweep of his novels additionally provided Michener with the broader framework that allowed him to draw out

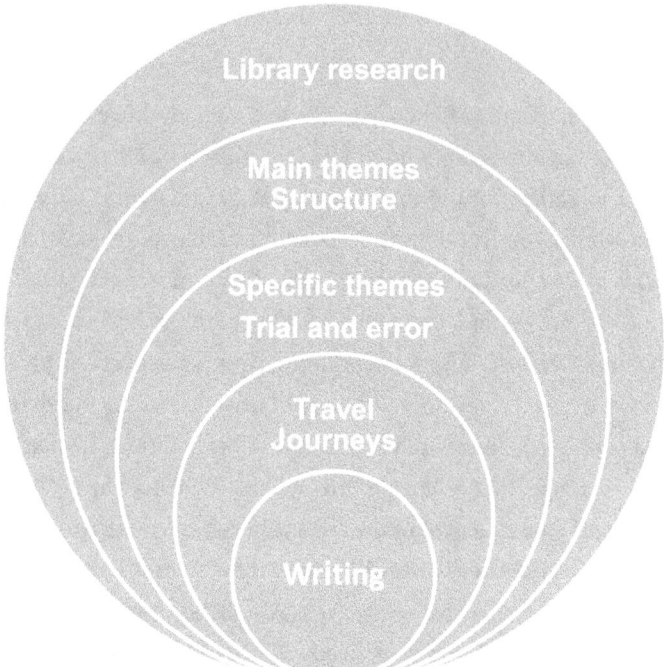

Figure 7.1 Michener's conceptualization of researching and writing a novel. Visualized by R. Witcher from verbal account in Kings (1978: 95).

the wider significance of these local-scale scenes. The ability of *The Source* to advance beyond the scholarly narratives of its day can be seen as a result of a combination of a traditional archaeological mindset – logical and empirical – with the use of imagination and creativity, giving Michener wider insight and the freedom to express this through invented characters.

If *The Bee Eater* illustrates how general archaeological themes can be explored through fictional techniques, Level/Chapter XII, *Psalm of the Hoopoe Bird*, offers an example of how Michener demonstrates the benefits of going beyond, while also remaining faithful to, specific archaeological evidence. The chapter is set in 963 BC and follows the engineer Hoopoe in the age of the biblical King David. Although he provides no references or footnotes in the novel to document his sources or research process, Michener was clearly familiar with the regional archaeological literature. This is well demonstrated by the story in Level/Chapter XII of the construction of a tunnel by Hoopoe, to provide direct access from Makor to its only source of fresh water, a well located beyond the settlement's defensive wall. In the event of a siege, this tunnel would allow the inhabitants to hold out against the enemy. Michener narrates the conceptualization, construction and use of this tunnel in great detail. Much of what he describes in this chapter is based directly on an archaeological report (Lamon 1935) about a tunnel discovered at the site of Megiddo, located 35 km to the south of Makor's fictional location. Although a similar concept for securing the water supply of Jerusalem is mentioned in 2 Kings 20.20, the specifics of Michener's account can only come from Lamon's report. Yet whereas the latter limits itself to description of the tunnel's form and reconstruction of the building sequence, Michener elaborates on the motivations, decisions and methods of the builders, going well beyond the limits of standard archaeological narratives, while remaining entirely compatible with Lamon's account. The chapter, for example, explores not only the technical planning and construction of the tunnel but also how Hoopoe conceives of the project, builds community support for it and the social and political effects that its successful completion brings about. In doing so, Michener commits to paper a series of considerations that archaeologists may entertain about the material evidence but which are omitted from scholarly accounts because they extend beyond strict evidential limits. Yet if, as archaeologists, we are to understand why and how the tunnel was built, we also must advance beyond pure description and the logical ordering of construction phases. In creating a plausible scenario for the building of the tunnel – regional political instability, technical knowledge, group debate and consensus about the building project – Michener develops a narrative that is amenable to evaluation, alongside other accounts, of its relative strengths and weaknesses in explaining the archaeological evidence (Gibb 2020).

Michener's use of Lamon's account of the Megiddo tunnel is entirely compatible with the archaeological evidence with the exception of the addition to the story of an inscription; no such epigraphic evidence has been recovered from Megiddo. The details of this inscription, however, correspond closely to the Siloam inscription from Jerusalem, which documents the construction of a water tunnel and is reported as one of the earliest, long Hebrew texts – exactly how Michener describes it in *The Source* (Reich and Shukron 2011). In narrating the story of the tunnel in Level/Chapter XII, and of the site of Makor more generally, Michener therefore combines evidence from different sites to create an archaeological 'composite' with which to advance his plot. This is an approach not dissimilar to that used by archaeologists who must often work with patchy or incomplete evidence. The standard plan of a Roman fort, for example, is pieced together using incomplete evidence from multiple sites, and Terrenato (2001) demonstrates how the conventional narrative of the evolution of Roman villas in Italy is an idealized sequence based on a composite of phases excavated at many different villas, but undocumented in its entirety at any individual site. Makor is therefore not *a* tell, but functions metonymically as *the* Tell, standing for all such sites. Makor plays the same role geographically as Ur's lineage plays genealogically. The site and Ur unify the narrative in such a way that local-scale histories are intertwined with global themes in a single coherent whole. The objectives and techniques of the archaeologist and the novelist can therefore be closely aligned, even if the resulting narratives are presented in different written forms and for audiences with differing expectations.

As with his chapter on the adoption of agriculture, Michener's account of Hoopoe's tunnel engages closely not only with archaeological evidence but also with archaeological ways of thinking by integrating different scales of analysis, the exploration of multiple perspectives and historical causation, and the primacy of human agency in large-scale processes. Above and beyond its treatment of the past, the novel is also highly sensitive to questions about the creation of knowledge through archaeological practice and alert to the dangers of the politicization of archaeological information in the service of nationalism or religious extremism. Throughout, the three directors of the excavation bring the insights and prejudices of their different backgrounds to bear on the creation of a historical narrative for the newly founded nation state of Israel. Michener exhibits an archaeological mindset, taking 'facts' and building narratives consistent with the evidence and giving the data historical meaning and trajectory by imputing human motivations; in doing so, he also uses the techniques of fiction both to think through and present the results. By putting himself empathetically into the shoes of the people he seeks to portray, Michener operates in a way that is more similar to the approach of archaeologists than the latter might admit. Michener's readers will not find his novels populated by particularly empathetic characters (Hayes 1984: 217); what he demonstrates, however, is the role of empathy in the *creation* rather than the portrayal of those characters. As such, he offers an example of the importance of empathy to the writer (or archaeological researcher) rather than the reader. The presentation of the results in the format of a novel rather than a site report should not suggest that Michener's aims and methods are totally distinct from those of the academic archaeologist (Elphinstone and Wickham-Jones 2012). The value of studying a novel such as *The Source* lies not in identifying where it deviates from conventional archaeological thinking but in how it illuminates the strengths and weaknesses of archaeological narratives.

Conclusions

The title of this chapter draws inspiration from Sir Mortimer Wheeler's report on his excavations at Maiden Castle, an Iron Age hillfort in Dorset. So clear, he claims, was the archaeological evidence he uncovered that 'something less than imagination' was required to reconstruct the Roman storming of the hillfort (Wheeler 1943: 61). The evidence, he asserts, effectively spoke for itself. His reconstruction of the Roman attack is a rightly famous piece of archaeological narrative writing, but it clearly also blends the archaeological and the literary, interweaving archaeological finds with earlier textual narratives (Tacitus) and literary tropes (tragedy) (for further discussion, see van Helden and Witcher 2020b). Contrary to Wheeler's claim that the archaeological evidence spoke objectively, the material and literary are intimately interconnected in this text, each inspiring and imitating the other in equal measure. A long archaeological tradition has drawn on the techniques and the texts of the writers of fiction, no less than the craft of archaeology has offered rich metaphors and materials for creative writers. In this chapter, we have drawn attention not only to the risks – some more substantive than others – of archaeology engaging with fiction but also more importantly to the many benefits and opportunities that arise. We do not suggest that all attempts to think about the past using fictive techniques should end with the publication of fictional texts, nor – alert to the cream-bun syndrome – that the use of these techniques should become standard or even commonplace. Such techniques must be deployed judiciously and with clear purpose. Yet there is scope to use these approaches more ambitiously than they have been used to date. Currently, fictional techniques tend to be called upon at the end of the archaeological research process to facilitate the dissemination of the results to wider audiences. But as the example of Michener's *The Source* suggests, fictive techniques can be employed profitably as part of the research process itself, as a valid means of integrating evidence, identifying gaps in understanding, analysing logical connections and causation, addressing social and political concerns, building emotional links with the past and more besides – in short, by making our ideas about the past 'actually work' (Elphinstone and Wickham-Jones 2012: 536). By recognizing the shared aims, methods and forms that connect archaeology and literature across the borderline of fact and fiction, we argue that we can write archaeological narratives that are simultaneously more creative and more rigorous. Through experimentation and emotional connections, we might also find more satisfying or even more fun ways to engage with the past. Without doubt, fictional narratives and the exploration of empathy will need to be embedded within a rational, hermeneutic framework of critical evaluation. But the same applies to any archaeological interpretation or narrative. Fictive techniques are compatible with a variety of theoretical approaches and should be used to complement, not replace, them (van Helden and Witcher 2020b).

In many ways, the structure of Michener's *The Source* mimics the hermeneutic position that we advocate. The novel tacks between scales large and small, between 'grand narrative' and the biographies of individual characters, and between the events of the past and of the present from where we must attempt to interpret them. More than just an effective example of the genre of historical fiction, Michener's book embodies a wider archaeological stance. Fittingly, it also provides an example of the provisional nature of our hermeneutic position as archaeologists. In his description of the schematic cross section that illustrates the excavation of the site, and which introduces the novel's final chapter, Michener writes: 'Observe also that the monolith to El, perhaps the most significant of the remains buried in the tell, will be missed by the excavators' ([1965] 2014: 965). Despite their exhaustive efforts, the archaeologists are denied – perhaps in perpetuity – the full story of Makor. That privilege is reserved for the novelist and the reader.

References

Attridge, D. (2004), *The Singularity of Literature*, Abingdon: Routledge.

Barkan, L. (1999), *Unearthing the Past: Archaeology and Aesthetics in the Making of Renaissance*, New Haven, CT: Yale University Press.

Bernbeck, R. (2004), 'The Past as Fact and Fiction: From Historical Novels to Novel Histories', in S. Pollock and R. Bernbeck (eds), *Archaeologies of the Middle East: Critical Perspectives*, 97–121, Chichester: Wiley-Blackwell.

Bernbeck, R. (2015), 'From Imaginations of a Peopled Past to a Recognition of Past People', in R. M. Van Dyke and R. Bernbeck (eds), *Subjects and Narratives in Archaeology*, 257–76, Boulder: University Press of Colorado.

Childe, V. G. (1936), *Man Makes Himself*, London: Watts.

Collingwood, R. G. (1937), 'Review of "R. Klibansky and H. J. Paton (ed.), Philosophy and History: Essays Presented to Ernst Cassirer"', *The English Historical Review*, 52 (205): 141–6.

Connah G. (2010), *Writing about Archaeology*, Cambridge: Cambridge University Press.

Cunliffe, B. (2017), *On the Ocean: The Mediterranean and the Atlantic from Prehistory to AD 1500*, Oxford: Oxford University Press.

Elphinstone, M. (2020), 'Voices from the Silence', in D. P. van Helden and R. E. Witcher (eds), *Researching the Archaeological Past through Imagined Narratives: A Necessary Fiction*, 54–69, Abingdon: Routledge.

Elphinstone, M., and C. Wickham-Jones (2012), 'Archaeology and Fiction', *Antiquity*, 86: 532–7.

Fagan, B. (2010), *Writing Archaeology: Telling Stories about the Past*, 2nd edn, Walnut Creek, CA: Left Coast Press.

Ferguson, N. (1998), 'Introduction', in N. Ferguson (ed.), *Virtual History: Alternatives and Counterfactuals*, 1–90, London: Papermac.

Flannery, K. V. (ed.) (1976), *The Early Mesoamerican Village*, New York: Academic Press.

Fleming, A. (2006), 'Post-Processual Landscape Archaeology: A Critique', *Cambridge Archaeological Journal*, 16 (3): 267–80.

Gadamer, H.-G. ([1960] 1990), *Wahrheit und Methode: Grundzüge einer philosophischen Hermeneutik*, Tübingen: J. C. B. Mohr (Paul Siebeck).

Gadamer, H.-G. (1994), 'Truth in the Human Sciences', in B. R. Wachterhauser (ed.), *Hermeneutics and Truth*, 25–32, Evanston, IL: Northwestern University Press.

Gear, W. M., and K. O'Neal Gear (2003), 'Archaeological Fiction: Tripping through the Minefield', *SAA Archaeological Record*, 3 (5): 24–7.

Gerbault, P., et al. (2014), 'Storytelling and Story Testing in Domestication', *Proceedings of the National Academy of Sciences*, 111 (17): 6159–64.

Gibb, J. G. (2000), 'Imaginary, but by No Means Unimaginable: Storytelling, Science, and Historical Archaeology', *Historical Archaeology*, 34 (2): 1–6.

Gibb, J. G. (2020), 'Entering Undocumented Pasts through Playwriting', in D. P. van Helden and R. E. Witcher (eds), *Researching the Archaeological Past through Imagined Narratives: A Necessary Fiction*, 148–67, Abingdon: Routledge.

Gill, J., C. McKenzie and E. Lightfoot (2019), '"Handle with Care": Literature, Archaeology, Slavery', *Interdisciplinary Science Reviews*, 44 (1): 21–37.

González-Ruibal, A., P. A. González and F. Criado-Boado (2018), 'Against Reactionary Populism: Towards a New Public Archaeology', *Antiquity*, 92: 507–15.

Gottschall, J. (2012), *The Storytelling Animal: How Stories Make Us Human*, New York: Mariner.

Graves, R. (1934), *I Claudius*, London: Arthur Baker.

Green, M. C., and T. C. Brock (2000), 'The Role of Transportation in the Persuasiveness of Public Narratives', *Journal of Personality and Social Psychology*, 79 (5): 701–21.

Green, M. C., J. Garst and T. C. Brock (2004), 'The Power of Fiction: Determinants and Boundaries', in L. J. Shrum (ed.), *The Psychology of Entertainment Media: Blurring the Lines between Entertainment and Persuasion*, 161–76, Mahwah, NJ: Erlbaum.

Green, C., and R. Gilchrist (2015), *Glastonbury Abbey: Archaeological Investigations 1904–79*, London: Society of Antiquaries of London.

Grethlein, J. (2010), 'Experientiality and "Narrative Reference," with Thanks to Thucydides', *History and Theory*, 49 (3): 315–35.

Grethlein, J. (2014), '"Future Past": Time and Teleology in (Ancient) Historiography', *History and Theory*, 53 (3): 309–30.

Grethlein, J., and L. Huitink (2017), 'Homer's Vividness: An Enactive Approach', *Journal of Hellenic Studies*, 137: 67–91.

Harris, O. J. T., and C. N. Cipolla (2017), *Archaeological Theory in the New Millennium: Introducing Current Perspectives*, Abingdon: Routledge.

Hayes, J. P. (1984), *James A. Michener: A Biography*, Indianapolis: Bobbs-Merrill.

Hobden, F. (2020), 'Spartacus: Blood and Sand (STARZ, 2010): A Necessary Fiction?', in D. P. van Helden and R. E. Witcher (eds), *Researching the Archaeological Past through Imagined Narratives: A Necessary Fiction*, 238–54, Abingdon: Routledge.

Hodges, R. (2017), *The Archaeology of Mediterranean Placemaking: Butrint and the Global Heritage Industry*, London: Bloomsbury.

Hopkins, K. (1999), *A World Full of Gods: Pagans, Jews and Christians in the Roman Empire*, London: Weidenfeld and Nicolson.

Joyce, R. A., R. W. Preucel, J. Lopiparo, C. Guyer and M. Joyce (2002), *The Languages of Archaeology: Dialogue, Narrative, and Writing*, Oxford: Blackwell.

Kavanagh, K. E. (2020), 'Writing Wonders: Poetry as Archaeological Method?', in D. P. van Helden and R. E. Witcher (eds), *Researching the Archaeological Past through Imagined Narratives: A Necessary Fiction*, 184–209, Abingdon: Routledge.

Kings, J. (1978), *In Search of Centennial: A Journey with James A. Michener*, New York: Random House.

Lamon, R. S. (1935), *The Megiddo Water System*, Chicago, IL: University of Chicago Press.

Lekson, S. H. (2018), *A Study of Southwestern Archaeology*, Salt Lake City: University of Utah Press.

Michener, J. A. ([1965] 2014), *The Source*, New York: Dial Press.

Michener, J. A. ([1974] 2007), *Centennial*, New York: Dial Press.

Noël Hume, I. (1964), 'Archaeology: Handmaiden to History', *North Carolina Historical Review*, 41 (2): 215–25.

Patton, M. (2020), 'Beyond Archaeological Narrative: Imagined Worlds of Neolithic Europe', in D. P. van Helden and R. E. Witcher (eds), *Researching the Archaeological Past through Imagined Narratives: A Necessary Fiction*, 70–87, Abingdon: Routledge.

Pluciennik, M. (2015), 'Authoritative and Ethical Voices: from *Diktat* to the Demotic', in R. M. Van Dyke and R. Bernbeck (eds), *Subjects and Narratives in Archaeology*, 277–86, Boulder: University Press of Colorado.

Pollock, S. (2015), 'Wrestling with Truth: Possibilities and Peril in Alternative Narrative Form', in R. M. Van Dyke and R. Bernbeck (eds), *Subjects and Narratives in Archaeology*, 55–81, Boulder: University Press of Colorado.

Praetzellis, A. (2015), *Archaeological Theory in a Nutshell*, Walnut Creek, CA: Left Coast Press.

Ray, K., and J. Thomas (2018), *Neolithic Britain: The Transformation of Social Worlds*, Oxford: Oxford University Press.

Reich, R., and E. Shukron (2011), 'The Date of the Siloam Tunnel Reconsidered', *Tel Aviv*, 38 (2): 147–57.

Robb, J., and T. R. Pauketat (2013), *Big Histories, Human Lives: Tackling Problems of Scale in Archaeology*, Santa Fe, New Mexico: School for Advanced Research Press.

Shanks, M. (1992), *Experiencing the Past: On the Character of Archaeology*, Abingdon: Routledge.

Shanks, M. (2012), *The Archaeological Imagination*, Walnut Creek, CA: Left Coast Press.

Sidebotham, S. E. (2016), 'From the Mediterranean to South Asia: The Odyssey of an Indian Merchant in Roman Times', in K. S. Mathew (ed.), *Imperial Rome, Indian Ocean regions and Muziris: New Perspectives on Maritime Trade*, 75–82, Abingdon: Routledge.

Stueber, K. (2006), *Rediscovering Empathy: Agency, Folk Psychology and the Human Sciences*, Cambridge, MA: MIT Press.

Tarlow, S. A. (2001), 'The Responsibility of Representation', in M. Pluciennik (ed.), *The Responsibilities of Archaeologists: Archaeology and Ethics*, 57– 64, Lampeter Workshop in Archaeology 4, BAR International Series 981, Oxford: Oxbow.

Terrenato, N. (2001), 'The Auditorium Site in Rome and the Origins of the Villa', *Journal of Roman Archaeology*, 14: 5–32.

Tolkien, J. R. R. (1978), *The Lord of the Rings*, London: Unwin Paperbacks.

Trevelyan, G. M. (1913), *Clio, a Muse, and Other Essays Literary and Pedestrian*, London: Longmans, Green.

Van Dyke, R. M., and R. Bernbeck (2015), 'Alternative Narratives and the Ethics of Representation: An Introduction', in R. M. Van Dyke and R. Bernbeck (eds), *Subjects and Narratives in Archaeology*, 1–26, Boulder: University Press of Colorado.

van Helden, D. P., and R. E. Witcher (eds) (2020a), *Researching the Archaeological Past through Imagined Narratives: A Necessary Fiction*, Abingdon: Routledge.

van Helden, D. P., and R. E. Witcher (2020b), 'Introduction: Historical Fiction and Archaeological Interpretation', in D. P. van Helden and R. E. Witcher (eds), *Researching the Archaeological Past through Imagined Narratives: A Necessary Fiction*, 1–37, Abingdon: Routledge.

van Helden, D. P., and R. E. Witcher (2020c), 'Walking in Someone Else's Shoes: Archaeology, Empathy and Fiction', in D. P. van Helden and R. E. Witcher (eds), *Researching the Archaeological Past through Imagined Narratives: A Necessary Fiction*, 109–29, Abingdon: Routledge.

Wachterhauser, B. R. (1994), 'Introduction: Is there Truth after Interpretation?', in B. R. Wachterhauser (ed.), *Hermeneutics and Truth*, 1–32, Evanston, IL: Northwestern University Press.

Wallace, J. (2004), *Digging the Dirt: The Archaeological Imagination*, London: Duckworth.

Wheeler, R. E. M. (1943), *Maiden Castle, Dorset*, Oxford: Oxford University Press.

White, H. (1973), *Metahistory: The Historical Imagination in Nineteenth-Century Europe*, Baltimore, MD: Johns Hopkins University Press.

Wickham-Jones, C. R. (2020), 'The Cornflakes of Prehistory: Fact, Fiction and Imagination in Archaeology', in D. P. van Helden and R. E. Witcher (eds), *Researching the Archaeological Past through Imagined Narratives: A Necessary Fiction*, 38–53, Abingdon: Routledge.

Witcher, R. E. (2013), '(Sub)urban Surroundings', in P. Erdkamp (ed.), *The Cambridge Companion to Ancient Rome*, 205–25, Cambridge: Cambridge University Press.

Witcher, R. E. (2017), 'The Globalized Roman World', in T. Hodos (ed.), *The Routledge Handbook of Globalization and Archaeology*, 634–51, Abingdon: Routledge.

8

The death of the archaeologist: Imagining science, storytelling and self-understanding in contemporary archaeofiction

Anna Auguscik

In recent years, the relationship between archaeology and its public understanding, or between its self-understanding and its representation in popular fiction, has often been considered with reference to the archaeological imagination. Archaeologist Michael Shanks defines the archaeological imagination in his eponymous 2012 book as the impulse to 'recreate the world behind the ruin in the land, to reanimate the people behind the sherd of antique pottery, a fragment of the past' (25). For Shanks, this impulse is not one limited to archaeologists but as the title of his first chapter 'We are all archaeologists now' indicates, it is inclusionary, interdisciplinary and inherently modern. It is

> a creative impulse and faculty at the heart of archaeology, but also embedded in many cultural dispositions, discourses and institutions commonly associated with modernity. The archaeological imagination is rooted in a sensibility, a pervasive set of attitudes towards traces and remains, towards memory, time and temporality, the fabric of history. (2012: 25)

On his website Shanks suggests that this process is comparable to fiction, as imagining the archaeological is 'to bring alive the past-in-the-present, as in an historical novel, to cherish and work upon fragments of the past, what remains of the past in the present' (Shanks 2011). Indeed, the idea of the archaeological imagination has not only been theorized by archaeologists (cf. Schnapp, Shanks and Tiews 2004) but also proven fruitful in literary studies (cf. Wallace 2004; Sanders 2009; Warwick and Willis 2012; Reid 2017), as well as becoming a topic of narrative fiction. In Michael Ondaatje's (2000) novel *Anil's Ghost*, for example, the protagonist seems to anticipate Shanks in claiming that '[a] good archaeologist can read a bucket of soil as if it were a complex historical novel' (147). How does contemporary fiction about archaeologists contribute to debates about archaeology and its public? How does it imagine the relationship between the epistemological work done in archaeology and that of a novel? Does it matter whether the characters doing the imagining are archaeologists or members of a wider public? And what are the limits of the archaeological imagination?

The history of literary representations of archaeology is often dated back to a time before archaeology as a discipline came into being but when the archaeological imagination was already at work in literature (cf. Reid 2017). Early literary examples in English – Walter Scott's *The Antiquary* (1816) or Percy Bysshe Shelley's sonnet 'Ozymandias' (1818) – do without archaeology as a scientific practice or the archaeologist as a character. Instead, they deal with the objects of archaeological study (historical landmarks or statues, and the ruins thereof), often read as reminders of the evanescence of individual life or the ephemerality of entire empires (cf. Janowitz 1984). In later Victorian literature archaeology acts as a metonym for colonialism (see H. Rider Haggard's 'imperial Gothic' novels, most notably in *King Solomon's Mines* (1895)) and as a metaphor for the hidden or the secretive (notable in detective and crime fiction such as Charles Dickens's *The Mystery of Edwin Drood* (1870) and the writings by Edgar Allan Poe, Wilkie Collins and Sir Arthur Conan Doyle). The archaeological imagination of the nineteenth century was linked to various subject positions – antiquarians, travellers, adventurers, colonialists, detectives – but not yet to the archaeologist.

The literary interest in archaeology as a profession only became established in twentieth-century fiction as the discipline of archaeology developed, an interest filtered through Freud's conceptualization of psychoanalysis which he explained to one of his patients as an archaeology of the mind: 'The psychoanalyst, like the archaeologist in his excavations, must uncover layer after layer of the patient's psyche, before coming to the deepest, most valuable treasures' (Gardiner 1971: 139). The 'stratified' psyche becomes connected to 'the physical strata uncovered by disciplines such as archaeology and geology' (Dobson and Banks 2019: 1) as novels from Agatha Christie's *Murder in Mesopotamia* (1936) to Margaret Drabble's *The Realms of Gold* (1975) combine earlier Victorian concerns such as the discipline's connections to colonial history, with an exploration of how, in Poirot's words, a 'journey into the past' becomes '[a] journey into the strange places of the human soul' (Christie [1936] 2001: 301). The archaeologist protagonist's own psychological excavation is the focus of *The Realms of Gold* where the novel's interest lies less in the (post)colonial implications of her protagonist's digs in Egypt than with her personal development from depression and loneliness to settling into a house charged with family history. The discipline of archaeology acts as a symbol for Frances's understanding of the layered personalities among those she takes care of, as well as, finally, her own 'self-excavation'.[1]

However, the metaphorical use of archaeology to represent modern self-understanding has been problematized within twenty-first-century fiction in ways which raise questions about the archaeological imagination, subjectivity and the power of interpretation. This chapter explores the archaeological imagination of twenty-first-century fiction through an examination of two novels, Barry Unsworth's *Land of Marvels* and Sarah Moss's *Cold Earth*, both published in 2009. It argues that these contemporary 'archaeofictions'[2] renegotiate both the metonymical and the metaphorical use of archaeology by representing archaeologists as 'complex scientist characters' (Kirchhofer and Roxburgh 2016: 151). Placing them centre stage, the novels reveal the blind spots of archaeologist protagonists who are prone to establishing false continuities by identifying with their object of research and building narratives in order to fill gaps or turn fragments into something 'whole'. Driven by ambitions to carve out a place in the history of famous archaeologist explorers – or at least to acquire tenure – and ignoring their immediate, contemporary surroundings, the archaeologist characters in these novels seemingly excavate themselves by exploring the 'other'. The archaeologist narrator or focalizer, at first 'storifying' the found objects, completing or even rewriting their presumed history, instead becomes the object of other characters' stories by the end of these novels, the archaeologists dying, ironically, as a consequence of their obsession with protecting and preserving. Their withheld position as those having a last word thus becomes a critique of whose imagination is being prioritized: Who imagines, in what subject positions and what difference does it make? Each novel offers a different answer to this question through a doubling of their archaeologist protagonists as both subjects and objects of imagination. In the case of *Land of Marvels* – a historical expedition narrative about an early-twentieth-century excavation in the Middle East – questions of imperial power and colonial knowledge are inextricable from the heroic age of exploration. In contrast *Cold Earth*, a realist novel with gothic elements about a contemporary expedition to Greenland, emphasizes an everyday perspective on field work but includes the history of heroic explorers as part of the expedition members' self-understanding.

Heroic archaeologists

Barry Unsworth's *Land of Marvels* (2009), set in the spring of 1914 at an excavation site in Mesopotamia, begins with the perspective of self-taught archaeologist John Somerville,[3] whose dream it has been to follow in the footsteps of his hero and real-life archaeologist, Sir Austen Henry Layard (1817–1894). In the third year of his first expedition as leader, Somerville's dig hasn't produced any major new insights apart from one 'piece of ivory, which had no context – so far at least – and therefore no meaning' (26). Somerville's search for the meaning of the unknown object is paralleled by his search for his own self-narrative – one which he seeks to attach to available narratives which prove problematic. In her article on archaeology in postcolonial literature, 'Digging Far and Deep', Gesa Mackenthun observes that postcolonial writing often employs heterotopic and heterochronic tropes in order to rewrite past perspectives laden with 'late-imperial mythology' (2014: 5). She theorizes archaeological digs represented in Ondaatje's *Anil's Ghost* and Unsworth's *Land of Marvels*, as 'nodal sites in the rhizomatic structure of empire where many of its economic, geopolitical, and scientific energies conjoin and interact' (Mackenthun 2014: 12). In my reading, I will expand the focus on archaeological sites to the archaeologist character's attempts at self-excavation. Not only is Somerville's identity shown to be as fragmented, layered and trenched as the mound, but, in the end, instead of being hailed for completing the story of the found object, it is his story that is used for other characters' narratives.

The archaeologist and the excavation site, Tell Erdek, become 'nodal sites' for multiple layers of historical and archaeological struggle: Somerville's choice to excavate this particular mound is based on his mentor's promise that it is situated 'at the borderlands of empire' (25) and this is where his archaeological imagination has led him:

> It appealed to his imagination as strongly now as ever to think of the powers that had marched and countermarched across this land of the Two Rivers: Sumerians, Babylonians, Hittites, Assyrians, Medes, Chaldeans, all bent on conquest, all convinced they would last forever, building their cities and proclaiming their power, empires following one upon another, their only memorial now the scraps that lay below ground, which he and his like competed in digging for. (23–4)

Set just before the outbreak of the First World War, the novel's Mesopotamia is also a region in which various nations – the struggling Ottoman Empire, the older Empires of Britain, France and Russia, as well as emergent German and US global interests – are competing to exert an influence. As the story progresses, the characters bear witness to the major shift from colonial imperialism to 'economic imperialism' (286), cemented with the final re-naming of Mesopotamia as 'Iraq' (287) – the novel's final word. These historical and current conflicts are reflected at Tell Erdek and the expedition house, which is the site of a large cast of characters who represent various conflicting and coinciding interests. Somerville's aim to understand the archaeological context of the site and give meaning to his findings is continually interrupted by various forces which threaten both the mound and his career. The construction of the Baghdad railway, sponsored by Deutsche Bank, is advancing onto the mound itself, while the sand surrounding it shows signs of harbouring vast oil reserves which bring an American geologist and various international institutions backing his explorative research to the scene. The site is also a possible contender to the coordinates of the Garden of Eden, identified by a pair of 'biblical archaeologists' (228). The local young Bedouin Jehar stokes Somerville's fears about the approaching railway in the hope of earning a large sum of money in exchange for information on the progress of construction. The financier Lord Rampling uses the archaeologist's increasingly desperate situation for his own (and secondarily, British) advance. Matters are made worse when Somerville's wife, Edith, losing her admiration for her explorer husband, elopes with the more adventurous American geologist. In the end, Somerville dies in a spectacular explosion alongside Jehar, unintentionally destroying the very site he vowed to protect and inadvertently turns into the 'jumping mouse, or jerboa … a creature that had reached legendary status' as a small harbinger of havoc on excavation sites by digging holes and thus disturbing layers and 'was an accustomed joke' (12) between the archaeologist and his assistant Palmer. The novel does not, however, end with his death but is concluded by an 'afterword', which states that 'what chiefly remained' of Somerville, Jehar and the Assyrian king Sin-shar-ishkun whose bones were destroyed in the flames 'was a story' (282) and that those involved in the expedition continued to reflect upon and interpret their legacy.

Land of Marvels rewrites archaeology's metonymical function as colonial discourse by problematizing Orientalist stereotypes and exploring how evaluations of imperialism are contingent upon power dynamics. The novel underscores the hypocrisy of the colonial enterprise through its archaeologist characters who look down upon local people while coveting their objects. Somerville is 'searching for treasure' (5), the components of which 'would have to be packed on the surface and made ready for transport to London' (268) where his initial interpretations would have to be tested in 'labs' (54) and presented to The Royal Society (274). His sense of entitlement and superiority is repeatedly demonstrated in his relationship with Jehar. The archaeologist's imperial gaze that views Jehar as animalistic and uncivilized is exposed through a reversal: it is Somerville who feels 'under observation' (29) by the other 'man's gaze' (6), his 'predatory intentness' (23) or the 'gaze of a savage' (75). While Jehar is aware that Somerville 'thinks I am a lesser than he' (161), it becomes clear that their relationship is one of interdependence, a keen observation repeatedly made by Jehar rather than Somerville: 'their two lives were closely intertwined' (29), 'their destinies were linked' (32). Jehar proves not only more observant but also calmer: for example, while the archaeologist is prone to 'speculations' (36), his informant displays a more rational approach, not stepping into the pitfalls of speculations, as he says, 'better the vacant mind' (29). Yet, Jehar's is not the story of a reversal of power, and the moment he believes his deal with Somerville to blow up equipment central to the German railway project to be 'an agreement between gentlemen' (273) is also when he seals their tragic fate.

The archaeologists' imagination of their work and of the past is shown to be entangled with contemporaneous discourses of empire. In a debate between Somerville and his assistant Palmer about the status of the Assyrian ruler Ashurbanipal who 'took an army on an expedition' and whom Somerville admires for being an 'empire builder', Palmer quickly corrects Somerville's assessment to 'large-scale raider', prompting Somerville to compare Ashurbanipal to Cecil Rhodes in Africa as he admits that it is '[n]ot easy to draw the line' (61). As the archaeologists develop their ideas about the empires they research, their reflections are imbued with the colonial struggles surrounding them: In one instance, their dialogue discloses the value they ascribe to Assyrian in contrast to Syrian artwork: 'It's a thousand years too early. There was no ivory in circulation then, none that we know of' (11), Palmer claims, and Somerville continues: 'There might have been some local carving in ivory, though none has come to light. But I don't think it is Syrian work in any case. It's too refined, too ceremonious somehow' (11). Archaeological value is tied to the powerful Assyrian Empire, not to the more recent, far less imperial Syria.

Such conclusions are also the result of the way the fictional archaeologists imagine their discipline. While the novel represents the practice of doing archaeology (the circumstances of leasing the excavation site and the particular methodology of cutting trenches; the hierarchal structure of the groups digging at the mound; the gender division with certain minor tasks assigned to women inside the expedition house), the characters also imagine archaeology – as the text explicitly points out, through storytelling. The scientific questions pertaining to the archaeological findings and the methodology of working out their significance for the understanding of Assyrian history, as well as the history of archaeology itself, are not peripheral but plotlines with their own arc of suspense. At first, the progress of the archaeological insights is communicated through Somerville as focalizer and many of the ideas about the findings are developed in dialogues with his assistant Palmer, particularly when it comes to dating and chronology, which inspire and motivate him: '[h]e enjoyed speculations of this kind' (12). Increasingly, however, as Somerville escapes from the enclosing railway and other interests surrounding him, he seeks a space of his own which he finds by withdrawing to the site of his findings – at first the layers of the hill and later the tomb shaft at its foot – and into his imagination. His inner turmoil leads him to ponder various histories as stories. He is in awe of the Assyrian kings and their power: 'it was the Assyrians who had made a conquest of his imagination, theirs the empire that had seemed to him a paradigm of all empires' (124); he 'elaborated the story he had begun to tell himself from the moment of finding the piece of carved ivory. This story began with the second Assyrian king to be called Ashurnasirpal, the first of them all to boast of his power to inflict suffering' (164). He contemplates the history of archaeology as scientific discipline, beginning with Sir William Matthew Flinders Petrie's methods and culminating in a long line of the 'great men' of archaeology in order to position his own scientific career within that history. He aspires to 'go down in the annals of archaeology . . . with . . . Layard, Rassam, George Smith' (258). Archaeology 'had been his consuming passion. In an age of explorers and empire builders his hero had been an archaeologist, Henry Layard' who 'had excavated Nimrud' and 'uncovered . . . Nineveh' in what Somerville repeatedly acknowledges as 'an immense addition to human knowledge' (27). It is no less than 'the story of humanity' (83) to which he, too, hopes to contribute as he cannot help but detect 'similarity of circumstance between Layard and himself' (28): 'he too would reveal to the world a splendour from underground, long unsuspected'.

Somerville's very identity, then, is intricately bound up with his object of archaeological study and his imagination of it, but the ensuing self-narrative is often false; there is a large gap between whom Somerville imagines himself to be and how others imagine him. This tension becomes apparent in Somerville's relationship with his wife Edith. Edith is not interested in 'broken pots', 'fragmented and dispersed' but is instead attracted by the 'promise of beauty', 'finished form', 'the original vessel complete in every part' (20). She wants her husband to be 'a digger and searcher, a man of action' (50) and finds details of archaeological knowledge, specifically the history of cuneiform letters, 'boring' (52). When he confides in his wife, exposing his fears about the advancing railway but also his plans to fight back and use his connections to the ambassador, she is ecstatic to see him stick to his 'dream of exploration and discovery', a moment in which she deems him to be 'truly yourself' (84). Yet while such heroic discovery is what Somerville aspires to, he has to admit that 'he knew . . . that the man lying between her thighs had ceased very early in their life together to be truly himself' (84). Somerville ends up proving a 'disappointment' (20), both to himself and to his wife, because his identity is, in fact, as fragmented and partial as his archaeological finds, 'the structure of his character was loosening somehow into incongruous components' (143). Like the Assyrian identity thieves who 'risk the curse of the god Sin by stealing his name or denying it' (267), Somerville's own sense of identity is at risk, as he desperately tries to maintain his delusive self-narrative, 'to repair this disappointment, restore [Edith's] faith in the heroic ideal' (84) through his work in which he imagines that '[h]is own name would be made now, his own identity confirmed' (267).

Through the prism of Somerville's attempt to construct an identity, Unsworth demonstrates the limitations of archaeological storytelling, of constructing a whole from fragments, when such storytelling is bound up with (colonial) power and control. Susceptibility to stories is not a mark of positive distinction in the novel. While Palmer and Patricia's relationship is based on 'deflating high-flown sentiments' (46) – significantly, Palmer trusts numbers, that is, the price of metals, rather than editorials when it comes to making predictions about the advent of war – Somerville and Edith's relationship begins and ends with storytelling. Their marriage is threatened when Edith perceives another to be the better storyteller and her husband's conversation as the 'paler imitation of Elliott's narrative style' (142). The novel unpacks storytelling as what all characters do – archaeologist or not – and explores where they are most at risk of succumbing to the seductive power of stories. The character which perhaps most clearly emerges as a storyteller is Jehar, 'the fabulist' (70). Not only does he tell stories as messenger to Somerville but stories are also his chosen means to secure the attention and love of his Ninanna. Jehar understands that while stories give him 'power over her', reflecting that 'it was as if by subjugating her with his words, he were laying hands on her body', as storyteller, he is also 'a subject chieftain' – power goes both ways (158). While he finds most inspiration in stories (cf. especially his story of 'two men dying when only one needed to die', 163), the narrator makes clear early on that he runs the risk of being 'under the spell of his own stories' (76) and, in fact, his biggest asset is also his downfall: 'Jehar began to pay the price for having turned his life into a story' (276). A character who is portrayed as significantly more worldly, cunning and matter-of-fact but for whom storytelling is also the means to earn his living and more is Lord Rampling – whom the text repeatedly suggests as foil for Jehar. Not only does Rampling value the gift for storytelling in others (Richard, a dragoman, tells him a story 'thereby earning goodwill and extra payment' (151)), he uses stories for his personal gain by manipulating others on the basis of their own self-narratives. For example, in his conversation with the ambassador whom he needs to dupe Somerville, Rampling quickly understand that 'his guest's resentment stemmed less from a concern for Somerville than from a sense of wounded dignity' (95), upon which he changes his rhetoric from morals to politics and steers the topic to 'the vital interests of the British Empire' (96). But Rampling, too, is not immune to narratives, for nationalism and colonial relations, while creating powerful narratives, also undermine the stories which the characters (and archaeology) tell. Despite his earlier reminder that 'wrapping ourselves up in the Union Jack will not protect us' (110), he is tricked by Elliott precisely when he partakes in the national narrative of British superiority over Americans. All of a sudden, he is prepared to view the geologist's trick as 'a moral issue', reasoning that it would have been comprehensible for the American to assume a false identity in order 'to explore for oil on behalf of the British government' but that it is altogether a different thing now that 'the man had doubled, possible trebled his reward', 'strik[ing]' a blow at the foundations of commercial practice on which European civilisation was based' (179).

While Somerville wants to 'rewrite the final chapter of Assyrian history' (267), after his death, he becomes the object of other characters' stories in the final chapter of the novel, the afterword. In a final self-referential turn, the archaeologist's storytelling is continued beyond his control by non-archaeologists and archaeologists alike: there is a public debate about the authenticity of photographs made of the archaeological findings in 'the press', the events are adapted in the form of a 'novel' and even among scientists 'the story survived the scepticism' (282). The archaeologist's story is used by other characters to suit their own narratives: Somerville, 'achieved a sort of posthumous heroism in Edith's eyes' (282), as she 'grew to believe that she had always supported him' (283). Even Palmer and Patricia speculate about what might have happened (281). Just as Tell Erdek has a different meaning to different characters at the beginning, Somerville's death is interpreted in accordance with other characters' needs. At the height of his interpretation of Assyrian power, Somerville observes that at 'the apex of power' the Assyrian king Shalmanezer would desecrate the corpses of those he had killed and thus 'punish his enemies beyond the grave' (167). In a way, the afterword has a similar effect. With his ending echoing Schliemann's use of dynamite at Troy, Somerville is punished for a variety of individual, scientific and expedition-related mistakes: for not sharing his insights with his assistant and keeping them 'in secrecy' (60); for instigating public understanding of archaeology through passion rather than reason and falsely believing that other characters 'shared his passion for the history of the Assyrian Empire' (113); for coveting Mesopotamian treasures but feeling 'no slightest kinship with the people of the place or with the land that stretched around him' (145); for losing 'trust [in] the evidence of his senses' (169) and no longer opting for knowing facts but choosing 'to believe' (274). In *Land of Marvels*, the idea of 'archaeological imagination' is also expressed in the particular narrative trajectory reminiscent of other examples of archaeofiction (e.g. Michael Ondaatje's *Anil's Ghost*): an initial investment in an archaeologist character, followed by his death which does not mark the ending of the story – this time, with an emphasis on the power of retelling his story as focalized by and tied to other characters' narratives in the afterword.

Interpreting archaeologists

Another example of a novel with such an archaeofictional narrative arc contributing to its framing of 'archaeological imagination' is Sarah Moss's *Cold Earth* (2009) which follows an archaeologist team on expedition to Western Greenland, where they excavate the remains of a Norse farm and mass grave hoping to find out what led to the ending of the medieval settlement. The Greenlandic summer proves a productive season for the team but is overshadowed by news from the outside, where an epidemic threatens the world population, as well as by inner tensions around major mistakes committed in preparation for the expedition. When the weather turns and they fail to make contact with the outer world, the team face their own imminent ending. Like *Land of Marvels*, *Cold Earth* represents the practice of archaeological digging as it brings into question the impulse – both archaeological and literary – to draw analogies between the expedition team and their research objects, here the Norse settlers. The archaeologists' professional concerns are in many ways similar to those of Somerville: The expedition's leader and postdoc, Yianni Papadatos, has secured £100,000 in the form of an ESRC grant, 'UK taxpayers' money for Greenlandic archaeology' (201), in order to bring out a team of five doctoral students, but he is constantly under time and funding pressure. The discipline is shown to be highly competitive as the archaeologists do not share their data, and Yianni is reproached by other archaeologist members of his team for his ambitions for 'professional advancement' (258). The novel includes other aspects characteristic of expedition narratives, referencing the history of heroic explorers (Franklin, Shackleton) and making recurring analogies of their journeys' 'tragic flaws' (such as burdening the team with the wrong people for the wrong reasons) with the contemporary dig: Yianni smuggles in one literature PhD student and is accused of 'using research funding to bring a friend along for the ride' (137). Like *Land of Marvels*, the novel ends with the leading archaeologist's death – this time from cold and hunger – a death which is also presented as the result of his mistakes and one which is narrativized by another character.

At first glance, the novel appears to bypass the 'burden' of disciplinary history, as its interest in Norse settlers has a different quality than the colonial machinery which accompanies early-twentieth-century expeditions in Mesopotamia in Unsworth's novel. Nevertheless, *Cold Earth* raises questions about what Mary Louise Pratt has termed '"contact zones," social spaces where disparate cultures meet, clash, and grapple with each other, often in highly asymmetrical relations of domination and subordination' ([1992] 2003: 5), both in terms of the medieval Norse settlement and the expedition team themselves. Discussing their theories of what may have happened to the settlers and why the colony ended, the archaeologists' interpretations vary from climate change-induced food shortage to more violent ends by raiders, even conflicts between Greenlanders and Inuit, which one archaeologist refers to as 'not the PC version' (44). The expedition members have their own brief moment of contact with local shepherds towards the end of the summer which they tragically fail to employ usefully: Instead of learning from local knowledge of seasonal farming and hunting, or even learning from their conclusions about their research objects, the team pay little attention to matters outside their expeditionary goals (and their various attempts at self-excavations) and subsequently face isolation and death by hypothermia and starvation, their fate reminiscent of earlier expeditions referenced in the text, including Franklin's search of the Northwest Passage (255). The team itself is an exercise in international, mostly transatlantic contact. While the non-archaeologist literary scholar Nina harbours anti-American sentiments based on a string of stereotypical expectations (most expressed against the lipstick-wearing pristine-looking Ruth and the good-natured Bible-belt stemming Jim), her own characterization – both self-defined and by others – is that of 'a mad Englishwoman' (11), 'normal, at least in an eccentric British way' (187). The lack of explicit reference to the British colonial context satirically reflects her own (and Britain's) wilful ignorance of the past, Nina's criticism instead aimed at Ruth when she makes a snide remark on US imperialist politics, 'No one ever welcomes an American presence' (192). The irony of the lack of acknowledgement of the British colonial past and archaeology's role within it is perhaps most explicit, however, in relation to Yianni's Greek origin. While the text focuses on his problematic display of incompetence and rising propensity to violence, it also implies a larger context is playing out. For it is a Greek archaeologist leading a British-sponsored expedition which disturbs the archaeological site, in a reversal of the historical British archaeological presence which contributed to a desecration of Greek cultural heritage, most notably the Parthenon. Yianni's increasing loss of self-control is represented as part of patriarchal hegemony, but it can also be read as a subtle revenge against Nina as the smug, self-entitled Oxford-educated Englishwoman who encapsulates a British, colonialist sense of entitlement.

Moss demonstrates through the novel's epistolary form how archaeological stories can vary according to whose imagination is being prioritized. *Cold Earth* introduces a diversification of archaeological perspectives and that of their public perception: each expedition's member is given one chapter in which they address someone from outside the expedition and characterize themselves through their own perspectives on their research objects and research team. The archaeologists' narratives are framed by a much longer introductory and, more significantly for this paper, ending chapter penned by the non-archaeologist expedition member Nina. The five archaeologists share some characteristics in contrast to the literary scholar, not least braving the simple life on a dig ('we were serious archaeologists, sacrificing ordinary comforts for our work' (207)). But they are also very particular 'complex scientist characters'. This is evident not only in their diverse research interests but also in their exchange of hypotheses in regard to the lot of the Norse settlers, conditioned both by their specific research foci (as represented by the topics of their doctoral theses) and by their characters as they emerge based on their letters, which often eerily mirror their scientific interpretations. The Scottish archaeologist Catriona, 'who paints and doesn't wash' (107) and is working on a thesis on '[e]arly medieval North Atlantic migration patterns' (17), is described as paranoid and easily scared by parallels between historical and contemporary epidemic outbreaks (45). She communicates her part of the narrative to a female flatmate who also turns out to be her love interest (263). Ben, 'from the North of England via Madison' (107), writes to his family at home but refuses to say final goodbyes. Working on '[c]ultivation and foraging in liminal settlement areas in Norway' (18), his character exhibits the most intense survival urge, prepared even to partake in cannibalism: 'I wouldn't kill but I'd eat' (269). The two Americans – Jim and Ruth – in some ways act as default counterparts to the British Catriona and Ben. Religious, family-oriented Midwesterner Jim is the physically and spiritually larger male whose generous notion of the Norse settlers' ending as having simply 'sailed away' (221) is in line with his trusting nature. The prematurely widowed Ruth, meticulous about her looks but with little patience with her team members, claims that the Norse, not prepared to learn from the Greenlandic Inuit 'died of conservatism' (109). Despite good evidence for new theories the site offers – 'the archaeology . . . is suggesting more interesting possibilities', including 'the pirate-raid theory' and 'potential to complicate recent thinking on Norse-Inuit relations' (110) – in the end, Ruth is not prepared to change her interpretation (217).

The critique of using archaeology for self-understanding as shown in my reading of *Land of Marvels* is somewhat more nuanced in *Cold Earth*, but the use of storytelling is similarly problematized. With its narrative structure and plural perspective, the text does not have to put the heft of archaeological representation on one character only but can use them individually to make different comments on the discipline and its practitioners. It falls to the forensic anthropologist Ruth to draw the most explicit identification of the research objects with her own situation. Here, the comparison of the corpse she excavates with her late boyfriend who died in a car accident (123) has a reparative function: she comes to understand that while her late boyfriend was her 'future' (133), she was only 'his present' (181). But it is with the expedition's leader that the novel comments on scientific hubris, ethics and storytelling. Like Somerville and his aim to throw new light on the history of the Assyrian Empire in *Land of Marvels*, Yianni hopes that the results of the expedition will allow him to advance Greenlandic history: 'I told you in the briefing papers that this is the site ... identified with the farm owned by Bjorn Bardarson in Bjornsaga. Late thirteenth century ... so if this was abandoned earlier [than the late fourteenth] we probably can tie it to the saga' (24–5). He, too, is under time pressure, 'We've got less than six weeks here' (27), and is in fear of his funding running out before he can make a mark on his discipline: 'There's no guarantee of another season's funding and anyway, it'd delay publications' (99). He, too, is ambitious, 'Yianni looked at the midden as if it held the keys to the kingdom or at least tenure' (70), and paranoid (especially about the equipment (cf. 68)). Even when faced with certain death after they fail to establish contact with the outer world and risk starvation, he vows not to participate in 'desecrating the site' (258). He does not want to be 'remembered as the guy who trashed his own site' (261) but, like Somerville, contributes to his worst nightmare. In the end, Yianni is not only held responsible for endangering the expedition (by himself as much as by other team members) but also made to pay the price: refusing to take shelter among the ruins, he dies of hypothermia. Ironically, while the others are rescued and do not 'end up leaving themselves' (15), Yianni's remains are both verbally reinterpreted and physically scattered over the land by the non-archaeologist character Nina.

In addition to the spectrum of archaeologist perspectives on their research objects as well as on their research team, the novel uses the voice of an outsider to directly comment on the nature of archaeological work as well as, indirectly, on the nature of this public commentary. Nina's perspective fulfils several functions. As a layperson to whom the archaeologists are forced to speak in non-jargon register, she becomes a mediator for the lay reader, though her filtering is revealed as decisively unreliable. As a humanities scholar she makes comparisons between archaeology and literature. When Jim explains that he chose archaeology over history because it's not 'just stories' and therefore 'more honest', she retorts – reminiscent of Michael Shanks – that '[a]rchaeology is reading, just earth rather than text' (64). Yet, she criticizes the archaeologists' attempts at communicating their science through such metaphors. When Jim tries to use other practices of reconstruction in comparison with his discipline, 'think of archaeology as being like mining, Nina. Or surgery', Nina is quick in a judgement which recalls the criticism of the field's colonial history also found in *Land of Marvels*: 'Sounds more like burglary to me' (212). As a literary historian, then, Nina stands for and highlights the novel's own emphasis on storytelling, not least in reference to her thesis on the 'influence of Norse Sagas on Victorian poetry' (17). Crucially, her research proves 'the imaginary nature of Iceland in Victorian poetry' (36). Just like Nina's Victorians, the archaeologists' differing interpretations of the archaeological findings suggest that there is some imagination involved in the picture of the Norse formed in their scientific hypotheses. In fact, there is an explicit awareness of the later exchange of theories as less scientific but fulfilling different functions: When Jim tells his version, Ben compliments him and hints at a universal and communal role of storytelling: 'Nice story, Jim … I guess this was what people did before TV' (221).

The non-archaeologist character's perspective and her reinterpretation of Yianni's perspective – 'some kind of reconstructive archaeology' (278) – point to the power of such reconstructions, problematizing the subject of the archaeological imagination. Nina's framing narrative of the archaeological perspectives is analogous to those perspectives' framing of Greenlandic history. Echoing their character-driven interpretations, the text highlights her position as commentator on archaeology as problematic. She is repeatedly referenced as representing the brooding humanist in allusion to C. P. Snow's two-culture divide, exhibiting 'arts and humanities' envy of social science research funding' (68), or 'still counting on her fingers' despite '[a]n Oxford PhD' (185). She is blasé about the discipline: 'I began to suspect that the practice of archaeology is less interesting than I'd hoped' (33) if not downright ignorant, particularly when viewed by Ruth: 'Nina, it's an archaeological dig. We came here to disturb them' (138). Using a concept of intellectual layers, she self-characterizes as 'too shallow for archaeology' (79) – resembling Somerville's Edith in Unsworth's novel. Despite being an expert on textual analysis and seemingly able to pair every expedition member with an apt Victorian novel (237–8), she proves to be a poor reader herself, (mis)reading both her own and others' characters, as the prismatic perspectives by other characters reveal. In addition to scattering

Yianni's remains over the land of the site, Nina is also responsible for making him the object of her storytelling. This is foreshadowed early on in the text when she claims that '[w]e want everyone to leave a story' (19), in response to the archaeologist's premonition that 'You can't just disappear the dead. That's the point about archaeology. People can't help leaving themselves' (15). While there is something conciliatory in Nina's last effort to address and remember Yianni, there is also reason to read this as part of a power struggle. The empowerment of speaking to and against someone who cannot respond is explicitly drawn out in another instance of communication. In her letter addressing a grief counsellor, Ruth feels empowered by the fact that the other cannot respond: 'You tried to make me tell another story but I'm talking now and you can't answer back' (106). Yianni, like Somerville in *Land of Marvels*, is not given the last word but becomes the object of Nina's interpretation trying to make 'sense of your life, … your work, or maybe your death' (277) as she throws his 'ashes onto the wind and watch[es] them drift and settle like dark snow on the pale flowers of West Greenland' (278).

Whose imagination, whose archaeology?

Both *Cold Earth* and *Land of Marvels*, while differing in spatial and temporal context, reflect upon the power of the archaeological imagination and the relationship between archaeology and its public. *Land of Marvels* is a historical novel which problematizes archaeological collaboration in imperial struggles while *Cold Earth* is less overtly interested in colonial history but hints at competing Anglo-American forces and the impact of nineteenth-century exploration narratives on contemporary researchers' self-understanding. The death of the archaeologist protagonist, whom each text builds up as a 'complex scientist character', marks an important recurring motif. This death does not coincide with the novel's ending but in each case is followed by a narrative aftermath in which the archaeologist's life and death is reinterpreted by other characters, a narrative structure which allows each text to revise both the historical colonial narratives with which they engage as well as the subjectivity of archaeological imagination. In the afterword to Unsworth's *Land of Marvels*, the extradiegetic, heterodiegetic narrator reports on the surviving characters' interpretations of the archaeologist's death, highlighting the appropriation of Somerville and his storytelling beyond his control. In *Cold Earth*, the non-archaeologist team member Nina is given more narrative space for a second and last chapter, in a novel in which all other characters are granted only one. Not only does she use this space to verbally contradict the archaeologist's prioritizing of more ancient history by claiming that '[w]e are history too' (278) but she also – by scattering his ashes – adds another archaeological layer over a site which he had refused to contaminate in his lifetime. In both novels, the privilege of interpretation is marked as a display of power and a form of discursive violence. Somerville is remembered differently by Palmer, the archaeologist, and by Edith, his wife. Nina's perspective is not only revealed as decidedly non-archaeological but also subjective (even unreliable as her interpretations of the events and of other expedition members are proven wrong in their respective sections of the novel). Hence, the archaeological imagination and interpretation also depends on a specific subject-position. Both novels link this to an archaeological obsession with public perception. Somerville and Yianni have a problematic, obsessive relationship with their publics. The former is preoccupied with his positioning in a long line of heroic archaeologists and his public image, while Yianni tries to add a public perspective to the team with Nina but loses patience when she does not participate actively or fails to understand the importance of the archaeological site. Through these characters, the novels question an all-pervasive, transhistorical or universal understanding of the archaeological imagination and instead emphasize its subjectivity and specificity. They are aware of but also problematize the metaphorical use of archaeology for modern self-understanding.

Literary representations of archaeology have been increasingly noted by archaeologists as a possible source for reflecting upon how the public may perceive them (Conkey 2002; Russell 2002; Moshenksa 2017). In this chapter, I have proposed that archaeofiction may also contribute to how archaeologists perceive their discipline. Indeed, the beginning of archaeologists' interest in fictional representations of archaeology coincides with major shifts in the history of the discipline from professionalization through developing rigorous methods and scientific instruments (or New Archaeology in the 1960s), to the emphasis on subjectivity, influenced by postmodernism and sociocultural anthropology, or post-processual archaeology from the late 1970s and early 1980s (cf. Thomas 1976; Evans 1983). At times, the question of just how much archaeologists should pay attention to fictional archaeologists has become the cause of academic dispute. In a 2008 special issue of the journal *Antiquity*, Cornelius Holtorf and Kristian Kristiansen heatedly debate the question 'Should archaeology be in the service of "popular culture"?' Archaeofiction will not solve such discussions over the importance of contemporary popular culture for archaeology but it may add the question 'whose archaeology?'. It is not the place of fiction to side with either celebrating the archaeological imagination as part and parcel of modernity and independent from the discipline of archaeology (cf. Shanks 2012) or with attempts at 'reclaiming archaeology' from its various metaphorical use by modern thinkers from Freud to Foucault (cf. González-Ruibal 2013). However, fiction can provide a space to imagine various constellations of archaeological imagination, with changing subject positions and changing power relations. Having its own narrative turn in the 1990s, archaeology has reached the phase of critically embracing the connection between 'epistemology and literary production' (Lucas 2018; cf. also Van Dyke and Bernbeck 2015). While this has been largely done by focusing on archaeological writing as a crucial element of assembling knowledge, a closer look at contemporary archaeofiction adds critical perspectives on imagining archaeology as scientific discipline, its use of storytelling as well as both individual and modern self-understanding.

Notes

1 The term has been previously used by Karen Sanders in an analysis of Anne Michaels's 1966 novel *Fugitive Pieces* to describe the activity of a protagonist metaphorically digging into their past (2009: 75).
2 The term 'archaeofiction' has been used to conceptualize literary writings about archaeology whose function is seen as 'expanding the archaeological imagination' (cf. Conkey 2002: 167). Archaeologists have also used it to describe: (1) myths and legends within the discipline: either long-held presumptions discredited as unscientific at some point or notions previously deemed in contempt but redeemed due to new findings (much of contemporary astroarchaeology); (2) an

educational method, that is, playful excavation of objects consciously placed or hidden for didactic purposes (cf. Masson and Guillot [1994] 2002).

3 The fictional character may well have been inspired by John Somerville Birch (1861–1913), a highly regarded diplomat in Egypt who was in charge of irrigation works.

References

Christie, A. ([1936] 2001), *Murder in Mesopotamia*, London: Harper Collins.
Conkey, M.W. (2002), 'Book Review: Expanding the Archaeological Imagination', *American Antiquity*, 67 (1): 166–8.
Dobson, E., and G. Banks. (2019), 'Introduction', in *Excavating Modernity: Physical, Temporal and Psychological Strata in Literature*, 1–8, New York: Routledge.
Drabble, M. ([1975] 1977), *The Realms of Gold*, Harmondsworth: Penguin.
Evans, C. (1983), 'Wildmen, Pulp and Fire: Archaeology as Popular Fiction', *Archaeological Review from Cambridge*, 2 (1): 68–70.
Gardiner, M. (ed.) (1971), *The Wolf-Man by the Wolf Man: The Double Story of Freud's Most Famous Case*, New York: Basic Books.
González-Ruibal, A. (ed.) (2013), *Reclaiming Archaeology: Beyond the Tropes of Modernity*, London: Routledge.
Holtorf, C. (2008), 'Academic Critique and the Need for an Open Mind (A Response to Kristiansen)', *Antiquity*, 82: 490–92.
Janowitz, A. (1984), 'Shelley's Monument to Ozymandias', *Philological Quarterly*, 63 (4): 477–90.
Kirchhofer, A., and N. Roxburgh. (2016), 'The Scientist as "Problematic Individual" in Contemporary Anglophone Fiction', *Zeitschrift für Anglistik und Amerikanistik*, 64 (2): 149–68.
Kristiansen, K. (2008), 'Should Archaeology Be in the Service of "Popular Culture"? A Theoretical and Political Critique of Cornelius Holtorf's Vision of Archaeology', *Antiquity*, 82: 488–90.
Lucas, G. (2018), *Writing the Past: Knowledge and Literary Production in Archaeology*, London: Routledge.
Mackenthun, G. (2014), 'Digging Far and Deep: Archaeological Sites, Dislocations, and Heterotopoi in Postcolonial Writing', in J. Kuortti (ed.), *Transculturation and Aesthetics: Ambivalence, Power, and Literature*, 3–13, Amsterdam: Brill/Rodopi.
Masson, P., and H. Guillot ([1994] 2002), 'Archaeo-Fiction with Upper Primary-School Children 1988–1989', in B. L. Molyneaux and P. G. Stone (eds), *The*

Presented Past: Heritage, Museums and Education, trans. P. Planel, 375–82, London: Routledge.

Moshenska, G. (2017), 'Archaeologists in Popular Culture', in G. Moshenska (ed.), *Key Concepts in Public Archaeology*, 151–65. London: UCL.

Moss, S. (2009), *Cold Earth*, London: Granta.

Ondaatje, M. ([2000] 2011), *Anil's Ghost*, London: Vintage.

Pratt, M.L. (1992/2003), *Imperial Eyes: Travel Writing and Transculturation*, London: Routledge.

Reid, J. (2017), 'Archaeology and Anthropology', in J. Holmes and S. Ruston (eds), *The Routledge Research Companion to Nineteenth-Century British Literature and Science*, 357–71, London: Routledge.

Russell, M. (2002), 'No More Heroes Any More: The Dangerous World of the Pop Culture Archaeologist', in M. Russell (ed.), *Digging Holes in Popular Culture: Archaeology and Science Fiction*, 38–54, Oxford: Oxbow Books.

Sanders, K. (2009), *Bodies in the Bog and the Archaeological Imagination*, Chicago: University of Chicago Press.

Schnapp, J. T., M. Shanks and M. Tiews (2004), 'Archaeology, Modernism, Modernity: Editors' Introduction to "Archaeologies of the Modern" a Special Issue of Modernism/Modernity', *MODERNISM/modernity*, 11 (1): 1–16.

Shanks, M. (2011), 'The Archaeological Imagination', *Michael Shanks – Archaeologist*, 17 December. Available online http://www.mshanks.com/archaeology/the-archaeological-imagination/ (accessed 8 October 2019).

Shanks, M. (2012), *The Archaeological Imagination*, Walnut Creek, CA: Left Coast Press.

Thomas, C. (1976), 'The Archaeology of Fiction', in J. V. S. Megaw (ed.), *To Illustrate the Monuments: Essays on Archaeology*, 310–19, London: Thames & Hudson.

Unsworth, B. (2009), *Land of Marvels*, London: Windmill.

Van Dyke, R. M., and R. Bernbeck (eds) (2015), *Subjects and Narratives in Archaeology*, Boulder: University Press of Colorado.

Wallace, J. (2004), *Digging the Dirt: The Archaeological Imagination*, London: Duckworth.

Warwick, A., and M. Willis (2012), 'Introduction: The Archaeological Imagination', *Journal of Literature and Science*, 5 (1): 1–5.

Index

aDNA 11, 23–5, 27–8, 30, 34, 36, 38, 41
Africa 2, 37, 48, 128–31, 135, 209
African 3, 37, 71–2, 74, 130, 165–6
agriculture 128, 153–4, 156, 189–90, 194
Albert Memorial 126–9, 133, 135, 140
ancestral 12, 50, 53, 79
ancestry 3, 37
ancient Egypt 119–22, 124–5, 127, 132, 139
ancient Egyptian
   antagonists 140
   architecture 127
   art 130
   artefacts 14, 123, 125, 127
   civilization 129
   dead 139
   deities 130
   encounters 127
   engineering 135
   hieroglyphs 119–20
   language 120
   magic 124, 130
   motifs 119
   myth 128
   mythology 128
   power 130
   presence 120, 122, 140
   Ptahmes 133
   queen 123, 130
   royalty 126, 133
   servant 130
   space 119
   style 127
   themes 139
   traces 139
   writing 120
ancient world 137, 177
Anil's Ghost 204, 206, 213
anthropology 72, 221
antiquarian 127, 148, 160, 167
antiquity 119–20, 130, 135, 150, 221
archaeofiction 203, 213, 220–1

archaeogenetics 11, 23–4, 26–7, 30, 34, 40
archaeological
   accounts 15, 178–81, 191
   artefacts 96, 103
   concerns 4, 80, 121
   context 98, 207
   data 49, 73–4
   fiction 6, 103
   findings 3, 209, 212, 218
   imagination 10–11, 13, 16, 105, 109–12, 203–5, 207, 213, 218–21
   interpretation 7, 191, 196
   investigation 8, 11, 23, 31, 188
   knowledge 2, 12, 16, 178, 183, 210
   methods 5, 8, 74
   narratives 4, 12, 178, 182, 184, 193, 195–6
   objects 8, 10, 104, 188
   perspectives 74, 215, 218
   practice 25, 146, 169, 182, 194
   record 46, 53, 95, 98
   report 193
   research 5, 15, 100, 178, 180, 183, 185, 190, 196
   science 9, 76, 80, 85
   site 178, 189, 215, 220
   sites 14, 24, 145, 183, 206
   stories 13, 97, 215
   writing 15, 178–9, 183, 221
architecture 13, 120–1, 127, 139
artefact 104, 128, 133, 169
artefactual fictions 96–7, 103–4, 109
artist 28, 38, 87–8, 125, 133, 168
Assyrian 207–13, 217
autobiographical 71, 101, 124

Barbados 75, 85
Beard, Mary 2–3
Beatty, Paul 11, 36–8, 42
Before Adam 12, 45, 50–4, 59–63
bioarchaeology 6, 7, 10–11, 27, 72, 88

biological 8, 30, 32, 41, 77
biology 31, 33
black
  people 1–2, 153
  writers 77, 79
Boothby, Guy 14, 120–2, 132–3, 136–40
Boutin, Alexis 3, 7
Bristol 2, 13, 74–6, 88
British Empire 14, 120, 122, 138, 212
British Museum 124–5, 128, 132, 165
burial
  grounds 15, 75, 88
  mounds 98, 145, 152

Cardiff 13, 106, 108
care 61, 71, 87–8, 89, 168, 205
ceremony 26, 40–1
Christian 164–5, 177, 189
chronology 28–9, 150, 209
civilization 129–30, 133, 152–4, 156, 160–1, 167
Cleopatra's Needle 119, 133–4, 136–7, 139–40
climate change 95, 214
cognitive revolution 47–8
Cold Earth 16, 205–6, 213–16, 219–20
colonial
  assumptions 10
  context 215
  discourse 208
  enterprise 208
  history 14, 205, 218–19
  imperialism 207
  implications 205
  Italians 180
  knowledge 206
  machinery 214
  narratives 219
  New York 72
  past 16, 215
  plundering 122
  power 211
  present 10
  relations 212
  statues 88
  strategy 15
  struggles 209
  violence 52
colonization 9, 122, 132, 139

compassion 61–2
conflicts 154–5, 207, 214
contemporary
  fiction 16, 38, 73, 97, 204
  writers 11, 24
creative
  writers 8, 13, 72, 74, 76, 195
  writing 12, 73, 77–8, 85, 89, 100
cross-disciplinary 2, 77, 90

decolonize 15, 165
Detroit Post 14–15, 146, 149, 151, 156, 158, 164
digital 13, 105–6, 108, 110–12
digital technology 13, 105, 110–12
disease 138, 155
DNA investigation 25, 29, 35
Dorchester 145–6, 148, 160, 167
Dorset 14–15, 145, 148–50, 160, 167–8, 195
Duffy, Carol Ann 11, 36, 40–1

earthworks 14–15, 98, 145–52, 156–62, 168–9
economic 32, 38, 104, 146, 153–7, 165–6, 183, 206–7
Egyptologist 120, 123, 125, 128
Egyptology 122, 125, 128
eighteenth century 5, 9, 151
emigration 155
emotion 79, 83, 88, 101
empathy 4, 12, 61–3, 178, 182, 185–8, 194–6
England 15, 97, 120, 126–7, 145, 148, 159, 168, 179, 216
enslaved
  Africans 72, 74, 91
  people 71, 73–4, 77–8, 83, 88–9, 181
environment 4, 52, 73, 74, 76, 101, 105, 110
Epipalaeolithic 188–9
ethics 8, 26, 79, 84, 89–90, 166, 217
ethnology 150, 156–7
Eurasia 47, 49, 61
Euro-American 154, 155, 168
Eurocentric 153, 163, 165–6
European 31, 53, 153, 155, 164–5, 212
Evaristo, Bernardine 1, 4
expedition 16, 206–9, 213–15, 217–18, 220
experimental 13, 38, 76, 102–3, 177

facts 4, 45, 53, 63, 86, 90, 96, 150, 178, 191, 194, 213
fantasy 14, 121–2, 140
fictional
    archaeologists 209, 221
    literature 15, 178
    narrative 11, 177, 180–1, 183–4, 196
    scenes 177, 183
    texts 139, 195
fictive
    narrative 180
    techniques 15, 177–8, 181, 183–6, 195–6
Foucault, Michel 7, 72, 121–2, 125, 134
fragments 7, 14, 30, 72, 87–8, 106, 140, 203, 205, 211
Freud, Sigmund 7, 50–1, 72, 204, 221
frontier 140, 154
future 33, 41, 88, 95, 154, 168, 178, 180–1, 185, 217

Gamble, Clive 49, 63
gender 36, 41, 190, 209
genealogical 40, 189
genetic
    analysis 24, 30
    science 23–4, 31, 42
geneticists 24, 31
genetics 11, 21, 27, 31, 34, 36, 38, 72
genocide 155, 157, 166
geographers 121
geography 14, 25, 101, 120–2, 125–7
geopolitical 9, 206
global 10, 85, 88, 105, 108, 110, 125, 163, 194, 207
gothic 98, 121, 132, 140, 204, 206
government 145, 152–4, 156–7, 165, 167, 212
Gran Canaria 75
Great Mound 145, 150–1, 157–9, 168, 170

Hardy, Thomas 14–15, 145–52, 156–60, 163–5, 167–9
heritage 26, 98, 105, 168, 215
heterotopia 121, 132, 134, 139, 140
hieroglyphs 119–20, 127
hillfort 14, 145, 195
historians 2–3, 31, 49, 63, 121–2, 140, 168, 179, 185

historical
    archaeology 6, 10
    causation 15, 178, 185, 194
    fiction 180, 182, 196
    investigation 24, 31
    legacies 103, 109
    narrative 178, 194
    novel 188, 203–4, 219
hominins 5, 12, 45–6, 48–50, 59–63
Homo sapiens 11, 24, 29–30, 32, 46–9
Hubbard, Bela 151–2, 157, 168
human
    agency 15, 178, 194
    body 32, 42, 77, 85
    evolution 12, 29, 31, 45–6, 48, 53, 63
    history 3, 11, 16, 24–5, 29
    origins 59, 63
    past 27–8, 45
    remains 4, 7–8, 11, 26, 77, 84–5, 166
    species 11, 23, 25, 29–30, 49

iconography 88, 120–1, 130, 135
identity 15, 26, 32, 36–8, 41, 156, 160, 167–8, 180, 189, 206, 210–12
imagined 34, 39, 40, 41, 79, 151, 180
immigrant 35
imperial
    anxieties 14, 122, 140
    centre 122
    gaze 208
    gothic 204
    hold 139
    idea 163
    impulses 10
    loot 139
    mechanisms 14
    mission 127, 138, 139
    mythology 206
    power 206
    relationship 137
    struggles 219
    Syria 209
imperialism 9, 145, 158, 169, 207–8
Indian 52, 145, 150, 154–7, 168, 170
indigenous
    artefacts 156
    communities 166
    culture 152, 157, 161
    cultural items 166

228 Index

earthworks 157-8, 169
genocide 166
lands 153-4
leaders 166
mounds 145, 168
people 152-7, 159, 166-7
population 15, 145, 150, 155
studies 166
tribes 145, 152, 154, 157
youths 154
inscription 120, 161, 193
Iron Age 14, 145, 195
Israel 157, 188, 194

Jackson, Valda 85, 87-8
Jewish 177, 188-9
journeys 13, 37, 97, 99, 103, 120, 122, 138, 214

Kendi, Ibram 152-4, 157
Kisuule, Vanessa 80

Land of Marvels 16, 205-6, 208, 213-14, 216-19
Latour, Bruno 33-6, 39
legacy 12, 24, 35, 97, 208
legislation 154-5, 167
Levy, Andrea 71
literary
  archaeology 72-4
  critics 49-50
  engagements 9, 74
  production 9, 221
  representations 12, 14, 53, 98, 204, 220
  scholar 1, 2, 12, 73, 89, 215
  scholarship 4, 7-8, 10
  studies 2, 4-5, 7-10, 23, 73, 76, 89, 122, 203
London, Jack 12, 45, 50-3, 59-63
London 1, 3, 14, 100-3, 109, 119-22, 124-8, 131-3, 135-40, 166, 208

Macfarlane, Robert 101, 109, 112
magic 124, 130, 137
magical 14, 124, 128
Maiden Castle 14, 145, 147-51, 157, 159-60, 164, 168, 195
map 31, 77, 101, 102, 106, 108, 187
material

culture 5, 7, 16, 73, 181, 183, 190
evidence 180, 193
remains 6, 28, 178, 182
traces 9, 182
materialism 23, 34, 36
materialist approach 32
materiality 9, 28, 31, 34-5, 40, 73
memory 7, 27, 50, 73, 76, 84, 100, 104, 152, 203
Mesolithic 53, 184
Mesopotamia 205-7, 214
Michener, James 15, 178, 182, 188-96
Michigan 145, 151, 159
migration 25, 216
Millgate, Michael 148-9
modern human 12, 46, 48-50, 53, 60
modernity 35, 46, 48, 54, 63, 135-7, 203, 221
monuments 119-20, 127, 133, 137, 139, 140
Morrison, Toni 71-2, 79
Moss, Sarah 16, 205, 213, 215
mound 145, 150-1, 157-9, 168-9, 188, 206-7, 209
multicultural 102
mummy 123, 125
Museum of London 1, 3
mythology 127-8, 140, 206

narrative archaeology 11, 15, 175
narrative
  form 12, 15, 178, 181
  structure 39, 99, 216, 219
nationalism 3, 4, 155, 163, 194, 212
Native American 15, 26-7, 52, 166
neanderthals 12, 46-50, 61
Neolithic 53, 145, 190
New Archaeology 5, 220
New York 27, 72, 100, 109, 153
Newton Plantation 75
nineteenth century 5, 9, 14, 52, 61, 103-4, 120-1, 125, 134-5, 137, 140, 145, 153, 162, 204, 219
non-fiction 97, 99, 101
North America 26, 51, 150, 157, 162, 164, 191
NW 102, 103

Ondaatje, Michael 204, 206, 213
osteological 8, 73

palaeoanthropological 46, 49, 53
palaeoanthropologists 45, 59
palaeofiction 12, 45, 49–51, 61–3
Palaeolithic 47, 53
performative 13, 95–7, 100, 104–5, 111
Petrie, William Matthew Flinders 125, 210
Pharos the Egyptian 14, 120, 132, 135, 138, 140
philosophy 32–3, 103, 188
plantation 71, 75
plot 53, 128, 137–8, 146–7, 158, 163–4, 189, 194
plundered 139, 150
poem 39–41, 80, 82–8, 180
poet 40, 80–4, 86–8, 163
poetry 10, 38, 81, 84, 98, 163, 218
policy 152–4, 157, 185
politics 180, 188, 212, 215
popular fiction 14, 203
postcolonialism 34
post-processual archaeology 5–6, 221
post-truth 95–6, 111–12
prehistory 6, 10–1, 23–4, 27–31, 53, 63, 189
prejudice 186–7
primates 60–2
primitive 50, 53, 60, 161–2
processual archaeology 5
psychogeographers 13, 109, 140
psychogeographical
   archaeology 14, 119–20
   literature 100, 104
   walk 13, 106
psychogeography 13, 95–7, 100–5, 109–11
psychology 30, 101

race 32, 36–8, 41, 50–2, 61, 71, 150
racism 2, 38, 51–2, 146
racist 41, 152–4, 156–7, 159
reconstruction 6, 7, 193, 195, 218
regulations 156, 167
relic 52, 150
Renaissance 9, 119, 180
Renfrew, Colin 28–30
reparations 166, 169
revolution 25, 47–8, 105, 152, 190
Roman
   archaeology 6
   army 145
   attack 195
   city 167
   Britain 2–3, 99
   Britons 2
   Egypt 183
   empire 138, 160
   emperors 180
   fort 160, 194
   galleries 1
   London 1
   road 98, 102
   skeletons 1
   soldier 2
   station 167
   statuette 161
   villas 194
   world 183
Romano-British 148, 160, 167
ruins 13, 167, 204, 217

savage 155–7, 160–1, 208
science fiction 45, 49, 61
scientific
   accounts 53
   analyses 10
   approaches 8,
   archaeology 7, 27, 73, 87
   career 210
   community 28
   considerations 61
   credentials 51, 63
   data 45, 95–6
   developments 8
   discipline 89, 210, 221
   discourse 34, 96
   evidence 1
   enquiry 63, 84
   fact 3, 45
   hubris 217
   hypotheses 218
   information 78
   inquiry 160
   instruments 220
   interest 139
   interpretations 216
   language 81
   methods 63, 150
   narratives 53, 60, 62–3
   observation 178
   opinion 95

papers 150
perspective 86
practice 204
process 84
projections 95
questions 209
rigour 51
team 75
techniques 11, 23, 28
technology 32
self-excavation 16, 205–6
self-narrative 206, 210–12
self-understanding 203, 206, 216, 219–21
sensory 79, 86–7
Shanks, Michael 5–6, 100, 104, 109–12, 203–4, 217
short stories 8, 10, 98, 147
Sinclair, Iain 101, 103
site report 178, 182, 189, 195
Situationists 101, 103, 105, 110
skeletal remains 1, 3, 74–5, 78, 81, 84
skeleton 1, 17, 26–7, 40, 78, 146, 151
slave trade 72, 76, 88
slavery 12, 71–6, 78–9, 83–4, 88–9
slaves 71–3, 75, 79, 89
Smith, Ali 11, 36, 38–9, 41
Smith, Zadie 102–3
Smithsonian 151, 157, 159
social media 10, 105, 107–8, 111–12
society 3, 32, 52, 124, 126, 138, 157
Sofaer, Joanna 7, 73
Solnit, Rebecca 100–1
Somerville, John 206–14, 217–20
species 11–12, 23–5, 29–30, 42, 46–50, 60, 62, 95, 155
stable isotope 1, 8
Stamped from the Beginning 152–4
statue 88, 127–8, 130, 132, 139, 204
Stoker, Bram 14, 120–8, 130–3, 138–40
storyteller 45, 211
symbolism 14, 120, 124, 127, 131, 139, 140

technology 13, 24, 32, 96, 105, 108–12
teeth 3, 72, 82–3
temporality 33, 35–6, 41–2, 203
territory 59, 101–2, 156–7, 165
testimony 62, 98, 108, 186
The Emperor's Babe 1, 4
The Jewel of Seven Stars 14, 120, 122–5, 127–8, 140–1
The Mayor of Casterbridge 145, 148
The Source 15, 178, 182, 188, 192–3, 195–6
themes 10–13, 77–8, 139, 188–9, 192, 194
theory 6, 32–4, 96, 104, 121, 146, 153, 155, 160, 181, 216
tradition 40, 63, 98, 100–1, 130, 157, 166, 178, 195
transhistorical 9, 36
transition 52, 59, 184, 189
tribes 145, 151–2, 154–7, 161
truth 3, 16, 26, 29, 34, 79, 81–3, 95–6, 111–12
twentieth century 5, 9–10, 47, 50–2, 72, 152, 179, 189–90, 204, 206, 214
twenty-first century 8–9, 12, 46
Twitter 2, 13, 106–7, 109

Unsworth, Barry 16, 205–6, 211, 214, 218–19

Victorian 14–5, 119, 121, 125, 134, 146, 165, 168, 204–5, 218
violence 52, 129, 215, 220
voices 3, 9, 38, 79, 82, 107, 165

Walkways and Waterways 13, 96, 106, 110, 112
Warwick, Alexandra 10, 96, 103–4, 109, 111–12
white
  settlers 152, 154, 157
  superiority 52, 154

www.ingramcontent.com/pod-product-compliance
Lightning Source LLC
Chambersburg PA
CBHW072148290426
44111CB00012B/2006